Agents of Neoliberal Globalization

Depictions of globalization commonly recite a story of a market unleashed, bringing Big Macs and iPhones to all corners of the world. Human society appears as a passive observer to a busy revolution of an invisible global market, paradoxically unfolding by its own energy. Sometimes, this market is thought to be unleashed by politicians working on the surface of an autonomous state. This book rejects both perspectives and provides an analytically rich alternative to conventional approaches to globalization.

By the 1980s, an enduring corporate coalition advanced in nearly synonymous terms free trade, tax cuts, and deregulation. Highly networked corporate leaders and state officials worked in concert to produce the trade policy framework for neoliberal globalization.

Marshalling original network data and a historical narrative, this book shows that the globalizing corporate titans of the late 1960s aligned with economic conservatives to set into motion this vision of a global free market.

Michael C. Dreiling is a sociology professor at the University of Oregon specializing in political and environmental sociology. He is the author of two books and numerous research articles, and is presently working on a comparative study of energy industry networks. Awarded Distinguished University Teaching in 2009, the Martin Luther King Jr. Distinguished Service Award in 2010, and numerous leadership awards in 2015, Professor Dreiling is also active in the nonprofit world to promote nonviolence, environmental care, and an economy that is fair for all. *A Bold Peace* – a feature documentary film coproduced with Matthew Eddy – depicts that vision of a better world.

Derek Y. Darves holds a PhD in sociology from the University of Oregon, where he focused on organizational theory, quantitative methods, the sociology of religion, and power structure research. Currently he is the Senior Data Scientist for a pension fund in New York City. An ordained Episcopal priest, he has contributed to several empirical reports on trends within the Episcopal Church and also serves part-time at a variety of churches in the Episcopal dioceses of Newark and New York.

Agents of Neoliberal Globalization

Corporate Networks, State Structures, and Trade Policy

MICHAEL C. DREILING

University of Oregon

DEREK Y. DARVES

Independent Scholar

CAMBRIDGE
UNIVERSITY PRESS

One Liberty Plaza, 20th Floor, New York, NY 10006, USA

Cambridge University Press is part of the University of Cambridge.

It furthers the University's mission by disseminating knowledge in the pursuit of education, learning, and research at the highest international levels of excellence.

www.cambridge.org
Information on this title: www.cambridge.org/9781107133969

© Michael C. Dreiling and Derek Y. Darves 2016

This publication is in copyright. Subject to statutory exception and to the provisions of relevant collective licensing agreements, no reproduction of any part may take place without the written permission of Cambridge University Press.

First published 2016

Printed in the United States of America by Sheridan Books, Inc.

A catalogue record for this publication is available from the British Library.

Library of Congress Cataloging-in-Publication Data
Dreiling, Michael C., author. | Darves, Derek Y., author.
Agents of neoliberal globalization : corporate networks, state structures, and trade policy / Michael C. Dreiling, University of Oregon, Derek Y. Darves, Independent Scholar.
New York, NY : Cambridge University Press, 2016. | Includes bibliographical references.
LCCN 2016026288 | ISBN 9781107133969
LCSH: Corporations, American – Political aspects | Corporations – Political activity – United States. | Neoliberalism – United States. | United States – Commerce. | United States – Foreign economic relations. | United States – Economic policy.
LCC HD2785 .D74 2016 | DDC 337.73–dc23
LC record available at https://lccn.loc.gov/2016026288

ISBN 978-1-107-13396-9 Hardback

Cambridge University Press has no responsibility for the persistence or accuracy of URLs for external or third-party Internet Web sites referred to in this publication and does not guarantee that any content on such Web sites is, or will remain, accurate or appropriate.

To our children:
Nalani, Nile, and Hana Dreiling
&
Rosalie Darves

Contents

Figures

Tables

Acknowledgments

This book emerges from a research trajectory begun by Michael Dreiling in 1998 that sought to explain how it is that large corporations achieved such a central role in the trade advisory system under the Office of the US Trade Representative. A strictly historical answer that focused on the 1974 Trade Act was unsatisfactory, given the politics of trade globalization during the 1990s, and elevated concerns about democracy and social inequality. Understanding how the 1974 Trade Act opened the avenues for more direct corporate involvement in the making of US trade policy was certainly an interesting question. But the strong correlation between the corporate appointees to advisory posts and their membership in leading corporate policy associations raised both substantive and theoretical puzzles about the *contemporary* exercise of power in the wider context of democracy and globalization. The mass protests and police counter-mobilizations in Seattle 1999 spoke to these stark issues.

Derek Y. Darves joined the research project in 1999 and mastered the issues as well as the quantitative methods, as presented in his 2006 doctoral dissertation at the University of Oregon. This book incorporates many of those wonderful analyses. Collaboratively, our work embarked on a project to bring a confirmatory network approach to macro-historical questions about corporate power and globalization. We acknowledge that such an endeavor is complex and likely to face real limitations. Any shortcomings to this project, we acknowledge, are our own. We take full responsibility for any errors in the logic or consistency of our presentation. Yet, numerous people have inspired and improved this project through their comments, support, and criticism. We share our appreciation for G. William Domhoff, whose comments at a 2007 conference encouraged us to pursue the project to the end. For this, we are grateful. We are grateful, too, for the insights and methodological guidance we received from Val Burris, Ken Hudson, Mark Mizruchi, and Caleb Southworth, all of which improved the many analytic strands that come together in this research.

On the whole, this book is an improvement on all of our previously published research on the subject, expanding theoretically and empirically in a number of ways. Some of the material in this book has also benefited from the review and editorial processes at two journals. Small selections of this book were published previously. Some portions of Chapters 3, 5, and 6 appeared previously in two published articles: Michael C. Dreiling and Derek Y. Darves, "Corporations in American Trade Policy: A Network Analysis of Corporate-Dyad Political Action," *American Journal of Sociology* 116(5): 1514–1563, © 2011 by the University of Chicago Press. Some selections from the following article also appear in Chapters 2, 3, and 6: Michael C. Dreiling, "The Class Embeddedness of Corporate Political Action: Corporate Leadership in Defense of the NAFTA," *Social Problems* 47(1): 21–48, © 2000 by the Oxford University Press. We thank the anonymous, external reviewers of an earlier draft of this book whose comments helped clarify our presentation of network graphics and tighten our theoretical conclusions. Many colleagues at the University of Oregon sat through a colloquium or two on this topic, and we thank them, both the faculty and graduate students who supported us on our respective paths in the Sociology program. In 2012, the University of Oregon granted Michael C. Dreiling a summer research award that helped bring the final manuscript together.

To our families, friends, and children, we say thank you! From Michael, a special word of appreciation goes to Yvonne Braun for the many years of intellectual and personal inspiration, love, and perseverance. From Derek, a special word of thanks to his parents Bonnie and Gil, who have taken interest in and supported this project for many years, and to his daughter Rosalie who provides endless inspiration and joy.

Common Abbreviations

AEI	American Enterprise Institute
BRT	Business Roundtable
CAFTA	Central American Free Trade Agreement
CBI	Caribbean Basin Initiative
CEA	Council of Economic Advisers
CED	Committee for Economic Development
CFR	Council on Foreign Relations
DOC	Department of Commerce
ECAT	Emergency Committee for American Trade
ERT	European Business Roundtable
FDI	foreign direct investment
FF500	*Fortune* and *Forbes* 500 directories
GATT	General Agreement on Tariffs and Trade
MNC	multinational corporation
NAFTA	North American Free Trade Agreement
NAM	National Association of Manufacturers
NICs	newly industrializing countries
OAS	Organization of American States
PNTR	Permanent Normal Trade Relations
STR	Office of Special Trade Representative
TACs	Trade Advisory Committees
TPA	Trade Promotion Authority
TRIMs	trade-related investment measures
TRIPs	trade-related intellectual property rights
USA*NAFTA	US Alliance for NAFTA
USCIB	US Council for International Business
USTR	Office of the United States Trade Representative
VFCRs	voluntary restrictions on capital outflows
WTO	World Trade Organization

I

Introduction

Laissez-faire was planned; planning was not.
  – Karl Polanyi, *The Great Transformation* (2001:145 [1944])

Several great shifts in the geography of global manufacturing occurred in the last sixty years. After World War II, US foreign economic policy contributed to a re-industrialization of Europe and Japan. Global shares of manufacturing capital moved outward from the United States following the war, generating robust conditions for Japan and Europe to boost exports in the decades to follow. Another major shift began with the de-industrialization of the United States in the 1970s and the acceleration of industrialization among numerous newly industrializing countries (NICs) that had previously engaged in strategic domestic industrial development (Dicken 2007). Over several decades, these global shifts – facilitated by trade liberalization, expanding multinational corporations, and the heightened role of finance – became nearly synonymous with globalization. Signaling this dramatic global movement of capital, the stock of worldwide foreign direct investment (FDI) as a share of total output increased from 5.92 percent in 1980 to 31.57 percent in 2010 (Fairbrother 2014). These multidecade processes culminated in China's becoming the largest manufacturing economy in the world by 2011. In each period, American trade policy had a direct role in these global shifts.

Initially, a policy of containment and market expansion in Europe and Japan – governed by the Bretton Woods framework – were significant features of economic globalization. The second wave of these transformations was characterized by increasing trade liberalization and a financialization of American capitalism.[1] Together, these developments uprooted manufacturing in America's industrial heartlands and propelled capital around the globe, a process that generated massive investment in China and numerous other NICs.

These broad features of globalization are well known. Variously depicted as the marvel of ordering a Big Mac in Kenya or with the dry recitation of trade growth figures, globalization is an enduring topic within both popular media and academia. In most of these accounts, human beings are presented as passive observers to a noisy revolution that appears, paradoxically, to be of its own making. Only rarely do the political roles of corporations and, specifically, the *class agency* of business leaders play a significant part within the broader narrative. This conceptual absence of class from the broader discussion comports with prevailing ideology but also limits our ability to describe (much less explain) the interactions between government and market actors in the historical spectacle of globalization. When viewed in this way – that is, as an impenetrable black box – the human and class-driven processes that underlie globalization are relegated to the shadows. On this point, while globalization is certainly larger than any single observer, we argue that its causal structure – the political logic that fashions its nodes of power and the course of future growth – is not so mysterious or diffuse as to wholly evade the investigator's lens. The primary purpose of this book, then, is to examine the important political role of American "corporate titans" (a group collectively referred to as "class agents") in the process of economic globalization. Chiefly of interest in this inquiry is the manner in which class actors forged enduring relationships with key national and international trade agencies in order to advance a *particular*, neoliberal vision of trade policy that would, ultimately, restructure the tapestry of modern capitalism.[2]

---

[1] In the introduction to his edited book on *Financialization and the World Economy*, Epstein explains that "financialization means the increasing role of financial motives, financial markets, financial actors and financial institutions in the operation of the domestic and international economies" (2005: 3). John Bellamy Foster, who has expressly linked the process of financialization to neoliberalism and globalization, argues that the financialization of capitalism represents "the shift in gravity of economic activity from production (and even from much of the growing service sector) to finance" (2007: 1). Our historical account identifies clear linkages between corporate advocacy for the liberalization of trade as well as finance from the 1970s forward.

[2] From the Caribbean Basin Initiative (CBI), to the North American Free Trade Agreement (NAFTA), the World Trade Organization, and more, American trade policy moved

Opening an inquiry into the political role of corporate actors involved in shaping globalization requires consideration of several related concerns. Most obviously, it requires a critical interrogation of the way that corporate leaders shape international markets through trade policy, closely interacting with state officials and institutions. No longer can the story of globalization be one of abstract "market forces" exerting quasi-natural laws on human societies. As Fligstein asserts, "globalization is not an impersonal force, but very much reflects the social and political construction of markets by firms and states" (2001: 222). But what does the political action of firms look like in the context of trade policy and globalization? If, as we qualify below, class political action is detectable from a rigorous social science approach, what does this mean for both theoretical and popular understandings of the relationship between government actors and market actors in reshaping the global economy?

Amid the global financial crisis of 2008, a new chapter in the history of neoliberal globalization emerged. Simple assumptions about markets as pure and neutral arbiters of economic transactions faced new challenges from beyond the pages of economic history and sociology. The apparent triumph of global capitalism came into temporary question, and with it, the reigning economic paradigm of neoliberalism.[3] From the left wing of US politics, a newly invigorated discourse of class and income inequality began to challenge corporate power with calls for greater accountability on Wall Street. The specter of the Occupy movement in 2011, with its sweeping critique of corporate power, took root in ways not seen in the United States since the 1999 World Trade Organization protests in Seattle. In response, proponents of neoliberalism heightened their demands for a market-governed society, further tax cuts, deregulation, trade liberalization, and more. From the GOP and Tea Party's politics of austerity arose a fresh defense of free market politics in the United States, as well as

---

markedly toward greater liberalization, hence the characterization of neoliberalism. Neoliberal markets, including the visions of international free trade, epitomize the classic-liberal utopia of an unregulated, free market society (see Polanyi 1944). Neoliberalism is thus defined as an encompassing perspective that claims that the "market allocates resources to all uses more efficiently than political institutions" (Przeworski 1990:15). See Harvey (2005: 4) for a "political-economic story of where neoliberalization came from and how it proliferated so comprehensively on the world stage" (see also Bourdieu 1994, 2005; Bourdieu and Wacquant 1992; Mudge 2008).

[3] When Alan Greenspan, then-chairman of America's Federal Reserve, and a leading spokesperson for financial market deregulation, announced in his 2008 Congressional testimony that there was a "flaw in the model of how I perceived the world works" (Kiel 2008), a quiet, but subtle crack was exposed on the edges of neoliberal ideology.

a reinvigorated denial of class as a structuring force in US society. These social tensions persist even as neoliberalism, as an ideology and a model for institutional restructuring, exhibits remarkable resilience.

Neoliberalism – which promises to efficiently generate wealth while disciplining states and bureaucracies with market forces – took shape over the course of decades. As a kind of governing philosophy, it has been offered, variously, as a remedy for economic stagnation, bureaucratic bloat, corruption, inflation, and more (Bourdieu 1999; Mirowski and Plehwe 2009; Mudge 2008). From the early 1980s onward, it provided the basic policy framework for "structural adjustment" in the global south, for "rescuing" the welfare state in the global north, and as a vision for a global economy unbound from centrally planned markets, dying industries, or rent-seeking interest groups. One cornerstone of this paradigm that remains mostly unchallenged among political elites is the principal of "free trade." Broadly speaking, neoliberalism and free trade have provided the ideological framework for most reciprocal trade agreements since the early 1980s, when President Reagan initiated a wave of new trade policies in February 1982 during a speech to the Organization of American States (OAS). There, Reagan unilaterally called for a Caribbean Basin Initiative (CBI) that would "make use of the magic of the marketplace of the Americas, to earn their own way toward self-sustaining growth" (quoted in Polanyi-Levitt 1985: 232).[4] This formulaic discourse of free markets, free trade, and personal liberty – hallmark features of Reagan's popular rhetoric – also captured what would later be acknowledged as core principles of an incipient neoliberal ideology that promised a restoration of US economic hegemony (Mudge 2008). Domestically and internationally, neoliberal trade proposals were generally presented in tandem with calls for privatization, deregulation, and a reduction in the size of government spending as a share of GDP.[5]

---

[4] The CBI was a unilateral program enacted into law on January 1, 1984. It was extended by NAFTA in 2000 to achieve parity with the larger, continental pact. It was the first of several tariff-reducing regional free trade programs in the hemisphere. Provisions in the act enabled US trade authorities to deny the reduced tariffs to countries judged to be under Communist influence or that had expropriated US commercial properties, hence the "free market" arrangements were quite political in their form, Office of the United States Trade Representative, CBI Page, Oct. 20, 2012, www.ustr.gov/archive/Trade_Development/Preference_Programs/CBI/Section_Index.html.

[5] A critical distinction is made between neoliberal "free trade" and open and fair world markets (see Chapter 3). As critics of neoliberal trade policy have argued for decades, the policy choice is not necessarily between protectionism and free trade. Instead, commonly recognized production standards are already part of the construction of world markets

Although a large and varied group of economists, policy wonks, and government leaders supported the general principles of neoliberal globalization, the "market fever" of the 1980s did not spread simply because certain individuals espoused free trade and domestic deregulation. The fact that many of these noncorporate actors assume a central role in many popular and academic accounts of this era does not reduce the many empirical problems with this view. In particular, the problem with this "triumphant" vision of neoliberal history is the manner in which the very *engines* of capital behind the market mania – globalizing corporations – *appear* as liberated historical agents acting out their market freedoms, not as class political actors foisting new institutional realities on the world. We contest this prevailing view and instead ask who liberated, or in Blyth's (2002) terminology, "disembedded," these markets from national social and political institutions? Was it the fever pitch of a new policy ideology acted out by government partisans and policy makers committed to its mantra? Or did the very economic actors benefitting from market liberalization act politically and concertedly to unleash it? And if so, did this coordinated corporate political campaign arise from a reorganized and newly emboldened economic *class*, or simply through ad hoc alignments created by shared organizational interests? Specifically, can we detect class political signatures on the wave of free trade policies, like the CBI, the North American Free Trade Agreement (NAFTA), or the World Trade Organization (WTO), that erected the institutional framework of neoliberal globalization?[6]

considered as "free trade" (Quark 2011), and phytosanitary workplace standards have been negotiated into the NAFTA and other agreements. The extension of market standards to include basic labor and workplace standards (already recognized in the ILO) or consumer and environmental protections need not diminish the ability to build open and fair markets. The difference, as critics of neoliberalism maintain, is between a neoliberal program of downward harmonization (a "race to the bottom" of labor, consumer, and environmental standards) versus a program of fair trade, with an upward harmonization of standards with market-enforceable mechanisms at the global or regional level.

[6] While "globalization" has been the subject of considerable debate, efforts to define the term and analyze its consequences have been stymied by the lack of a universally accepted conceptual framework within which to analyze it (Cohen et al. 2003: 313). Because the focus of this study is corporate involvement in US trade liberalization, it is probably sufficient to employ the most common meaning of the term, that is, growth in the global trade of goods and services. Even as we qualify the character of contemporary globalization as "neoliberal" and restrict our attention to the economic dimensions of globalization that pertain to the growth of international commerce, it should be noted that research on globalization encompasses a much broader range of cultural and social phenomena (McMichael 2012; Rupert 2003).

The answer to these questions and, in particular, the role of class agency within these macroeconomic shifts, is not simply a question of whether one likes Karl Marx or Adam Smith. Notwithstanding the recent tendency to equate the mention of class with "class warfare," it is our contention that removing class from accounts of recent economic history creates, at best, a narrow and distorted perspective on this important era. The primary purpose of this book, then, is to introduce and empirically validate a concept of class agency that deepens our understanding of both the trade policy-making apparatus as well as the neoliberal globalization "project" more generally. We believe that our approach, rooted in the "elite studies" and "power structure" research traditions, expands (and, in some areas, corrects) conventional explanations of neoliberal trade and globalization that emphasize market, institutional, and ideological factors, while neglecting to incorporate a concept of class political action.

Our general line of argument historicizes US trade policy and neoliberal globalization, highlighting the active and at times contradictory processes that shape the state and class relationships responsible for propelling institutions, like the WTO, into existence. Following McMichael (2001: 207), we concur that globalization is best understood as a *"historical project* rather than a *culminating process."* Treating neoliberal trade policies as part of a much larger historical project – made and remade by collective actors – offers a more realistic and empirically grounded framework for exploring the intersection of class and state actors in the political articulation of globalization.

Whereas much of the literature on globalization assigns an important role to the *economic* activity of multinational corporations, the force of their *collective* political agency in pressuring states to ratify trade agreements and enact institutional reforms is mostly attributed to narrow sectoral interests, like factor mobility, economies of scale, or various industry-specific characteristics.[7] This disconnect in the literature creates

---

[7] Exceptions include the relatively new genre of empirically oriented scholarship on transnational capitalist class networks (Carroll 2004, 2010; Kentor and Suk Jang 2004; Murray and Scott 2012; Sklair 2001, 2002b; Staples 2006, 2007). This research generally aims to empirically document and explain the organizational dynamics of transnational corporate boards and their interaction with transnational governance institutions, cultures, and production processes. Interest in the "transnational practices" (Sklair 2001, 2002b) of corporations and transnational bureaucrats certainly has a place in clarifying accounts of globalization and transnational institution building. This focus *beyond* the nation state, however, misses a crucial dynamic *within* national state institutions: globalizing corporations can penetrate and transform state agendas to advance transnational prerogatives (see Robinson 2004). Empirically, we direct our attention to dynamics within US state

a paradox for theories of globalization: on one hand, global markets are characterized as independent, impersonal forces governed by abstract rules that constrain states. In this view, global markets "act" on the state and governments consequently "react" to these impersonal economic forces. On the other hand, in the policy and international relations literature, state actors are viewed as the principal actors in the construction of global market institutions. State actors, in this view, ostensibly ascertain the economic interests of key industries and promote trade policies that strengthen the relative economic power of the country based on their rational-strategic evaluations. Paradoxically, state actors seem independently responsible for creating transnational institutions that mitigate or supersede the state's authority, from consumer safety to investor property rights (Boyer and Drache 1996; Dicken 2007; Strange 1996). Consequently, neoliberal globalization appears to advance in two steps, with states either following capital markets or markets expanding through states.

The broadly held assumption that the diverse economic interests of large corporations create "irreconcilable" political fractions contributes to this seeming paradox. In the extreme version of this perspective, competitive market dynamics are thought to create permanent divisions among corporations and their managing elite; only autonomous political elites holding the "unfettered" version of free trade orthodoxy are capable of creating rational systems to govern international transactions and capital flows (Block 1987; Lindblom 1977). Chapter 2 illustrates how the logic of this perspective – which emphasizes corporate political fragmentation stemming from economic competition – is rooted in epistemological orientations that view corporate political action through an atomistic, as opposed to relational, lens (see Emirbayer 1997). Corporate political action, within this framework, is reduced to a multiplicity of competing economic interests

---

institutions responsible for constructing transnational trade governance systems. We therefore invert the typical orientation of theories of global capitalism that focus on transnational and global processes and practices and bring attention to the active role of both state and class actors in constructing those transnational structures. We focus on the network embeddedness of US-based corporations and the interpenetration of these corporate power structures with trade policy processes within US government institutions, not transnational institutions. Our approach retains a distinct focus on measuring and testing forms of class cohesion among corporate political actors at the national level. The particular emphasis on measuring state-level outcomes for corporate political action also rests on a view that states matter, that transnational environments are suspended, in part, through the actions of states, and that explanations of corporate class power at the national level can be appreciably improved.

incapable of sustaining political unity to press broader classwide aims. When and if corporate solidarity prevails, it is conceptualized as a temporary, issue-based fix amid a larger sea of competitive flux. In the end, classwide business interests detach from the political behavior of corporations, leaving state actors and associated private regulatory agencies to determine international trade policy.

This perspective – where states direct a fragmented private sector toward trade liberalization – creates a rupture in political theories of globalization and, in particular, confuses the relative historic roles of class and state actors. This book presents an alternative thesis. Building on previous research, we highlight the *interaction* between state and class actors – measured, principally, through complex corporate, policy, and political networks – in the construction of global market institutions over time. Rather than assuming that the economic interests of corporations are simply "known" by state actors independent of corporate political action, and that these state actors are relatively "autonomous" from outside influence, we focus on how the two interact *politically* to advance a particular form of neoliberal globalization, one that defines the contours of an historical era. In this view, neither the political "shape" of globalization nor the "interests" of its primary actors are simple derivatives of reified macroeconomic theories or purely material concerns stemming from market interests. Instead, we argue that state and class actors work in concert, not singularly, to produce the trade institutions of neoliberal globalization, significantly altering the societies in which these markets are embedded.

Throughout this book we develop, test, and expand upon two interrelated bodies of literature concerning corporate political power and neoliberal trade policy. The first draws from elite studies in sociology and is concerned with the mechanisms and relative importance of the "intercorporate network." The part of this literature that is of particular interest for our analysis is the manner in which existing "nodes" in the intercorporate network (e.g., the Business Roundtable) have expanded their engagement with "the neoliberal project" and, in many instances, spawned new centers of influence within the trade-policy formation process (as with the various trade coalitions we discuss later).

The second body of literature we examine are those which incorporate a more strictly "interest group" conceptualization of corporate political action within the trade-policy formation and advocacy process. While corporate interest group coalitions (e.g., among firms in the same sector) are an important part of trade policy formation in the United States, in general we find these interest-centered accounts insufficient on two grounds. First, the concept of "interest groups" does not capture the unique power, resources, and bargaining position of large corporations in modern political systems. For example, institutionalist and interest group theories of corporate trade politics generally place sustained trade policy activism by large multinational corporations in the same category as gun or environmental advocacy groups. This, we think, betrays the historical significance of corporate collective action as well as the *incomparable* resources these organizations channel into the US political system. As the central hubs of capital, large corporations exert leverage within multiple social, economic, and political processes, impacting everything from labor markets to cultural aspirations. We take this to mean that as a starting point, a critical evaluation of the "interest group" concept – in this context – is warranted.

Collectively, the empirical observations presented in this book challenge "interest group" centered accounts of corporate advocacy for neoliberal trade policy. While sectoral interests are certainly an important driver of neoliberal policy activism among large corporations, our empirical models also highlight the influence of numerous unifying, intersectoral corporate and state associations.[8] The exclusivity, resources, and influence of these organizations, together with the dense social and political networks that connect the executives from many large US firms, warrants a careful juxtaposition of "interest group" and class-cohesion perspectives on corporate political behavior. In terms of US trade policy and, more generally, neoliberal globalization, we advance a restatement of *unified* corporate political action as *class agency*. This concept rests on the work of C.W. Mills (1956) and his understanding of the relationship between the corporate rich and the power elite.

It is our contention that a concept of class agency *enhances* institutionalist, historical, and interest group accounts of American trade policy and neoliberal globalization. A concept of class agency is presented in Chapter 2 that connects the uniquely resourceful characteristic of modern corporations with theories of organizational contingency, societal conflict, and institutionally specific political action over neoliberal trade policy.[9]

---

[8] Such as the Business Roundtable and the Advisory Committee on Trade Policy and Negotiations to the President (ACTPN).

[9] Prechel's (2000) research develops a theoretical framework rooted in a series of empirical investigations examining the historically contingent class organization of the steel industry. His work is discussed further in Chapter 2.

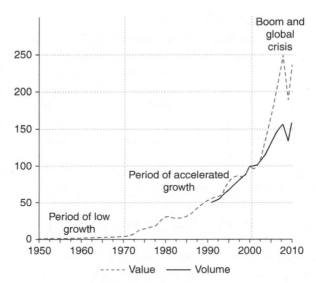

FIGURE 1.1 Long-Term Trends in Value and Volume of Merchandise Exports, 1950–2010 (Index Numbers, 2000 = 100)
From *Development and Globalization: Facts and Figures*, by United Nations Conference on Trade and Development, © 2012 United Nations. Reprinted with the permission of the United Nations.

NEOLIBERALISM, TRADE EXPANSION, AND CLASS AGENCY

A great deal of literature on globalization describes the growth of world trade as a purely economic phenomenon. Ostensibly, this growth possesses "a mind of its own" and takes states, localities, and organizations along for the ride. In much of this literature, growth in world merchandise exports (see Figure 1.1) is viewed as an important proxy for deepening networks of economic exchange and integration. While growth in the trade of goods and services is certainly an important part of globalization, concluding, as much of the literature on globalization does, that this growth is mostly a function of economics, not politics, is a mistake. To put the matter plainly: markets cannot exist apart from the active participation of states (Fligstein 2001; Polanyi 2001 [1944]). Whether one views the market and its various gyrations (e.g., toward more trade) positively or negatively is quite secondary to this basic observation about the role of the state and its important function with the project of neoliberal globalization.

The most straightforward manner in which states transform the conditions for international trade is through import and export tariffs (or taxes). Economists have long noted the negative relationship between tariffs and international merchandise trade. For example, Garret (2000), using World Bank data, found a strong negative correlation (−0.89) between annualized trade taxes for all countries and the total value of world trade. As tariffs steadily dropped from the 1970s onward, the volume of world trade expanded. While international trade flows linked to large firms were a key *expression* of this process, the genesis of these changes can be clearly traced, in many ways, to changes that occurred within *states*. Professional economists and technocrats often construct the specific rationales for market liberalization programs like NAFTA, but it is ultimately the authority exercised by the state that transforms trade rules (Fligstein 2001; Fourcade 2006). The substantial increase in world trade from the early 1970s to the present thus requires an understanding of the US trade policy literature.

Before embarking on a detailed review of American trade policy (see Chapters 3 and 4), however, we think it necessary to return to the theoretical problem, raised earlier, wherein trade liberalization is described, by some, as a process of state actors working in near isolation to create transnational institutions that supersede areas of their own nation-state authority. The difficulty, for us, stems from the manner in which these processes are described, specifically, the tendency to ignore corporate political involvement while accentuating the role of state technocrats and amorphous "market forces." While state actors are no doubt important, it is our contention that states – and their technocrats – cannot "know" the economic interests of corporations apart from corporate involvement in the policy formation process. Therefore, a reasonably thorough account of economic globalization requires an understanding not only of aggregate economic data or the intricate workings of state regulatory agencies, but also the complex, well endowed, and highly organized networks of corporate political power that exert influence at all levels of the policy formation process. Yet, outside of the sociological and political science research on an incipient transnational capitalist class (Carroll 2004, 2010; Sklair 2001; Staples 2006), little is said about corporations *collectively* shaping neoliberal institutions of trade and globalization (though books and articles on the power of economists and their ideas in shaping neoliberalism are easily found).[10] The absence of systematic accounts of corporate collective action

---

[10] Some notable exceptions are Silva's (2008) research on capitalist coalitions in Chile's neoliberal ascent, Fairbrother's (2007) and Thacker's (2000) in Mexico, and Carroll's research on Canadian and transatlantic corporate elite networks (2004, 2010). Research

in shaping neoliberal trade in the United States is somewhat puzzling. As is widely understood by historical institutionalists and economic sociologists, the market did not liberate or disembed itself. Instead, global markets were transformed by collectively mobilized corporate actors working *in concert* with state actors to facilitate more flexible responses to profitability crises and financialization in the 1970s and 1980s.

In the chapters to follow, a key theoretical component of our account of neoliberal globalization is *class agency.* As it stands, neo-institutionalist literature tends to avoid a critical theorization of class agency (see Campbell and Pederson 2001). Blyth's (2002) otherwise brilliant historical account of neoliberalism falls short in this area as well: while he does not develop a *theoretical* argument involving class, class actors, or class agency, he argues that "business was able to dismantle embedded liberalism" (201). Somewhat incongruously, he further argues that "disembedding liberalism was above all else, then, a struggle over ideas, a struggle that Democrats lost" (ibid.). His extensive reliance on business political action as a causal force within "disembedded liberalism" speaks more to the awkwardness of talking about class outside of Marxism than to the potential that, conceptually, *class agency* provides an appropriate and illuminating frame for describing this important causal factor, that is, "business."

Our integration of a class agency approach does not discount the importance of ideological factors, technological advances, and long-term trade and investment flows in shaping the context in which policies for trade liberalization and market governance occur (see Chase-Dunn, Kawano, and Brewer 2000; Dicken 2007; Goldstein, Rivers, and Tomz 2007). Instead, this project complements existing literature, which tends to posit market, technology, or policy ideas as *determinant,* while ignoring class forces that shape political and institutional responses to economic globalization. For example, Dicken's (2007) highly popular account of globalization, now printing a fifth edition, is an extensive study of the technological, economic, and geographic characteristics of the "global shift." In a superbly developed overview of the economic dimensions of globalization, transnational corporations are examined for their economic and administrative

by Babb (2009), and Fairbrother (2014) shows the importance of the economics profession in framing an ideological alternative for policy makers. This fascinating comparative work highlights the distinct contours and the transnational professional networks responsible for shaping neoliberalism in specific policy outcomes (see also Prasad 2006, 2012).

dynamics. Yet surprisingly, multinational corporations (MNCs) are por-
trayed almost entirely as singular, atomistic forces within their surrounding
political systems. Only "east Asian" firms are examined for their political
linkages, particularly in the case of the Japanese *keiretsu*, and then only to
dispute the "convergence thesis," which states that global corporations
adopt similar organizational features. Even in the chapter devoted to the
relationships between states and MNCs, there is little discussion of the
political organization and mobilization of MNCs within their countries of
operation. This focus on MNCs as economic rather than political engines of
change is a pervasive feature of Dicken's analysis and, indeed, much of the
globalization literature. Yet excluding the *political* force of MNCs, especially as collective actors, tends to reproduce the assumption that global
corporations are mostly fragmented actors incapable of sustained, coordinated policy activism. Increasingly, however, research on transnational
business networks confirm what Carroll and Sapinski observed in 2010
(502): "interlocks between corporate boards and policy boards ... mobilize
corporate directors as *a social category capable of political action.*" Because
these pervasive ties are measurable and function as a robust proxy for the
class associative processes we describe more fully in Chapter 2, class agency,
itself, can be viewed as an *empirically testable* component of neoliberal
corporate activism.

Investigating the role of corporations as individual and class political
actors remains especially pertinent to understanding the substantive historical shifts in trade that signaled a new era of global capitalism. While
still relatively uncommon, a few studies are attentive to the *political* force
of elite corporate actors in support of neoliberal globalization. Studying
the European context, Dahan, Dah, and Guay (2006), for example, argue
that the European Business Roundtable (ERT), formed in 1983, was the
most influential political actor in support of the Single Market Program in
Europe. Similarly, Fairbrother's (2007: 289) account of political support
for NAFTA in Mexico concluded that "neoliberalism ... can be *constructed* by a motivated state allied with a dominant faction of the
domestic capitalist class." Building on this literature, our study moves
beyond the case study approach and integrates confirmatory statistical
analyses to explain the dynamic of class and state agency in neoliberal
trade policy. These analyses, together with our historical overview, combine to illuminate distinct political events associated with the consolidation of neoliberal trade and transnational market institutions. As we will
argue in the chapters to follow, neoliberal globalization emerged within
a contested, class-inflected context, creating new sites for challengers to

corporate globalization (Smith 2008) while also expanding the transnational market mechanisms for global economic power.

IMAGINING A GLOBALIZED WORLD

While "ideas" about neoliberal globalization are insufficient, within themselves, to create the world of unfettered economic activity and capital mobility, they are particularly potent when linked with the resources and networks of economic and political elites. As Mudge (2008: 709) argues, it was precisely this kind of process – "ideas" connecting with an elite corporate class – that transformed neoliberalism "from a marginalized set of intellectual convictions into a full-blown hegemonic force." The force of these ideas was further augmented by repeated economic crises, "which weakened existing governments and rendered political elites amenable to a different system of thought" (ibid.). Locating the resonance of neoliberal ideology and ideas amid economic crisis is important as we consider historical forerunners of neoliberalism. Ideological support for free trade, lower wages, deregulation, and tax cuts resided front and center in the Business Roundtable and other corporate policy groups throughout the 1970s and 1980s, well *before* Ronald Reagan and other Republicans popularized the rhetoric.

In addition to the emerging ideals surrounding "liberated markets" in the 1970s, others note how world historical contingencies played an important part in neoliberal globalization. For example, there is little doubt that the crisis in the Soviet Union created political opportunities for accelerating the promotion and experimentation with neoliberal prescriptions already tested in the heavily indebted global South (e.g., privatization, increased FDI, and restrictions on public sector investments [Tabb 2000]). As others point out, the adoption of neoliberal economic policies within developing states involved both active coercion by international finance (via the International Monetary Fund's structural adjustment programs) and by the incorporation of neoliberal technocrats into leading government positions (Babb 2009; Campbell and Pederson 2001; Fourcade and Babb 2002). McMichael (2005: 596) argues that with "the collapse of the Cold War in 1991, the stage was set for a universal application of liberalization, under the leadership of the United States and its G-7 allies." With the conclusion of NAFTA (1994) and the creation of the World Trade Organization following the conclusion of the GATT Uruguay Round (1986–1994), a robust transnational apparatus to enforce market governance began to take shape. The possibility for newly "open" markets in Eastern Europe and Russia further consolidated neoliberalism as a global economic modality (Campbell and Pederson 2001).

Most literature on recent globalization history identifies the 1990s as a period where neoliberalism achieved global relevance. This would seem to be a reasonable conclusion given the extensive series of initiatives by the United States, the EU, and multilateral institutions to implement what Robinson (2004) refers to as a "revolution from above." From the Maastricht Treaty to NAFTA and the WTO, the liberalization of global markets accelerated in this period. At the same time, historical approaches tend to cast doubt on explanations that overstress the origins of neoliberal globalization in the 1990s (Harvey 2005; Mirowski and Plehwe 2009). With regard to economic policy in particular, the shift toward state-initiated liberalization began decades earlier. Economic historians and Marxists, for example, tend to locate these shifts toward neoliberalism within economic and structural crises in the late 1960s and early 1970s.

In *Capital Resurgent*, Dumenil and Levy (2004) situate the shift toward a neoliberal social order in the crisis of accumulation and profitability beginning in the late 1960s. This well-documented pattern of declining US profit rates, which continued into the 1980s, is also the basis for the argument that neoliberal restructuring reflected a (relative) ascent of finance capital and the trend toward financialization of world markets (Foster and Magdoff 2009; Howard and King 2008; Inoue 2011). While these arguments convincingly suggest that the structural crisis in capitalism compelled a re-ordering of social and class power as business sought ideological and political strategies to increase profits by cutting corporate taxes and labor costs, there are few empirical tests of class agency within this genre of historical scholarship. Instead, as in most Marxist accounts, the contradictory logic of capital accumulation is thought to foist upon history the need for deregulation and neoliberal market principles. Corporate class action is implied, but remains invisible or narrated on a case-by-case basis. While Dumenil and Levy (2004 & 2011), for example, offer an explicitly Marxist account of recent economic crises, their focus remains on the aggregate economic conditions of accumulation and, by extension, the impetus for abstract capital to liberate markets (and finance) in its search for renewed profitability.

We also recognize broad empirical variations in the ascent of neoliberal globalization, especially across the global North–South divide. Rather than an ideational, economistic, or state-centric explanation, our research expands on explanations that posit different globally structured paths for nations to move toward neoliberal globalization.

In Eastern Europe and the Global South, evidence seems to converge on the point that international financial institutions (IFIs: such as the International Monetary Fund, World Bank, and international banks), and sympathetic *state technocrats* – often Western-trained economists – worked with select factions of domestic business to implement neoliberal reforms (Fairbrother 2014). At the same time, paths to neoliberal trade and globalization for rich countries appear to have consistently involved active and robust business mobilizations alongside ideologically aligned state elites who challenge tax codes, union rights, and public welfare institutions (ibid.). These distinct paths to neoliberal globalization reflect, of course, the important structural chasms in the system of global capitalism during the time. Neoliberal prescriptions for a variety of economic and state fiscal problems were differentially institutionalized from an "outside-in" approach, as described by Babb (2000), and class-state collaboration was particularly common in the EU and United States. The research in this book formally tests the latter assertion.

Common to the variety of approaches discussed here is the dearth of efforts to operationally conceptualize class political agency in the context of neoliberal globalization. Any adequate grasp of neoliberal globalization demands an understanding of the political capacity of large, multinational corporations and, in particular, their work with state actors to transform state and market institutions. The historically specific fusion of corporate political networks to institutional spaces in the executive branch, as facilitated via an advisory system created by the 1974 Trade Act, is one important example. More are uncovered in the chapters that follow. The 1974 Trade Act offered new institutional opportunities for corporations to shape trade policy in an era of economic crisis, helping to define the wave of neoliberal trade projects that began in the early 1980s. Corporations, as we will show, did not function in a purely economic role in this process, but also in an intensely political one, helping to define and defend the signature trade blocs that made neoliberal free trade nearly synonymous with globalization. As our historical anecdote below suggests, this project of fusing corporate and state actors around a new trade policy apparatus began in the late 1960s.[11]

---

[11] The US trade policy apparatus and specifically corporate involvement in the industry advisory system are the subjects of our empirical tests in the chapters ahead. This historical reference, while illuminating the creation of new institutional avenues for corporate and state actors to work concertedly in shaping trade policy, also begins to contextualize the historical and empirical argument we advance in Chapter 4.

WHERE CORPORATE NETWORKS MEET THE STATE: AN ANECDOTE AND A BEGINNING

Signaling the rise of neoliberal trade policy (see Harvey 2005), we turn, now, to a little known political mobilization at the height of the Nixon Administration, one that reshaped the voice of large corporations and the authority of the president in US trade policy. Steel and textile industries, once comfortable allies in the postwar hegemony of Keynesianism, New Deal liberalism, and American global "free enterprise," now faced stiff import competition and began to demand new protections. As new economic competition from Japan and Europe in select industries elevated business conflicts over American trade policy, a new political moment was opening for economic conservatives who had been pressing against the New Deal and Keynesianism for decades (Domhoff 2013). By the late 1960s, interindustry splits created a political opportunity for leaders in the American Enterprise Institute (AEI) and other conservative groups to align with free trade globalizers. Describing this period, Chorev (2007) and Destler and Odell (1987) highlight the stark and growing divide between "internationalist businesses" intent on trade liberalization and the increasingly marginal voices of declining domestic industries, such as steel and textiles.

Concurrently, a number of public conversations – well documented in Barnet and Muller (1974a) – among corporate managers revealed a conscious understanding of globalizing corporations as a new force in history. "For business purposes," says Maissenrouge in 1971 (president of IBM), "the boundaries that separate one nation from another are no more real than the equator ... The world outside the home country is no longer viewed as a series of disconnected customers and prospects for its products, but as an extension of a single market" (quoted from Barnet and Muller 1974a: 14–15). These pronouncements reflected an understanding of relatively new constraints and challenges to the US economy that demanded new corporate and policy initiatives. As IBM's president opined, "In the forties Wendell Wilkie spoke about 'One World.' In the seventies we are inexorably pushed toward it" (ibid.: p. 13).

At the center of the push against protectionism and toward a "single world market" was the Emergency Committee for American Trade (ECAT), formed after a 1967 meeting between David Rockefeller, IBM's Arthur K. Watson,[12]

---

[12] Arthur K. Watson, son of IBM founder, was the president of IBM at this time, president of the International Chamber of Commerce (1967–1968), co-founder of ECAT, and would later serve as ambassador to France (1970–1972).

and several US "business leaders ... concerned that a new worldwide trade war was in the making" (ECAT 2008). Worried that new demands to restrict trade were passing through Congress and that retaliatory threats were being made between nations, these corporate leaders voiced an agenda for an open, multilateral trading system, even as they helped form alliances with industry leaders besieged by import competition. Some of their concerns were formulated in the 1971 report by Nixon's Commission on International Trade and Investment Policy, headed by Alfred Williams. Williams was a former president of IBM, and at the time of the commission's founding he sat on the boards of the Mobil Corporation, General Foods, Eli Lilly, and Citibank. As a member of this corporate inner circle, his perspective on domestic and international economic affairs was regarded as an asset to initiatives aimed at advancing multilateral trade liberalization.[13]

Though the Williams report contained recommendations that, today, would be thought of as outside the neoliberal banner, it suggested avenues for reform of the trading and international monetary systems that took into account existing domestic political institutions and constraints (Mundo 1999). The report had the effect of spurring debates in policy circles, such as the Council on Foreign Relations and the Committee for Economic Development (CED), which elevated promises of trade liberalization to new heights among large corporations, the ECAT, and the older US Council for International Business. By 1973, these efforts crystallized with the mobilization of business groups, including the newly formed Business Roundtable, and internal efforts by the Nixon Administration to open new opportunities for a strategic dialogue about trade in a changing global economy (Chorev 2007; Cohen, Paul, and Blecker 2003). During the debate over the 1974 Trade Act, ECAT assembled a coalition of major business associations to support the Nixon administration's "serious lobbying effort" (Chorev 2007: 85), assuring congressional passage of the 1974 Trade Act even as the Watergate scandal unfolded. Passage of this legislation, with the help of groups like ECAT, dramatically expanded the authority of the president in trade policy negotiations and formalized avenues for business participation while simultaneously diluting the authority of Congress. Most important for our discussion, the Trade Act of 1974 created a three-tiered system of trade policy advisory

---

[13] As a whole, the Williams Commission was composed of representatives from eighteen large corporations (from banking and manufacturing to agriculture commodity firms), three academics, and two union representatives.

committees that allowed industry representatives to provide direct policy input and recommendations to US trade negotiators.[14] This elaborate system of "private sector advisory committees" was established "to ensure that U.S. trade policy and trade negotiation objectives adequately reflect U.S. commercial and economic interests" (Office of the US Trade Representative 1994:114).

Fast-forward several decades to an April 2003 House Ways and Means Committee hearing and one discovers that, for its broad influence and organizational efficacy, the ECAT "can be justly proud of the many accomplishments of U.S. trade policy, including the Tokyo Round Agreement, the Uruguay Round Agreements, the North America Free Trade Agreement, Permanent Normal Trade Relations with China, and the GATT/WTO system itself" (ECAT: Press Release, April 9, 2003: 1). ECAT, usually with the Business Roundtable and the USCIB, led during every major transformation in US trade policy during the three decades prior. In addition, attempts to enact sanctions or insert "Buy American" provisions into government job stimulus bills, transportation bills, and more were fought aggressively by ECAT. Like other major corporate lobbying groups, ECAT has become a powerful fixture in Washington, DC. The US Trade Representative and other officials often serve as keynote speakers for the group's annual awards dinners celebrating free trade advocacy, such as Ambassador Susan C. Schwab's address during an ECAT award dinner on March 5, 2008:

It is hard for me to imagine a higher calling than what we as a nation can do through our trade policies to promote growth – at home and abroad – to expand the base of those who benefit from trade, and to help lift millions out of poverty ... Now is the time to work together to make our move.

But ECAT is not just a lobbying group; it is also an organization that mobilizes and, we argue, unifies the executives of some of the largest US corporations in their quest to engineer trade policy. Like their larger compatriot, the Business Roundtable (with whom membership is highly

---

[14] Also important in this Trade Act was the establishment of "fast track negotiating authority" for the president. This piece of legislation weakened congressional authority, compelling votes on negotiated trade agreements to a yes/no vote, without amendments, by a simple majority thereby altering the constitutional requirement of a supermajority for the approval of treaties. While Congress was restricting executive authority on other matters (War Powers Resolution, Budget Act, etc.) amid the deceptions of Watergate, "it is surprising," as Mundo (1999: 116) notes, "that Congress willingly turned over more authority to the president on trade policy."

correlated), ECAT's member participation in congressional committee hearings, appointments to executive branch posts, and public relations campaigns serve to bolster the influence and stature of the group and its corporate constituents. For example, recent chairman of ECAT, Harold McGraw III – also 2011 Chairman, president, and CEO of The McGraw-Hill Companies and chair of the Business Roundtable – commands prominent status among corporate executives. Networks between government and corporate policy groups, like ECAT, fuse the personal and corporate via executives like Harold McGraw III. Mr. McGraw III rose from his family connections in publishing and information services to become a corporate leader in ways that parallel Michael Useem's "inner circle" (1984). As chairman of the board and CEO of McGraw-Hill, in 2011 he also served on the boards of United Technologies and ConocoPhillips. His network connections included premier business associations as well as government appointments in the executive branch. In a span of a few years, Mr. McGraw III acted as chairman of the Business Roundtable, chairman of the Emergency Committee for American Trade (ECAT), board member of the US Council for International Business (USCIB), Vice-Chairman to the International Chamber of Commerce (ICC), and served as a long-time member of the Business Council. His span of elite connections through these groups place him in a unique social world, offering what Useem (1984) referred to as "business scan": that is, the capacity to perceive the interests of business not solely in terms of his own company – that is, through "company rationality" – but also through the lens of a "classwide rationality." As our network and statistical analyses explore in the aggregate, overlapping memberships in these nongovernment associations act as significant predictors for appointment to government positions. For example, Mr. McGraw served as a member of the State Department's Advisory Committee on Transformational Diplomacy and was appointed in 2009 by President Obama to serve on the top-tier of the US Trade Representative's advisory system, in the Advisory Committee for Trade Policy and Negotiations (ACTPN). In the chapters ahead, we apply a sociological approach to these corporate and state networks that draws from C. W. Mills' *Power Elite* (1956) and incorporates network analytic methodologies to explore and test the effects of corporate networks on numerous political outcomes related to trade policy.

To further illustrate the dynamics of these overlapping networks in trade policy formation, we plot a network graph of the forty-five largest ECAT members in 1998 and their connections to the Business Roundtable and to the government advisory posts on trade policy.[15] Analytically, the narrative above – including the reference to Harold McGraw III – stresses the importance of thinking about the social and political consequences of overlapping networks among corporations and their executives in the context of trade policy. Corporate policy networks that overlap with state agencies, especially the trade advisory committees created in the 1974 Trade Act, are the crux of our empirical analyses. Too often, trade policy studies fail to bring analyses of overlapping power structures to either explanatory or historical accounts of American trade politics. A better approach should draw on political theories that account for observations of overlapping networks between state and corporate arenas, relying on a relational epistemology, as found in the power structure tradition in sociology (Emirbayer 1997). Our primary theoretical argument in this book, tested in the chapters ahead, asserts that overlapping corporate networks, like the one depicted in Figure 1.2, produce social and institutional consequences that unify participants politically across organizational and institutional spaces.

For our purposes, herein lies an empirical fulcrum to explore and test assumptions about the confluence of class and state actors in the making of neoliberal trade policy in the United States. All forty-five companies in Figure 1.2 are members of the ECAT – an organization whose significance will become clearer in Chapter 4. Those companies in the lower left corner are isolates; that is, they are members of the ECAT but have no executives in either the Business Roundtable or as appointees to the trade advisory committee system in the US executive branch in 1998. Firms approximately in midsection of the figure share their common membership in ECAT with all firms in the graph, but also have a membership in the Business Roundtable *and* the trade advisory committee system, linking corporate and state institutional spaces via these overlapping memberships. Of the companies affiliated with the trade advisory system, all but four are also Business Roundtable members (in addition to their membership in ECAT). We measure the cohesiveness of this subgraph using a measure of its connectedness, which provides a weighted proportion of the pairs connected via a network path of any length.[16] The subgraph

---

[15] Note that the figure below was constructed from our 1998 data and some corporate names have changed since then. We discuss the methods for accounting for name changes and mergers in our population in Appendix 2.

[16] Each of these measures of network cohesion indicate a very well-connected graph. Density, the simplest of the measures, is the proportion of ties in the network to the total possible $[n(n-1)/2]$.

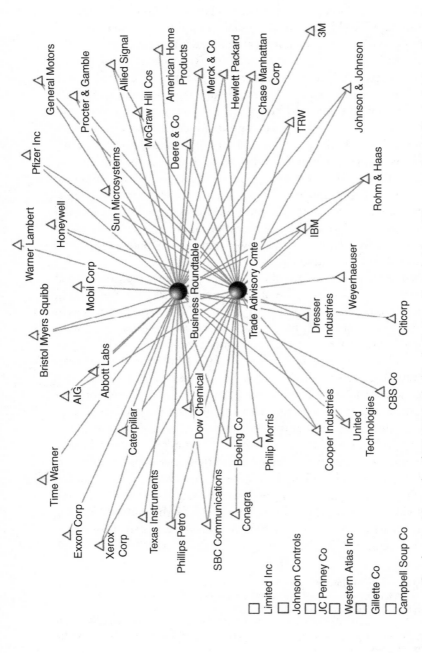

FIGURE 1.2 Overlapping Networks of ECAT Members in the Business Roundtable and Executive Branch Trade Advisory Committees, 1998

Plotted using Fruchterman-Reingold layout algorithm. **Connectedness,** *0.759;* **Compactness,** *0.396;* **Density** *0.058.*

has a connectedness score of 0.759, a compactness score of 0.396, with an average distance between nodes at 2.049 and a density of 0.058. Together, this suggests very little social distance between the parties.

This simple network heuristic identifies patterns consistent with the expectations of a class cohesion approach; that is, one that postulates that firms embedded in overlapping corporate policy planning networks exhibit greater *political unity* (Burris 2005, 2008; Domhoff 2006; Mizruchi 1992). Further, our key theoretical proposition in this book is illustrated: class-inflected corporate networks facilitate the creation of stable networks between corporate leaders and the state – networks that ultimately yield a concerted field of action responsible for the promotion of neoliberal trade policy.

To grasp this shift in trade politics, then, we must consider how the emergence of the 1974 Trade Act helped focus the political activity of large, globalizing corporations toward new structures within the state, facilitating a collaborative, class-state process of institutional change to respond to rising import competition, domestic stagflation, and declining US profitability. The passage of the 1974 Trade Act bridged new expressions of corporate policy activism with existing state projects to reform US trade policy. In doing so, it opened the possibility of fusing an agenda of trade liberalization with the incipient ideology of neoliberalism. Ultimately, it permitted highly organized corporations to forge a neoliberal trade agenda in concert with the state. On this newly minted institutional space, corporate advisors and presidential appointees established a nexus of power to pursue the work of social change, asserting – over the course of decades – a project to liberalize trade and construct multilateral market governance apparatuses that provide the skeletal structure of neoliberal globalization.

WHO RULES? A RELATIONAL INQUIRY

As the historical anecdote above suggests, new forms of corporate political action aimed at transforming US trade policy emerged in earnest during the early 1970s.[17] This was not an accident. As widely noted by

---

[17] Though it was not until the 1980s and 1990s that major transnational market governance initiatives like the NAFTA and WTO were instituted, demonstrable shifts in American trade policy began in the 1970s, particularly aggressive efforts by the United States to liberalize trade in financial services and agriculture in the Tokyo Rounds of the GATT negotiations (see Chorev 2007).

scholars and journalists, it was the early 1970s in particular when "business was learning to spend as a class" (Blyth 2002: 155; see also Akard 1992; Court 2003; Clawson, Neustadtl, and Weller 1998; Domhoff 2006; Edsall 1985; Harvey 2005; Peschek 1987). Well-funded think tanks, new corporate advocacy groups, targeted endowments to universities, and other activities characterized a well-documented push-back from corporate America, one that increasingly chimed the chords of deregulation, free trade, and shrinking the welfare state. The American Enterprise Institute (AEI) – a neoliberal think tank – rose to new prominence on the right just as the Business Roundtable shaped a new corporate political center, displacing the moderate-leaning Committee for Economic Development (CED) as the hub for domestic economic policy discussions. The reaction to the 1960s by economic conservatives was brash. Mizruchi (2013) and others have described this important moment in corporate elite history, a moment whose essence is well summarized by Justice Lewis Powell's "confidential" memo to the US Chamber of Commerce, which urged business to fight back against "The Attack on the Free Enterprise System":

the time has come – indeed, it is long overdue – for the wisdom, ingenuity and resources of American business to be marshaled against those who would destroy it ... independent and uncoordinated activity by individual corporations, as important as this is, will not be sufficient. Strength lies in organization, in careful long-range planning and implementation, in consistency of action over an indefinite period of years, in the scale of financing available only through joint effort, and in the political power available only through united action and national organizations (Powell 1971, confidential memo to US Chamber of Commerce).[18]

The strategic political organization of large corporations in the United States began afresh in this era, resulting in the founding of numerous bodies with lasting impact. From the conservative Heritage Foundation to the American Legislative Exchange Council, the population of corporate funded organizations made a well-documented rightward shift (Domhoff 2006; Mizruchi 2013; Peschek 1987). Most significantly for our research was the founding in 1972 of the Business Roundtable (BRT). Distinct in form and function from earlier corporate policy bodies, the BRT, as *Business Week* declared in 1976, acts as "business' most powerful lobby in Washington." As former chair of the Business Council, Edmund

---

[18] See historian Phillips-Fein (2009) for an extended discussion of Lewis Powell and his interpersonal networks. The full memo was cited from the online document, www.greenpeace.org/usa/en/campaigns/global-warming-and-energy/polluterwatch/The-Lewis-Powell-Memo/, accessed May 10, 2011.

Littlefield stated, "we leave the advocacy work to the Business Roundtable" (Edsall 1985:120–121).

According to Burris (1992a; 2008), the BRT remains the most central policy and lobbying organization in the corporate policy network. Indeed, the creation of the BRT marked an event of historic proportions, analogous to the role of the Business Council, the CED, and the Council on Foreign Relations (CFR) during the interwar years. Rather than adhering to Keynesian strategies of macro-economic regulation, the BRT endures as a tireless advocate of neoliberal strategies of market deregulation domestically, and free trade globally. As is detailed in later chapters, corporate policy organizations like the BRT played a pivotal role in promoting and defending a free trade policy agenda. Our statistical and network analyses validate their significance in trade policy and paint a portrait where membership in these groups significantly raises the likelihood of corporate activism in the policy-making centers of the state.

Given the trajectory of corporate political action in the 1970s and the broad push for trade liberalization, this book incorporates the tenets of a class cohesion model of corporate influence into a study of global trade politics. Mizruchi (1982) and Useem (1984) articulate these tenets quite well. While the corporation remains the primary site of action and decision making for a wide range of matters, the twentieth century witnessed an "institutionalization of intercorporate relations" (Mizruchi 1982: 187), such that the "transcorporate network becomes a quasi-autonomous actor in its own right" (Useem 1984: 195). Via board interlocks, extensive policy planning memberships, and direct participation in government policy making, highly networked corporate leaders exert a unique form of political influence in modern political processes. This "institutional capitalism" generates the capacity for classwide politics as a result of the social and political practices of an elite corporate "inner circle." Recent research on intercorporate networks and their political influence abounds, ranging from studies of an incipient transnational capitalist class to more traditional studies of corporate elite in specific policy projects, campaign expenditures, and lobbying (Burris 2008; Carroll 2004; Clawson, Neustadtl, and Weller 1998; Dreiling and Darves 2011; Moore, Sobieraj, Whitt, Mayorova, and Beaulieu 2002; Prechel 2000). Though some research suggests a decline in the cohesion of the corporate board network (Davis and Mizruchi 1999; Mizruchi 2013), other policy-planning and lobbying networks among corporate elite remain robust, dense, and cohesive during the time period where corporate board networks appear to be softening, or perhaps globalizing (Burris 2005, 2008; Carroll 2010; Dreiling and Darves 2011; Peoples

2006; Staples 2006). The empirical models in this book test the relative role of board of director networks, policy planning, campaign spending, and lobbying associations on three dimensions of corporate political unity, offering a much needed data-centered update to these questions.

We employ the network-analytic tools found in power structure research to illuminate the role of class agency in the development of neoliberal trade policy in the United States. From the passage of the North American Free Trade Agreement, to permanent normalization of trade relations (PNTR) with China, large corporations have played a consistent and observable role in the formation and passage of all recent trade initiatives of import. Thus, the general, motivating question of this book asks: *Do corporate networks facilitate class-embedded associations across policy events – and channel the resources of large US companies toward common, strategically defined political agendas within the state that advance the institutional conditions for neoliberal globalization?*

This question intersects a number of important theoretical issues in the social sciences. In particular, the degree to which the superior *economic* resources of corporations can be translated into *political* power has been the subject of much debate. While considerable division on this question remains, most analysts concede that corporate political power is greatly enhanced when corporations pursue their political objectives in concert with other companies (e.g., by contributing to the same political candidates or by joining the same business advocacy groups). By the same logic, as Mizruchi (1992) and others have demonstrated, corporate political power is diminished when firms pursue their political goals through competing strategies; that is, when business is politically fragmented.

In this study, our focus is on *objective* political cohesion among corporations, as opposed to economic or ideological motivations that may animate a *specific* firm's political behavior. This is an important distinction because it shifts our focus from *why* corporations act in a certain way politically to *whether and under what conditions* corporations engage the policy formation processes or display unified political behavior (Mizruchi 1992).[19] Business unity – as an outcome, in itself, to be explained – is an

---

[19] Mizruchi (1992) formulates an "objective" measure of corporate ties both because subjective motivating factors are difficult to observe and, more significantly, it is the *ties* themselves that create the social consequences of unity, regardless of the initial motivation for taking part in those associations.

important area for continued sociological inquiry, mainly because the effects of relatively unified corporate political action weigh heavy on democracy, regardless of the particular motive a single firm brings to the larger class effort.

Historical conditions vary sufficiently to warrant a theoretical framework that accounts for the contingencies that impact corporate political unity and disunity. Prechel (2000) elaborated an historical contingency model in his capital dependence theory. Briefly, Prechel argues that the political unity of corporations manifests contingently as class political action under historical conditions where economic crises impact a wide segment of capital. Because the social conditions for capital accumulation vary by sector, economic crises are not always uniform and may generate competing interests among class segments. But when economic conditions substantially affect capital accumulation, political divisions among business are overcome in new forms of class cohesion. The crisis in profitability in the American economy in the early 1970s is one example. Here, ample research documents a corporate mobilization to roll back taxes, wages, and social welfare in order to reduce costs and boost net revenue. Trade policy, in this case, was simply one (albeit very important) facet of these changes.

To be sure, the neoliberal rearrangement of capital on a global scale over several decades – together with the creation of institutions like the World Trade Organization or the NAFTA as methods to stabilize capital accumulation – did not happen automatically or without considerable planning. What actors fueled this transformation and how? Where did the NAFTA or the WTO come from? A fair amount of attention across a range of social science and theory – from geography and anthropology to political economy and sociology – has addressed these questions with the obvious assertion that state actors moved free trade policy. Our account expands on this by identifying concrete institutional channels by which *class* actors – not as abstract capital, but as concrete political agents – exerted unparalleled influence over US trade policy, particularly with investment rules, tariffs, and property rights. This research does not claim to identify the specific motives that animated individual corporate actors, but instead focuses on the genesis of concerted corporate unity in US trade policy over several years, from NAFTA (1993) to the Central American Free Trade Agreement (CAFTA).[20] During these years, a highly

---

[20] Throughout the book, we will denote the Dominican Republic–Central American Free Trade Agreement as CAFTA.

organized segment of the United States' largest corporations did act, in concert, to politically reshape the world. In addition, a neoliberal ideology framed the appeals of these corporate actors – in their public relations campaigns, their concerted and coordinated testimonies in Congress, and in their formal input to the US Trade Representative and Secretary of Commerce – and served as a rationale for action. This ideology, we posit, can only be understood within a historical context where the interests and political capabilities of corporate (class) actors are fused with a narrative of the free market that intersects with the real conditions of labor, commerce, and capital accumulation.

The theoretical context of this project can thus be located in two sociological problems: (1) elite power and its influence on democratic processes in the United States (cf. Domhoff 1967; Hunter 1953; Mills 1956; see also Dahl 1961); and (2) the indirect and direct roles played by class actors in advancing the transnational market governance institutions that form the backdrop of neoliberal globalization.

DATA AND ANALYSIS, IN BRIEF

Our research draws on scholarly arguments (Blythe 2002; Harvey 2005) that emphasize the important historical role of neoliberalism as an economic ideology and political initiative, one that arises in concert with the heightened mobility of capital globally and has supported the restructuring of many economies from the 1970s to present. We go further, however, in our identification of a specific empirical problem that allows us to assess the sources of intercorporate political unity as a conceptual anchor to larger questions about the capacity of large corporations to act as class actors – working in concert with state actors – to shape the policy frameworks that undergird neoliberal free trade policies. A central contribution of this research stems from the original data and the use of the most current tools for network analysis. Unlike most social science approaches to institutions and historical change, our data and methodology situates the actions of corporations, policy makers, and government agencies in a web of measured relationships. This type of network-focused investigation is well suited to the combination of statistical analysis and historical narrative that form the center of this book, from confirmatory testing to graph theoretic heuristics that describe the extremely large numbers of relationships (over 200,000) present within a web of political and historical change.

The empirical body of this book is framed by nesting a historical narrative in a quantitative analysis of corporate involvement in government policy-making environments related to a series of major trade initiatives in the United States. Illuminating the rise and passage of recent international trade deals, our historical narrative contextualizes a rigorous quantitative operationalization of corporate trade policy activism. These include the 1991–1994 initiative for the NAFTA, the 1994–1995 conclusion of the Uruguay Rounds (and the creation of the World Trade Organization), the 1998–1999 campaign to establish "Permanent Normal Trade Relations" with China, and, finally, the 2003–2006 initiative for a Central American Free Trade Agreement (CAFTA). Archival data and two original data sets provide a unique perspective on the ties between large American corporations and two branches of US government throughout these processes of erecting trade governance structures.

Rather than focus exclusively on the policy process or on single trade policy events, as is common practice in trade policy studies, we look at the series of trade agreements as moments within a larger historical process of trade liberalization. These path-dependent outcomes, from NAFTA to CAFTA, reveal aspects of the world-historical patterns of neoliberal globalization. Our quantitative analyses of corporate support for trade liberalization policies are thus nested within a larger historical argument, drawing analytically from historical sociology (Griffin 1993; Mahoney 2000; McMichael 1990). Our quantitative methodology uses two sets of data that cover three related periods of trade policy in the United States, including four cases of trade policy. The first taps into the corporate campaign to pass the North American Free Trade Agreement, 1991–1993. The second data set is a more comprehensive compilation of data tracing corporate involvement in trade policy in two time periods (1998 and 2003, including congressional testimony and public relations data into 2005) and captures corporate political behavior, individually and collectively, across three distinct political settings: (1) testimony before Congress at international trade policy hearings, (2) participation in temporary business alliances that promote trade policy initiatives such as NAFTA, and (3) policy consultation to the government through influential federal advisory committees. Together, these data are the most comprehensive accounts of corporate involvement in the formation and passage of US trade policies to date.

Answers to the core questions arise by analyzing corporate political action in two distinct ways. At the firm level, various organizational and network determinants of corporate *participation* in trade policy formation and advocacy are analyzed. At the dyadic (paired) level, our analysis models the organizational and network determinants of corporate *political unity*.[21] Corporate political action and the similarity of political action are modeled in three domains of the trade policy arena: (1) congressional testimony at US trade policy hearings 1993–2004, (2) participation in temporary trade policy alliances, and (3) common participation in government trade policy advisory committees.

These three political settings measure corporate political behavior in a number of institutional spheres, from industry alliances in Washington, DC, to executive branch consultation and congressional testimony. Drawing hypotheses from economics, sociology, and political science, our research models "organizational" and "class cohesive" predictors of corporate involvement, individually and collectively, in each of these three political settings. Organizational variables measure the influence of *firm* characteristics, such as product market, geographic location, subsidiary operations globally, capital intensity, and size, on political behavior. Network variables, by comparison, measure firm *relations* to outside companies through, for example, shared directors (board interlocks), participation in prominent policy groups, and the formation of temporary political alliances.

The organizational and network attributes of these firms contrast two (generally construed) explanatory models of corporate political behavior, "atomistic" and "structural." Atomistic models, usually associated with interest group theories of corporate political action, focus on the attributes of corporations – without reference to the constraints and opportunities created by outside actors – to explain political behavior. Structural or relational models common in class cohesion theories, in contrast, highlight how the *relations* between and among corporations generate political and institutional isomorphism. While both structural and atomistic perspectives (typically) assume that organizational self-interest influences firm political behavior (Mizruchi 1992), the atomistic approach also assumes that actors evaluate choices independent from one another, without reference to other actors (Burt 1983a). The structural perspective views this assumption as both problematic and limiting, and argues that the decisions made by actors are influenced by social structural constraints.

While the focus of this book is on the *structural* factors that influence corporate political behavior, it should be noted that we are not claiming

---

[21] Dyads refer to pairs of corporations (see Mizruchi 1992). Variable construction, data sources, and sampling procedures are outlined in greater detail in Chapter 4.

that the organizational factors highlighted by atomistic interest group perspectives are unimportant to corporate political behavior. In fact, the hypothesized predictors of firm-centered explanatory models often reinforce the structural perspective (Mizruchi 1992). Neither the atomistic nor the network-structural approach alone provides a comprehensive account of corporate political behavior. The perspective advocated here postulates that both intra- and interorganizational dynamics give shape to corporate political behavior and govern the potential to act in concert, as a class force.

To summarize, our research offers new data and vistas for two important areas of social science research. First, comparatively little research analyzes the trade policy activism of the protagonists of neoliberal globalization, the large multinational corporation. Likewise, in the fields of economics and international relations, much of the extant trade policy literature focuses on how *state* actors respond to the amorphous "constraints" imposed by international markets, such as by promoting trade regimes that protect foreign investment and minimize international transactions costs (Destler 2005; Krueger 1995; Rodrik 1997). In much of this literature, trade policy is thought to be outside the scope of traditional interest group politics because, for historical reasons tracing back to the 1934 Reciprocal Trade Agreements Act, it is generated by "autonomous" executive branch actors (Chorev 2007; Woods 2003). The focus on state actors also follows from the common assumption that business is intensely divided on trade policy issues. While there is some historical evidence to support this assumption (cf. Bauer, Pool, and Dexter 1972), much of this evidence is based on an earlier period in US economic history, when big business was palpably divided into "internationalist" and "domestic" producer segments (Woods 2003).

This research also makes a unique contribution to the literature on interfirm networks and corporate political activism (Domhoff 2006; Mintz and Schwartz 1985; Mizruchi 1992; Useem 1984). Although a number of important sociological studies have analyzed the political behavior of large corporations, much of this research uses cross-sectional firm- and executive-level data from the 1970s and 1980s. In addition, many of these studies focus, primarily, on certain segments of big business, such as banks (Mintz and Schwartz 1985) or manufacturing enterprises (Mizruchi 1992). One of the contributions of our research is that it integrates a variety of data sources to study firms from an array of sectors during three time periods, 1993, 1998, and 2003. Although the structure of our data does not constitute a time series, we are nonetheless able to model some aspects of time dependency in the dependent variables, strengthening causal inference.

In summary, our specific empirical problem allows us to develop a multicausal explanation for the sources of political unity among large corporations as a conceptual anchor to larger questions about the capacity of large corporations, in concert with state actors, to initiate collective political action and shape the trade policies that undergird the turn to neoliberal globalization.

OUTLINE OF CHAPTERS

The organization of this book is presented in seven chapters. Chapter 2 situates our argument in the sociological literature concerned with corporate political action and influence. We engage the epistemological frameworks that underlie much of the theoretical tensions in this literature. Within this literature review, we identify two broadly defined explanatory models to guide this study: atomistic and relational – or class cohesion – theories of corporate political action. From that literature, a theory of class agency is presented.

In Chapter 2, our focus links theories of corporate political action to political-economic and institutional theories of trade policy and global capitalism, offering a critical sociology of trade policy. Therein we propose a framework for assessing the relationship of corporate political unity and class agency within the historically and institutionally specific channels of trade policy making. Building on trade policy literature and incorporating insights from theories of global capitalism (Carroll 2004; Robinson 2000; Sklair 2000, 2002), we argue that a focus on explaining transnational institutions should not abandon class political agency at the level of national states. Instead, our data and analyses unveil mechanisms through which corporate class agency works in concert with state actors to construct the transnational institutions that enable the "transnational practices" that Sklair describes to unfold. In the course of developing this argument, we review the literature on US trade politics and globalization. Several shortcomings in the literature are then considered, especially pertaining to its explanation of *corporate* involvement in trade policy formation. Briefly, our argument is that, whereas corporations are *assumed* to be important actors in nearly all accounts of trade politics and economic globalization, very little research adequately conceptualizes the mechanisms of corporate influence over the policy-formation process. Further, an adequate conceptualization of corporations as collective political agents of globalization is absent in historical accounts of the emergence of neoliberal globalization. This shortcoming in the literature, we argue, can be traced to the preponderance of atomistic organizational theories in the social sciences (as reviewed in Chapter 2), particularly in the interest group theories of corporate trade policy action. Building on this literature review, the final section of Chapter 3 develops several testable hypotheses that are examined in Chapters 5 and 6. These chapters explore individual and collective corporate activism in the trade policy arena, with particular attention to the class-based modes of corporate association and political power.

Chapter 4, "Forging a neoliberal trade policy network, 1967–1994," advances an historical argument concerning the emergence of a corporate "neoliberal trade policy network" aimed at transforming US trade policy, one that would culminate not only with the World Trade Organization, but with the permanent normalization of free trade with China. A fresh account of a common story told about trade politics is presented. We bring new focus to the founding of the ECAT and the overlap of their leadership in both the Johnson and Nixon administration's trade and commerce appointees. Twenty years later, ECAT, the BRT, and a few others are heavily involved in the trade policy apparatus of the Bush and Clinton administrations during the NAFTA campaign. Network heuristics are presented that illuminate the interorganizational characteristics of numerous business policy organizations in the NAFTA (1994) campaign, highlighting the network structure of key corporate policy organizations as they interface with key appointments and decision-making events in the US trade policy system. This historical network argument substantiates a key theoretical supposition proposed in Chapter 3: that the advance of neoliberal globalization cannot be adequately explained without attention to the class political agency of large US corporations engaged in multidecade trade policy activism. From this historical narrative, the 1960s conflicts between industries challenged with steep import competition (steel and textiles) and globalizing industries in electronics and finance reveal an intraclass dispute in which corporate leaders advanced free trade over protectionism. A new set of priorities among corporate elite took shape in this era, *forging a new coalition* of class political leaders around the deregulatory and supply-side demands of corporate conservatives with the free trade ambitions of CEOs at globalizing corporations. Neoliberalism took shape as both domestic and global policy initiatives, fusing free trade and domestic deregulation. Given this historical context, we explain why a robust network model of corporate political action can help answer questions about class agency and the dynamics of class-state relations in a changing world system. Origins of the US trade advisory system and corporate groups with lasting influence are intertwined ever since 1967–1974. Later, a historical network analysis of corporate leaders reveals a close institutional overlap among corporate members in the Trade Advisory Committees to the President and those corporate leaders that mobilized to defend the NAFTA (1991–1994). These arguments substantiate a series of statistical tests presented in Chapters 5 and 6. Specific methods for analyzing the quantitative data are discussed in Appendices 1 and 2.

Chapter 5, "Inside the state: corporate participation in trade policy," presents the results of several models of firm-level *participation* in trade policy formation and advocacy. We build from the Chapter 4's historical and network narrative of corporate political action in the campaign for NAFTA with our second data set, introducing several models of corporate participation in trade policy making around the WTO (1995), China PNTR (1999), and CAFTA (2005). Grouping firms at the two-digit industry code level, organizational, political, and network sources of participation are examined in three hierarchical nonlinear models (HNLMs). Unlike previous studies of corporate policy activism, which group firms from an array of industries within a single model, the application of HNLMs allow us to model participation such that each industry has a unique mean affiliation level (intercept). Membership in prominent policy groups, temporary trade policy alliances, board interlocks, PAC expenditures, and firm size all positively correlate with the odds of firm participation in the advisory committees.

Chapter 6, "Fusing Class Agency to a State Trade Policy Apparatus," presents a model of dyadic corporate political unity in the trade policy arena. Unlike Chapter 5, the unit of analysis becomes *all possible dyadic* relations within the network, and the outcome is not participation by single firms per se but the political unity of pairs within the group. This stochastic network approach has the advantage of allowing for a more granular specification of shared corporate ties, for example, through direct *and* indirect board interlocks or involvement in specific policy organizations. Results from these analyses largely confirm the main hypotheses presented in Chapter 3: ties through board interlocks and policy organizations significantly influence corporate political behavior across the three distinct political environments, even when controlling for organizational factors. These class-based networks among corporations prove to be very influential in unifying large corporations as they advocate for changes to US trade policy. An extended discussion of those results serves for a revisit of theories concerning the role of class actors in shaping the institutional framework of neoliberal globalization.

Chapter 7 concludes the book with a discussion of the main findings and argues for a robust theory of class agency to account for the political construction of neoliberal trade institutions. A return to our theoretical argument for class agency specifies how corporate political unity, measured as objective relationships between firms engaged in shared political aims, activates the latent class power of an intercorporate network amid the transformation of global capitalism. This framework clarifies the historical roles of state and corporate actors involved in shaping the institutions of neoliberal globalization. Given the historical argument advanced, we consider the role of national-level class networks as a necessary precondition for deepening transnational capitalist class networks.

2

Corporate Political Unity and Class Agency

> For they are in command of the major hierarchies and organizations of modern society. They rule the big corporations. They run the machinery of the state and claim its prerogatives.
>
> – C.W. Mills, *The Power Elite* (1956: 3–4)

SOURCES OF INTERCORPORATE UNITY

For most of the twentieth century, the political behavior of large corporations fascinated social scientists and political observers. This interest produced an impressive array of scholarly literature on corporate power, class organization, and the nature of the state. Very important strands of political theory orbit around the question of whether or not moments of organized corporate unity reflect modes of class formation and cohesion or indicate a coincidence of otherwise competing economic interests manifest as political pressure groups. This rather simple juxtaposition, whether intercorporate unity forms as a result of class-based modes of association or forms as a convergence of issue-based interests, has tremendous theoretical as well as political importance. When unified, the resources of large corporations (and business more generally) have the potential to dominate the state and crowd out other societal interests. For this reason, the type and extent of corporate political unity occupy the center of theoretical questions relating to democracy and modern states. Are there accounts of corporate political unity that can answer questions about the political role of large corporations in shaping the institutions of neoliberal trade and globalization?

Assuming that state actors (and technocrats) play an authoritative role in the making of neoliberal trade policy is not too contentious. Government officials, economists, and others played important and strategic parts in the major trade policy initiatives that are explored in Chapters 5 and 6. Because corporate collective action remains largely invisible in accounts of neoliberal institution-building, our primary challenge lies in specifying a theoretical framework that accounts for the repeated observations of extensive business involvement in US trade policy. To bring corporate political action from the shadow of explanations of neoliberal trade and globalization, some interrogation of common assumptions about business political action is necessary. For this reason, explorations of organizational theories of corporations lie ahead, identifying distinctions between a view of corporations through an atomistic lens – as isolated entities pursuing specific company interests in a market – versus a structural lens that considers the interconnected and overlapping interests of corporations. While the structural framework does not in itself depict class actors, the interconnected context of corporate political action, as demonstrated in research, does. Throughout this chapter, our intention is twofold: first, to consider how contrasting theoretical perspectives suggest different operational factors that drive the political interests and behavior of corporations in the modern world, and second, how existing literature supports a theory of class political agency within the context of trade policy.

WHEN CORPORATIONS ARE NOT A CLASS: THE ATOMISTIC PERSPECTIVE

In the early 1900s, the US economy was dominated by handful of large corporations, whereas only a few decades earlier most US firms tended to be small, operating in fiercely competitive, low-margin industries. As Berle (1952: 25) notes, during the first half of the twentieth century as few as 135 firms controlled 45 percent of all US industrial assets and accounted for nearly 25 percent of *global* manufacturing volume. According to Lamoreaux (1985: 87), this transformation from small to large producers occurred as "manufacturers formed consolidations to escape the severe price competition that developed during the depression of the [eighteen] nineties in certain types of industries: capital intensive, mass-production industries in which firms were closely matched and in which expansion had been active." As a result of these mergers, large, mass-production firms became increasingly central to capitalist industrial development in the United States. In tandem with their impressive economic power, these corporate titans also came to dominate American politics.

On the political front, these economic changes led many to question whether the political influence of business would be greatly increased by market concentration. Several, such as Dahrendorf (1959), Domhoff (1967), and Mills (1956), argued that the goliath firms that emerged from the merger wave could support historically unparalleled levels of political coordination; in effect, they reflected a new mode of class formation and power. Conversely, Berle (1952) contended that the disunification of the capitalist class following the separation of ownership from control had lasting impact on organizational behavior; specifically, strategic objectives that followed the logic and needs of a firm's primary market(s) would take precedence over the interests of any "capitalist class" or groupings of individual capitalists. A consistent point of debate was the impact, organizationally, of stock dilution and the rise of a professional managerial class. Dahrendorf (1959 [1994]: 82–83) succinctly expressed what became perhaps the majority viewpoint when he wrote that the "roles of owner and manager, originally combined in the position of the capitalist, have been separated and distributed over two positions, those of stock holder and executive." This understanding of large corporations supported a more general understanding of firms as both isolated (from other firms) and controlled, primarily, by a professional managerial class. Consequently, companies were now seen as largely autonomous from certain outside influences that once dominated their operational processes (e.g., bank indebtedness, family ownership, and independent producer suppliers/distributors) (Berle 1952; Chandler 1977; Dahl 1970; Galbraith 1971).

Though perhaps not the primary focus of this literature on firm control, these general claims about manager-run corporations actually supported a "pluralist" view of the state, because it was argued that the power of capitalists, and their raw economic interests, could no longer be easily unified politically given the tremendous power of inward-focused, non-owning corporate managers. Ostensibly, the ascendant managerial class would anchor the firm in long-run strategic objectives, increase productive efficiency, and enhance the overall welfare of society. Berle (1952: 28), writing years after he co-authored *The Modern Corporation and Private Property*, echoed this view:

The mid-twentieth-century American capitalist system depends on and revolves around the operation of a relatively few very large corporations. It pivots upon industries most of which are concentrated in the hands of extremely few corporate units. Materially, the community has profited mightily. The system of large-scale production and mass-distribution carried on by means of these large institutions can fairly claim the greatest share of credit. The face of the country has been changed. Poverty, in the sense that it is understood elsewhere in the world, in America is reduced to minimal proportions.

Given the tremendous influence of Berle and Mean's (1932) thesis, later inquiries – even critical and Marxist studies – had a similar tendency to conceptualize corporate influence as a product of firms pursuing their specific company interests (Baran and Sweezy 1966; Dahl 1967; Galbraith 1971). On balance, this implied that researchers directed little attention to extrinsic structural factors influencing corporations within the larger intercorporate context. While Berle (1952: 20) acknowledged that large firms exert considerable noncoordinated influence on "small businessmen," little attention was given to the *relations* among the largest corporations and, by implication, the ongoing potential for class-oriented political associations and power.

As Mizruchi and Schwartz persuasively argue (1987: 4), this "managerial thesis" effectively provided historical justification – by social scientists no less – for a weak corporate elite and a politically innocuous view of the corporation; that is, a view that conceptualized firms as relatively isolated, competing units. The central tenet of this burgeoning perspective – that large corporations are invulnerable to major external constraints – became a key underlying assumption that, in turn, shaped many strands of political *and* organizational theory (ibid.).

However, while this atomistic conceptualization of firms – common among economists and managerialists – may have described some producers well, several theorists argued that such a perspective was not applicable to the large, complex organizations that came to dominate US capitalism (Burt 1983b; Mizruchi 1982; Zeitlin 1974). Of particular interest, the impact of relational variables (social ties, interlocks, etc.) on corporate governance and political action was generally ignored by the managerialists (Domhoff 1978; Mintz and Schwartz 1985; Mizruchi 1982). Zeitlin's (1974) analysis of ownership and control proved a decisive turning point. He showed that the major shareholders of large corporations, though no longer composed primarily of wealthy individuals or families, were now simply banks and insurance companies. Moreover, the composition of corporate boards reflected those financial interests much more so than the non-owning managers. Hence, Zeitlin (ibid.) and other critics of the kind of atomistic approach central to the managerialist perspective identified several ways in which much of the existing literature had failed to assess the complex relationships that impact the behavior and structure of large corporations.

In response to this debate, and with added clarification on the limits of managerial autonomy, two distinct strands of research concerning class, corporate elite, and corporate governance developed from the mid-1970s onward. The first strand expanded on Zeitlin (1974) and continued to focus on the relationship between ownership and the controlling influence of *external* shareholders on corporate management – the issue of control, particularly by the financial sector. Another related approach arose from the power elite tradition that was building momentum in the wake of C.W. Mills's (1956) influential work, *The Power Elite*, which was published not long before his untimely death in 1962. Within the latter framework, a structural approach to the study of elites developed among New Left intellectuals who then paved the way for an explicitly network approach to corporate power in the United States, one that expanded the scope of inquiry beyond board interlocks to the policy and political behavior of corporations. Thus, as the debate about managerial control shifted to questions of *intercorporate* governance and control, a structural network approach was needed to assess further questions about the collective political power of corporations and what would, today, be termed "the one percent." Rising from this debate, a "power structure" approach established a firm-centered alternative to the managerial and pluralist models of corporations and corporate elite. But first, before we turn to these approaches, we examine where the literature went by adopting a structural analysis of corporate control with an increasingly sophisticated approach to studying board of director interlocks.

EMERGENCE OF A STRUCTURAL PERSPECTIVE ON CORPORATE CONTROL: BOARD INTERLOCKS

During the nineteenth and early twentieth centuries, board interlocks were rampant in the corporate community. When families owned a controlling interest in a given firm, it was common to fill the majority of board positions with family members (Domhoff 1990: 40). Likewise, many of these family-dominated enterprises were highly interlocked with outside firms that, in turn, were similarly dominated by individuals either from their own or another wealthy family. The merger wave of 1895–1904 transformed the positional bases of familial dominance within the US economy and brought large banks and trusts into the center of the conversation (Mizruchi 1982). Mizruchi (1992) and Scott (1997) reference the Congressional Pujo Committee, which was set up in 1912 to examine how the influence of banks and large trusts undermined market competition. This was the first reference to an interlocking board of directors in the United States. Interestingly, this report and its conclusions resonated with the Marxist theory of financial control that was emerging at that time.

Several theorists contend that in addition to transforming ownership structures within large corporations, the merger movement of 1895–1904 reconfigured the structure of relations among firms within the corporate community (Domhoff 1990: 40–43; Mizruchi 1982; Useem 1984). Early twentieth-century Marxists identified this major transformation in capitalism, and Hilferding's *Finance Capital* (1981 [1910]), in particular, served as a precursor to later analyses – including Lenin's (1916) – linking finance to monopolization. New attention was placed on the role of banking and family trust companies, where the boards and interests of leading capitalists converged with the ongoing concentration of industrial and financial capital. Hilferding's analysis provided a theoretical framework that explained this new corporate structure. The primary shareholders of capital in the financial system, as individuals, families, holding companies, and so on, also served as directors and executives in the largest financial institutions. In this way – that is, by controlling the system of credit – financial capitalists could coordinate and control wide sectors of the corporate world with their extensive network of board interlocks.

Eventually, the process of economic consolidation in many early twentieth-century industries fundamentally altered the function and discretionary quality of the corporate board; they became, as Domhoff (1990:36) argues, apparatuses that embodied "the intersection of organized bureaucracies and social classes." Elite corporate executives were increasingly selected on the basis of criteria other than family of origin, and functioned less *qua* arbiter of familial interests (in terms of the protection of family property and the increase of its profits) and increasingly as an institutional representative explicitly directed toward the needs of the organization. Through these revolutions in corporate culture, norms geared to the protection of the "organization" as an entity, indeed as a "person" in its own right, became the primary facet of managerial duty (Fligstein 1990; Mills 1956; see also Coleman 1982). Useem (1979) argued that under this organizational climate, firms increasingly came to function as meritocracies, where one's family of origin as a basis for occupational advancement began to decline in importance relative to education and employment history. With advances in formal network methodology, analyses using corporate board interlock data were applied to explore the implications of these transformations.

What became apparent through network analyses was that managerial reorganization, though historically important, did *not* remove the pervasiveness of interfirm ties that first developed through familial directorship networks. In fact, even though families became a less significant nodal attribute within the overall network, the "reach" of a typical firm (i.e., the extent to which it is connected to other firms through a formalized relationship) was remarkably stable over time (Bunting 1983; Mizruchi 1982). However, the overall density of the corporate network (in terms of the total number of existing connections) declined abruptly during the twentieth century (Mizruchi 1992: 63). As Mizruchi (1992) notes, the decline in network density was largely a result of fewer individuals occupying positions on six or more board positions. Given that most corporations maintained at least one interlock with firms to which they previously had many connections, researchers concluded that the effects of family ownership on interlock density had become less significant, although their institutional function – as conduits of information and resources – was most likely maintained. Did the mid-century transformations change the system of financial control?

Pressing questions remained and Marxist analysts led the way. Baran and Sweezy (1968: 30), for example, expanded on Sweezy's earlier research to explain how several firms could come under "common control" when power is exercised through a financial institution *or* a "family fortune." Sweezy's (1953) research identified the first large-scale network of "interest groups" among the largest American corporations. This study and related strands of research reinforced a theory of financial control, prompting a range of further research on interlocking directorates and bank control of nonfinancial corporations (see Mintz and Schwartz 1985; Glasberg 1987). Zeitlin's (1974: 1107) seminal research on this subject, discussed earlier, demonstrated that proprietary ownership is not essential to exert considerable influence on the actions taken by a firm. Mizruchi (1982: 30), too, acknowledged the legal separation of ownership from control and challenged the hypothesis that a legal separation would ensure corporate autonomy from markets, banks, and other firms.

Impressive international investigations on corporate interlocks began by the late 1970s and established a social science framework that linked innovations in network methodology with structural analyses of corporate control. John Scott (1979; 1991) is among a group of European scholars whose work addressed questions of control through a structural lens, positing that "control through a constellation of interests" enabled otherwise dispersed ownership to influence decision making on the boards of large publicly traded corporations in the United States and UK. For decades, his network approach set a new bar for the study of corporate elite, class, and corporate power. Scott (1997:15) argued that industrial capitalist societies moved from "personal to impersonal forms of ownership and control ... structured largely through an impersonal system of finance capital." His work established an empirically grounded critical framework for thinking about how the financial control of large shareholders (through financial or family fortunes) produce direct control over board decisions.

Scott's most recent work, with Murray (Murray and Scott 2012), applies his broad network conceptualizations of corporate relations to research on a transnational corporate class, a research initiative that originated among a group of European scholars. Along with John Scott, Frans Stokman, Rolf Zeigler, Meindert Fennema, and others helped first bring a structural analysis of ownership and control of the corporate elite to several European countries and then set the foundation for researching a transnational board network. Fennema and Nijhoff's (1982) classic study set the stage for the study of transnational banking control through interlocking boards.

Empirically, the most complete treatment of the issue of financial ownership and control came in 2011, from research conducted by physicists, not social scientists. In late 2011, a group of systems analysts published a groundbreaking study of global corporate ownership, showing that "nearly 4/10 of the control over the economic value of TNCs in the world is held, via a complicated web of ownership relations, by a group of 147 TNCs in the core, which has almost full control over itself" (Vitali, Glatfelder, Battiston, and Montoya 2011: 6). This dense cluster or "super-entity" (Vitali et al. 2011) of corporate ownership is centered within the world's largest financial institutions and produces a social and organizational network that parallels the imagery presented by the Occupy Wall Street movement. The study went viral and Glatfelder has received popular and academic acclaim for this research, some of which is summarized in his "TED Talk"[1] on corporate control. Interestingly, many of the postulates raised by Fennema and Nijhoff (1982) nearly thirty years

[1] www.ted.com/talks/james_b_glattfelder_who_controls_the_world.html, accessed April 8, 2016.

earlier are validated by this big data analysis. Although Vitali et al.'s (2011) research is perhaps less theoretically grounded than this earlier work, their research provided an important boost to the expansive research underway on a transnational capitalist class. Among other things, their network approach ultimately proved helpful in empirically documenting (among tens of thousands of transnational corporations) the mechanisms in ownership relations that affect board of director decisions.

The theory of financial control remains persuasive, and recent evidence suggests that the relations between financial capital and corporate control take form in specific "variations of capitalism" (Scott 2012). Data and analyses have been gathered well into the 2000s, both nationally and transnationally (Berkowitz and Fitzgerald 1995; Carroll 2012; Mizruchi 1982; Murray 2006; Peetz and Murray 2012). While the findings of this work are generally consistent, as Scott (1991) and Scott, Stokman, and Zeigler (1985) point out, there is no universal pattern to the relation between boards and capital control beyond the British, US, and German corporate systems.[2]

The general shift from a firm-level unit of analysis to larger corporate networks encompassing hundreds of firms produced a new field of social scientific inquiry, one concerned not only with the locus of organizational control but also interdependence, corporate political behavior, and the extensive "policy network" that surrounds large firms (Domhoff 1978; Mizruchi 1992; Mizruchi and Schwartz 1987; Useem 1984). The principal tenet of this "intercorporate" perspective was that "in order to understand how businesses operate it is necessary to explore the relationships among them" (Mizruchi and Schwartz 1987: i). An important area of research that emerged from this developing perspective was the literature on "resource dependence." In continuity with earlier, atomistic models of organizational behavior, resource dependence analysts typically emphasized the "primacy" of organizational interests and rejected models that conceptualized organizations as "settings" to facilitate the interests of a broader class or group of capitalists (Pfeffer 1987: 26). That is, the resource dependence perspective posited that organizations possess a set of interests that are autonomous from the particular concerns of individuals but, crucially, *are* constrained by the actions of outside actors, such as the state. In this view, interorganizational behavior is most influenced

---

[2] Moreover, as Domhoff (1967) pointed out, the board interlock network is only one way in which the corporate rich unify and exercise political influence. In the next section, we consider the significance of the policy network on corporate class cohesion.

by "patterns of resource and transaction flows, not issues of family or class solidarity, or even managerial interests" (Pfeffer 1987: 29). As Mizruchi (1992) summarizes, the primary assertion of this perspective is that corporations operate in turbulent environments that impel them to co-opt sources of uncertainty originating outside the organization. Firms may seek to co-opt their sources of production inputs or finance through several "mediating mechanisms," such as joining the boards of the firms on which they are dependent or engaging in horizontal or vertical mergers to reduce product or factor market competition.

In a widely cited study, Burt (1983a: 9–10), for example, found evidence that corporations form various "structural bridges" (such as board interlocks) to mediate the uncertainty created by dependence on suppliers, distributors, and financial institutions (see also Mintz and Schwartz 1985; Pennings 1980: 109). Firms, according to Burt, seek to co-opt their sources of dependency for product or finance through several "mediating mechanisms," such as board interlocks, stock ownership, and horizontal or vertical mergers. Developing a measure of "market constraint,"[3] Burt (1983a: 45), for example, found that "the crucial determinant of an industry's profit margin is the extent to which supplies are purchased from establishments in many sectors of the economy. To the extent that establishments in an industry purchased supplies from a single sector ... their industry had a low profit margin."[4]

This research, while significant (in particular, for its methodological sophistication), was mostly silent about the nature, scope, and efficacy of corporate political behavior. Yet large firms, particularly since the 1970s, became an indisputably central part of the US policy formation process. As Mizruchi (1992) postulated, what was needed was a multilevel model to assess the *specific conditions* under which elements of social structure can be shown to influence the political and economic behavior of large

---

[3] "Market constraint" is a measure of the dependence of one industry on another for sales or purchases, weighted by the concentration of the latter.
[4] A related study by Pfeffer and Salancik (1978: 166) examined the use of board interlocks as a mechanism to reduce competitive uncertainty and found that "the amount of interlocking is positively related to the level of [industry] concentration, and negatively related to the difference in concentration from an intermediate [interlocked] level." This finding, they argued, suggests that higher levels of industry concentration increase the market power that intermediate suppliers can exert on their customers. To maintain organizational autonomy, firms join the boards of input suppliers to stabilize transactions and minimize market constraint. Pennings (1980: 157) similarly found that several proxies for "organizational effectiveness," such as return on assets and price earnings ratios, were positively correlated with the number of interlocks a firm had to financial institutions.

corporations. His research (ibid.; 1982), as well as work by Useem (1979) and Zeitlin (1974), went far toward disproving the idea that large firms are not influenced by their social, economic, and political associations with both other companies and the government. Much of this research attributed great importance to the controlling function of company boards of directors and, in particular, board interlocks formed among large firms – even as board of director control was increasingly transferred from owners to managers. It was argued that intercorporate networks of overlapping directorships are both a source of organizational power and the result of operational constraints imposed by outside firms. These networks among large corporations, as Useem (1979) would aptly portray, integrate executives across multiple boards, creating the basis for a shared social perspective: a "classwide rationality" that emerges from a large yet logical "transcorporate network."

Although the resource-dependence perspective marked a considerable advance in organization theory, it has often been criticized for its limited specification of the social processes by which proxies for "embeddedness," such as interlocking directorates, intervene to influence organizational behavior (see Mizruchi 1996: 288–295 for a review of this literature). For example, it is often unclear whether interlocks created for co-optative purposes (such as loans and inputs of production) originate from the supplier or the customer.[5] Others argued that board interlocks embody complex social processes that transcend transactional constraints, processes that include the creation and reinforcement of a shared class identity (Domhoff 1971; Scott 1979). Sonquist and Koenig (1975: 198), for example, argued that interlocks, in addition to their various organizational and control functions, may also serve "to promote upper class cohesion, self-consciousness, and consensus on social issues."

The ambiguity surrounding the functions of the interlocking directorate prompted several analysts to argue for the need to study their actual behavioral consequences (Granovetter 1985; see also Mizruchi 1996). Important work by Useem (1984) offered a critical, if tentative, resolution to this dilemma, although the findings of his research were not supportive

---

[5] While several analysts found statistically significant correlations between the number of a firm's board interlocks and its profitability, bank indebtedness, and the likelihood it would receive bank financing, the actual processes that generated these correlations were often limited to bivariate statistical inference based on observed correlations (Mintz and Swartz 1985; Mizruchi 1982; Pennings 1980; Pfeffer and Salancik 1978). More recent research has not always replicated the findings of earlier studies (see Pfeffer 1987 for a discussion of this literature; see also Useem 1984).

of several predictions of the resource-dependence perspective. Using data obtained from 127 interviews with top US and UK corporate executives, Useem formulated a perspective on the sources and consequences of intercorporate networks that emphasized the totality of interfirm relations rather than pairwise ties between companies.

In contrast to resource-dependence theory, Useem's "inner circle" perspective argued that the primary function of the interlocking directorate is to provide executives with a general "scan" of the business community, *not* a specific corporation. In this formulation, corporate actors join the boards of several firms and business interest groups to gain a transcendent "scan" of the corporate community. For example, one executive in his study remarked:

If you serve on, say, six outside boards, each of which has, say, ten directors, and let's say out of ten directors, five are experts in one or another subject, you have a built in panel of thirty friends who are experts who you meet regularly, automatically each month. You're joining a club, a very good club. You can sit down with [another outside director] and you can say, "well what do you know about this kind of pension fund, what do you think about this kind of profit sharing, or what do you think about this or that" (Useem 1984: 56).

Another executive similarly commented on the usefulness of board interlocks in expanding the personal network of a CEO: "You're damn right it's helpful to be on several boards. It extends the range of your network and acquaintances, and your experience. That's why you go on a board, to get something as well as to give" (ibid.: 47–48).

With few exceptions, Useem (1984: 53) found that most interviewed executives considered it an impropriety to use one board position to promote the interests of another company. Since this finding was not congruent with the predictions of resource-dependence theory, Useem (1984: 45–46) argued:

The logic of the interlocking directorate, I found, was not reducible to particularistic, pairwise ties between firms, but rather originated in an entirely different business consideration, and one that is far more likely to generate a diffusely structured network. The central dynamic lies instead in efforts by large companies to achieve an optimal "business scan" of contemporary corporate practices and the general business environment.

An important consequence of interlocking directorates, Useem (1984: 61) argued, is that executives with multiple connections come to share a vision distinct from that of other, less connected business leaders. Of particular note, these more embedded executives typically take a more active role in promoting their politics. Interlocking directorates thus have the unplanned consequence of generating a "communication network that inevitably helps a segment of the corporate community identify its members' shared political interests" (Useem 1984: 211). The most embedded executives within the communication network (the inner circle) function as a unifying segment that transcends interfirm and sectoral rivalries (Useem 1979: 62). These inner circle executives and their associated firms sit at the apex of corporate political activism of many kinds. Statistically, they are more likely to participate in state advisory committees, political parties, nonprofit organizations, and various media events; moreover, their position as leaders within these multiple spheres of influence places them in a uniquely powerful position within the corporate community (Useem 1984: 61).[6]

Useem's study raised many important questions, yet concrete models of shared political activism – that is, beyond case studies – were needed to assess whether networks relating to corporate control also unified corporations politically. As interesting as developments in the study of who controls the corporate board have been, our argument does not rely on making an explicit connection between ownership and control because we are not operationalizing a concept of class control over the modern corporation. Rather, our focus is on how corporations act collectively to exercise class agency and shape trade policy. Recall that most of the literature on ownership and control was developed to rebut claims associated with the managerial thesis – that is, owners no longer control large corporations and thus corporations could no longer act solely from the motives of their capitalist owners. Many of the methods, and some hypotheses we pursue later, relate to this literature, particularly those related to the function of board interlocks. The scholarship emerging from this debate, while important in setting the foundations for a structural analysis of business, does not generally model how *intercorporate* relations impact specific political outcomes.

Instances of political cooperation – lobbying, campaign and PAC donations, revolving door appointments to government office – among large companies and their executives abound, suggesting that politically active corporate elite constitute a class subset (Domhoff 1967, 1970; Jacobs 1999; Mills 1956: 123, 143–146, 292–297; see also Mizruchi 1992: 17–19). Thus, our inquiry, with its focus on corporate policy activism, needs to incorporate another trajectory of scholarship, one

---

[6] See Mizruchi (1996) and Carroll and Sapinski (2011) for two very good reviews of the literature on corporate interlocks.

that expanded the political-organizational framework undergirding notions of "class cohesion" by linking the board network with the policy arena. In this literature, class is a political concept operationalized through the study of intercorporate networks and corporate political action.

THE NETWORK APPROACH TO CLASS COHESION

If more connected executives and their companies are generally more politically active than those with few outside corporate connections, this raises the question of why network position uniquely influences corporate political behavior. Whereas resource-dependence theory tends to emphasize the organizational imperatives driving economic behavior (such as growth and profits), social class, class cohesion, and power structure research employs a broader concept of corporate, class interests. Within the class cohesion framework, "network" and "class" are closely related concepts.[7] "Network" refers to the interorganizational ties created by board of director interlocks, policy planning organizations, foundations, think tanks, and various social clubs (Domhoff 2006; Useem 1984). Mills (1956: 123) articulated this relationship most explicitly, arguing that interlocks among the new economic elite created a social milieu where specific property interests translated into a wider, unified view of the political interests of the propertied class.

A network approach to class cohesion begins with the assumption that *economic* interests, in isolation, do not directly translate into a specific class agenda. This is because corporate "economic interests" are complex and contested – even among capitalists. Nonetheless, the articulation of a broader class interest is possible within the complex matrix of social and political ties that structure elite corporate networks. For example, Domhoff (1967; 2014), like Mills (1956), does not suggest that "owners" are the only "class actors," but instead argues for a conceptualization of class that is dynamic and takes shape within specific social contexts and institutional power structures. While that power structure is buttressed by the support and resources of the corporate rich – broadly speaking – it

---

[7] A key concept in this literature is network embeddedness, which refers to the density of firm ties to outside boards of directors, business associations, foundations, and state advisory committees. In contrast to theories that emphasize firm attributes to explain corporate political behavior, the class cohesion perspective tends to emphasize how network embeddedness facilitates broad political coordination among businesses.

cannot be crudely reduced to a basic, one-to-one correspondence between ownership and politics. In this way, class dominance is a function of the power structure of the corporate rich and their pervasive influence, but not necessarily the political action of *individual* capitalists. The important question, then, is what social processes inform and unify the interests of the propertied class and what is the role of corporate elite in that process.

By directing the resources of a corporation toward a common political agenda – an agenda materially anchored in the funding of key founda-tions, in various corporate membership dues, in government service, and through direct contributions to multiple policy groups – the resulting interwoven relationships promote an expansive *"classwide"* business interest. That is, a form of class consciousness among business elite – as in the Marxist notion of a class "for itself" – may be constructed (Marx 1972; Useem 1984). Certainly, as others have suggested, a commonality of material interests – where business is seen to form a class "in itself" – is sufficient to produce political cohesion regardless of any broader concern for the business class (Mizruchi 1992). That said, from the network perspective, whether business cooperation arises from organizational and social affiliations *or* from shared economic interests (or both) does not change the social consequences of intercorporate, unified political action (Mizruchi 1989: 404). In any such arrangement, unity among corporate elite results in a political force that far outweighs any other societal interest and can therefore dominate politics. Mizruchi (1992), for example, argues decisively that corporate political action is best under-stood in terms of the relations and the networks that corporate actors are embedded in rather than in terms of narrow economic self-interest. Similarly, Useem (1984: 212) suggests that intercorporate networks embody processes more complex than a simple cementing of resource-exchange in support of efficient transaction; they also have the conse-quence of producing an "inner circle" that can "serve as a vehicle for the promotion of the interests of business in general." The social consequence of those interlocks is at least as important as the reason they formed in the first place. Together, these connections form part of a broader commu-nication network that links various segments of business resulting in strategically defined policy initiatives. The intercorporate network thus describes a complex web of interfirm ties *as well as* a specific, historically contingent social formation with political consequences; a cooperative business class segment that transcends the economic concerns of specific industries (Domhoff 1990; Mills 1956; Mizruchi 1989; Useem 1984; Zeitlin 1974).

While myriad social, economic, and political organizations link together prominent firms and executives, class cohesion research typically focuses on two main sites of ongoing interfirm communication: the "board interlock" and "policy planning" networks.[8] The first site – interaction within the board of director interlock network – most elementally involves the sum of interfirm ties created by shared directorships. These ties are thought to influence corporate political behavior through two main mechanisms: information and social cohesion. Specifically, board interlocks produce variable access to *information* about other companies and sectors. As a network of communication, the interlocking directorate "discourages the specific and fosters the general" (Useem 1984: 55). Executives who sit on multiple boards weigh the organizational interests of several corporations and industries when lobbying for or against a specific legislative policy. Thus, these corporate elite are more likely to pursue political objectives that enhance the welfare of the broader corporate community, while executives with few or no board ties will tend to limit their political activism to issues that directly affect the particular firm they represent.

Board interlocks also generate *social cohesion* that facilitates the mobilization of resources toward political objectives generally favorable within the circle of closely bound executives (Useem 1984: 62). Groupings of similarly situated executives will tend to respond to conflict or political uncertainty in a similar manner – they display greater similarity and unity in behavior (Mizruchi 1992). While the interlock network, in the main, functions to connect *individuals* from different corporations, it is often argued that these ties also expand the *organizational* capacity for coordinated political action by corporations. Further, scholars have argued that the political actions of major individual stockholders in privately held and publicly traded corporations take distinct form from the political action of corporations. Burris (2001) mostly settles this issue, explaining the significant and observed differences between the political campaign contributions of individual capitalists and corporations (both of which, no doubt, reflect the deep impact of social networks).

The second major site of interfirm communication is often referred to as the "policy planning network." Among the numerous business advocacy groups that make up the policy planning network, several rise to the forefront in terms of the central role they play in integrating a vast

---

[8] While there are several thousand business lobby groups in the United States (Vogel 1989), business unity researchers typically utilize the term "policy planning network" to refer to a handful of prominent business advocacy groups. We examine them in Chapter 4.

constellation of corporate interests. These include the Business Roundtable, the Business Council, the American Enterprise Institute, and the Conference Board (Burris 1992a: 129). The pervasive influence of large firms within these organizations is evinced by the fact that they are directed by an "overlapping network of corporate elites" drawn from large US manufacturing, service, and financial companies (Burris 1992a: 130). Among individuals who serve on two or more policy planning boards, 90 percent are top corporate executives (Burris 1992a: 127). The corporate policy planning network has consistently clustered along two major ideological divides, with a moderate and a conservative faction discernibly grouped by corporate memberships over several decades (Burris 1992a, 2008; Domhoff 2014). Some of the groups in the corporate policy planning network have shifted as historical alliances were regrouped.

Domhoff (2006) argues that the main function of the major policy discussion groups (such as the Business Roundtable) is to channel the interests and resources of their members toward common political objectives. It is one among several mechanisms by which members of the corporate rich control the policy process and reproduce the institutions and interests of a power elite. Within the policy organizations, frequent interaction allows members to gauge their mutual political capacities (Useem 1984: 72) and promotes a more broadly conceived political perspective; participants are more likely to support policies favored by the plurality of members within the organization (Burris 1992a; Dye 1990). The ostensibly academic nature of the policy recommendations generated by organizations such as the Business Council also allow these actors to channel corporate interests into the political system under the auspices of unbiased, "technical recommendation." Given that state actors frequently rely upon the legislative recommendations of these organizations, the policy network functions as a strategic site of corporate influence within US politics (Domhoff 1990 163; Dreiling 2000: 38; Dreiling and Darves 2011; Useem 1984: 76–85). By coordinating the political activities of multiple segments of business, the policy network is central to the formulation of a common set of business "interests" and the transmission of these interests to the highest levels of government (Burris 1992a; Dye 1990).

Together, board interlocks and elite social and policy groups form a relational context that functions, in discernible ways, to shape and bind class political interests of the corporate rich with the leaders of large corporations. This nexus between board interlocks, policy groups, and various forms of corporate political activism (such as political donations) has been the subject of a number of empirical studies. Examining Useem's inner circle hypothesis, for example, Clawson and Neustadtl (1989) found that highly interlocked firms were more likely to make PAC donations to incumbent candidates and less likely to make contributions to ideologically conservative candidates. Building on Useem's (1984) hypotheses, Clawson and Neustadtl argued that their findings were consistent with the view that more bounded executives are less likely to display highly conservative political tendencies (such as in their political donations or business association memberships). However, they interpreted this finding to be suggestive that "highly interlocked firms displayed the *least* classwide rationality in their 1980 political contributions to candidates for Congress" (Clawson and Neustadtl 1989: 767), and further wrote:

We believe the explanation for this finding is that the most and the least interlocked firms have differing orientations toward electoral politics. The most interlocked firms differ from the least interlocked because they have many channels of communication, many means of discussing and resolving political disputes, and are the most likely to be members of various policy planning organizations. In these ways, they are able to develop policy *outside* the realm of partisan political activity; the policies they develop become accepted by leading members of *both* parties.

Clawson and Neustadtl's argument is that inner circle executives will pursue classwide interests through business associations; thus, when executives enter the campaign finance system, they do so with these broader interests.[9]

A related study by Mizruchi and Koenig (1991) examined the dyadic similarity of corporate PAC contributions. They found that industry concentration, Business Roundtable membership, firm size, and indirect interlocking through financial institutions were significant predictors of the degree to which a dyad of firms in the same industry contributed to the same political candidates. In their interpretation, the strong effects of

---

[9] With a slightly larger sample of firms, Boies (1989) tested "organizational" and "social class" accounts of corporate political behavior by modeling the *Fortune* 500's 1976 and 1980 PAC receipts. He found that defense contractors and firms with a larger aggregated value of mergers and acquisitions between 1960 and 1979 had larger PAC receipts in the two election years. His findings disconfirmed the purported "free rider" problem, he argued, because more concentrated industries were not significantly more likely to make large PAC contributions. Boies also found that firm affiliation with the Business Council increased 1976 PAC receipts by $8,070, but had no discernible impact on 1980 PAC receipts. His control for network indicators, however, was limited to firm participation in the Business Council (BC); he did not include a measure for director interlocks or Business Roundtable membership, as had other researchers (Clawson and Neustadtl 1989).

the network variables indicate that firms with similar relations to other firms will typically perceive their interests in similar terms, even in the absence of direct communication (Mizruchi and Koenig 1991: 310). Similar to Dreiling (2000), Mizruchi and Koenig interpreted their results to be supportive of Useem's inner circle hypothesis, adding further that "concentration, indirect interlocking, and size ... may be capturing processes similar to those tapped by Business Roundtable membership" (Mizruchi and Koenig 1991: 308). The significant effects of industry concentration, according to Mizruchi and Koenig, support the hypothesis that collective action among large corporations is more readily attainable in industries with fewer actors and concentrated resources (see also Olson 1965). As they write, "the observed contribution patterns strongly suggest that firms' political decision making does not occur in a vacuum. Nearly 50 percent of the variation in the similarity of firm contribution patterns among members of the same industries can be accounted for by firms' embeddedness in economic, inter-organizational, and social networks" (Mizruchi and Koenig 1991: 310).

Burris (2005) demonstrates that shared boards of directors among corporate elites significantly impacts their political behavior, showing that "on average, the top officers of large corporations are linked to roughly a third of all other top officers of large corporations through chains of interlocking directorships of no more than four or five links, and that linkages of this distance are significantly associated with similarity of political behavior" (278). Those effects apply to both direct and indirect interlocks, suggesting complex social processes that reinforce political similarity in campaign contributions. Individual executives from different firms who share board links are demonstrably more unified in their political behavior as a result of those shared social ties.

For our purposes, class formation, even if only as a class faction, is a *consequence* of converging concentrations of capital in large corporations and the social overlap of these corporations and their executives in multiple institutional spheres. Like Useem's research, Burris (2005) further elaborates the class embeddedness of firms and executives, concluding that "[not] only are firms that are linked through common directors more likely to engage in cohesive political action, but the directors who create those interlocks among firms are also, as individuals, likely to exhibit similarities of political behavior" (Burris 2005: 273). From a class perspective, an "inner circle" develops a "classwide rationality" that guides the political behavior of highly interlocked, influential corporations (Useem 1984).

Given the apparent role that board interlocks played in the political cohesion of corporate elite in 1980, it is worth considering how those interlocks work decades later. Few studies replicate the analyses conducted by Burris, but Mizruchi (2013) presents evidence that objective levels of network cohesion have changed in recent decades. For this reason, we cannot portray corporate networks in static terms. Nor can we present board of director ties as the primary source of political cohesion among corporate leaders. Other institutional settings – within the state, financial markets, the policy network, or transnational networks – shape the context in which corporations and their executives act socially and politically. Still, research on the political action of *corporations* – as organizations articulating the decisions of a corporate elite – has demonstrated both the embedded nature of corporate political action as well as the way in which this activity is relatively distinct from the political behavior of individual capitalists or questions of whether or not owners control the actions of an executive management team.

SHIFTING CONDITIONS OF CLASS COHESION: LOOKING FOR UNITY IN THE WRONG PLACES

While recent evidence suggests a decline in the total density of board ties, as well as the diminishing importance of large banks within the interlock network (Mizruchi 2013; Mizruchi and Davis 1999), other analyses show that board networks are simultaneously transnationalizing (Carroll 2004, 2010; Kentor and Jang 2004; Murray and Scott 2012; Nollert 2005; Sklair 2001; Staples 2006, 2007). This growth in global board of director exchanges reflects the historically specific context in which intercorporate relations operate – for example, corporate interlocks are today both more sparse *and* more global than they were twenty years ago. These shifts do not mean that intercorporate networks, as a general concept, have become irrelevant. Nor do they mean that observations of less unity among the board of director network nationally equate to less unity in *all* corporate networks. It simply means that our proxies for embeddedness must reflect the changing environments in which intercorporate networks form.

Four decades of research on corporate networks confirm that transitions occurred in the 1970s, again in the 1990s, and again within the present era with the transition toward a more "global" board network. Thus, research must remain attuned to the historically contingent, shifting dynamics that shape the corporate network. Changes in the types of networks that corporations participate in must also be considered.

While it is true that board of director networks have become less dense in the last three decades, the US policy planning network appears to be somewhat more stable. Burris (2008) shows how, over three decades, the corporate policy network has shifted in meaningful ways, even though the Business Roundtable and Business Council consistently form the center of the network. The relative stability of these loci of corporate political activism means, among other things, that the corporate elite need not rely on corporate board memberships to organize politically. In fact, the policy planning network may best match the motivations of corporate executives to channel political influence to the state. Other research has shown how corporate policy planning organizations are structurally central to broader elite networks that include foundations, charities, corporations, and state advisory committees (Moore, Sobieraj, Whitt, Mayorova, and Beaulieu 2002). Staples (2012), for example, turned attention to the CEOs in the US Business Roundtable and found a high concentration participating in transnational networks, and that the boards of the firms they run are much more multinational on several dimensions in 2005 than in 1993.

Historical shifts in networks do occur, just as history frequently brings new players to the scene. During the early 1970s, for example, newly created policy organizations (e.g., the Heritage Foundation and the American Legislative Exchange Council) pulled the center of gravity in the corporate policy network in the direction of conservative free market thinking (Burris 2008). Of course, the formation of the Business Roundtable was pivotal, as the new organization proved critical to what Mizruchi (2013) terms a "vigorous counteroffensive" by corporate elite. The mobilization, which is well documented, culminated in a heightened attack on labor unions, environmental and workplace regulations, Keynesianism, and the New Deal.[10] The Business Roundtable played a key role in this corporate "counteroffensive." The corporate mobilization led to the election of "Ronald Reagan to the presidency and a shift (which has continued to the present) away from activist government policies and toward the more *laissez faire* economic policy now referred to as 'neoliberalism'" (Mizruchi 2004: 607). The success of this corporate offensive over several decades, according to Mizruchi, had the paradoxical effect of undermining two social forces – labor and the state – that had

---

[10] As Domhoff (2013) and many others show, the attacks on labor unions were not new and that the corporate moderates in the CED had a long history of challenging labor unions in the postwar era. The intensity of the attack on labor unions is what changed.

previously "disciplined the business community and contributed to its longterm focus." The consequence of this "unchecked power" of business was a more reckless executive class (Mizruchi 2013). On this point, Mizruchi (2013) laments the demise of the moderate segment within the American business class during the decades that followed the "vigorous counteroffensive."

A short-term, self-interested focus of corporate leaders now guides corporate leaders in several areas of national public policy. Unlike in the postwar years, Mizruchi is correct in explaining that we no longer find a commitment among America's corporate elite to, for example, robust public education. Partisan and industry division is apparent on the environment and climate change. With respect to health policy and the Affordable Care Act, divisiveness in politics became endemic, though the BRT endorsed it. But is this the result of a class fracturing? We would posit, joining Mizruchi, that many corporate elite abandoned initiatives promoting the greater public good in direct proportion to the absence of stronger labor unions and an activist state. Does that mean that corporate elite actors are unable to forge political unity and bring class agency to other projects? We do not think so. It is plausible, in our view, that these recent orientations are more a function of domestic differences about neoliberal policy than deep fractures among the corporate elite *per se*. More importantly, the general decline of political "moderation" that perhaps once characterized the public behavior of many corporate leaders is not, *ipso facto*, evidence of a generalized decline in corporate unity. In fact, in recent years corporate political action has been *highly unified* in its push to liberalize trade and globalize the economy. Mizruchi (2013) did not grapple with this particular empirical puzzle, with research showing corporate unity on NAFTA and China trade liberalization (Dreiling 2000; Dreiling and Darves 2011) and an expanding social science literature on transnational corporate board and policy networks (Carroll 2004, 2010; Kentor and Jang 2004; Murray and Scott 2012; Nollert 2005; Sklair 2001; Staples 2006, 2007, 2012). Our present research shows that while less unity may be apparent on some national policy matters, *corporate unity has remained steadfast in the project of neoliberal globalization*.

Claims of business competition and fragmentation are not new. These views must, however, be properly contextualized. During much of the period after World War II, academic sociologists and political scientists rarely examined features of social and political unity among corporate elite. C. Wright Mills (1956), of course, exposed the limitations of the prevailing academic images of corporations during his career. Mills offered neither an embrace of the managerial thesis nor a defense of the idea of a united, propertied group consisting of a few families. Instead, Mills (1956: 147) offered an explanation of class – one that we endorse – that accounted for the institutional transformations of American culture, politics, and economy while also positing a nuanced understanding of business ownership, the socialization and networking of upper management, and the nature of authority and power within major American institutions:

Sixty glittering, clannish families do not run the American economy, nor has there occurred any silent revolution of managers who have expropriated the powers and privileges of such families. The truth that is in both these characterizations is less adequately expressed as "America's Sixty Families" or "The Managerial Revolution," than as the managerial reorganization of the propertied classes into the more or less unified stratum of the corporate rich.[11]

Mills' insight may be applicable to the present study even though major themes of the contemporary context differ. Specifically, a reorganization of corporate authority *does* appear to be underway. Although divisions among firms are perhaps more likely to find public expression nowadays – particularly as they relate to issues such as sexual identity – most of these divisions are situated within a mostly uncompromised framework of ongoing support for lower corporate taxes, lower wages, deregulation, and a major rollback of labor unions. Of particular note, given the impact of international trade on all these issues, corporate collective action to advance neoliberal trade agendas has persisted under both Republican and Democratic administrations despite significant, widespread public opposition.

This unity on the question of trade policy persists to this day. In early 2015, for example, yet another highly contested neoliberal trade deal was being promoted by President Obama (who, incongruously, promised to renegotiate NAFTA in 2007 as a presidential candidate). The same corporate groups that led every trade initiative studied in this book led the lobbying and promotion of the Trans-Pacific Partnership (TPP) from 2013 to 2015. Thus, it can be said that a high level of corporate unity concerning neoliberal trade policy persists in the United States even as American

---

[11] Mills is referring to the prominent views on American business in the years after the Depression. Lundberg's (1937) study of *America's Sixty Families*, 1937, is contrasted with the view of a publicly minded managerial class taking the reins of business and guiding corporate behavior, generally, toward a higher, public good (see Berle and Means (1932[1969]).

corporate elites abandoned some of the moderation that may have stabilized the postwar New Deal social compact – a compact predicated on the power of organized labor and the legitimacy of the state. Nonetheless, and as will be clear in the following chapters, the absence of corporate moderation in national policy for health care, tax reform, fiscal deficits, or the environment does not mean that today's corporate elite lack political coherence; it may simply mean that among the leadership, priorities have changed.[12] In fact, advocacy for neoliberal trade policy has clearly been a priority, as Chapters 4–6 will demonstrate.

AN EXPANDED CONCEPTUALIZATION OF CLASS AGENCY

Class has long been considered a central theoretical problem within social theory. Overall, the social science and historical literature does not support the notion that the abstract economic interests of owners neatly translate into a specific class program (an analytical assumption that historical sociologists have abandoned both in reference to the politics of owners *and* workers). Yet class is not only an economic concept, but a sociopolitical one as well. Class political action, for historical sociologists, is articulated (not mirrored) through the material interests of owners and corporations – or for that matter, workers and unions. In short, institutions imbue and shape economic interests within actual historical and relational contexts. Recognizing this does not require the abandonment of the concept of class. Instead, class interests and class political action are not *assumed* to reflect strict material interests, but emerge, instead, within a dynamic and contested sociopolitical context.

Making sense of how classes form, mobilize, and act on shared interests remains a critical problem for study in a world marked by growing economic inequalities and conflict. Yet – perhaps surprisingly – political and economic sociologists do not seem as eager to embrace the challenge of applying class theory to today's political and institutional questions. A focus on institutions has successfully drawn attention to contests over power and ideas within organizations, but the same rigor has not been applied to actions and ideas that cut across institutions, where macro-structural cleavages – like class, race, nation, and gender – and micro-interactions intersect within the social order. In the next chapter, for

---

[12] For an extended contrast between a class and corporate dominance approach and Mizruchi's (2013) "fractured-elite" argument, see Domhoff 2014.

example, we find a near absence of class – or even the more minimal notion of corporate collective action – in the popular explanatory frameworks applied to American trade policy.

This book considers the problem of corporate political action seriously and asks how explanations of trade liberalization, and neoliberal globalization more generally, tend to evade empirical tests of a class framework. The problem is striking because the theoretical and empirical research on corporate networks offers a lens for clarifying the relationship between historical dynamics of class and specific instances of corporate political action in a variety of contexts, especially in trade and globalization. Though the corporate network literature clearly retains some ambiguities, the track record has been ambitious and nothing short of impressive. More generally, research on economic elites, from local to national and transnational corporate contexts, reveals complex and overlapping networks of executives, corporations, and political institutions. A clear pathway for the study of class agency and elite organizational milieus has been established: both Marxian and Weberian frameworks grasp how economic power is transformed into political power in the course of class political action. Innovative research has begun to fill the conceptual gap between what Mills (1956) refers to as "the corporate rich" and the role of corporations in class political action (Burris 2001). Indeed, an operational framework for the study of class agency exists in the social sciences, and the network approach to corporate cohesion discussed above offers explicitly class-based concepts to apply to multicausal, historical explanations for the rise of neoliberal globalization. Below, we offer a conceptualization of class and class political action grounded in the empirical literatures on class cohesion and corporate unity.

TWO BROAD CONDITIONS FOR CLASS AND CLASS AGENCY

Prechel's (2000, 2003) historical contingency model establishes the contours of a macrohistorical framework for thinking about corporations, class, and the state. The theoretical and empirical approach developed here builds on Prechel (2000), but also Domhoff (2013), C.W. Mills (1956), Mizruchi (1992), and Scott (1997). These theoretical developments, in turn, are applied to an assessment of the trade policy and globalization literature in the next chapter.

To understand the historical mobilization of corporate leaders in the 1970s, and the sustained role that corporations played in the development and implementation of neoliberal trade institutions over several decades, a concept is needed that addresses this unique form of collective action. What follows is not a reconceptualization of class, but instead a consideration of class and class cohesion as the context within which specific forms of corporate political action become *class agency*. Borrowing from several strands of class theory, a specific argument is shaped about the relationship between corporate political action that arises from specific, intercorporate relationships, and class political agency.

We begin by drawing the parallels between Mill's conception of a propertied class and Scott's conception of a corporate "class . . . rooted in the large enterprises that constitute the system of impersonal possession, along with the entrepreneurial capitalists whose large personal shareholdings give them a continuing role in the business system" (1997: 280). This definition, which we operate from, links privately held or single shareholder global corporations like Koch Industries, WalMart, and Dell with the more broadly dispersed shareholder systems found in General Electric, BankAmerica, and Xerox. Corporations fit similarly into the class system for Mills, where "corporations are the organized centers of the private property system: the chief executives are the organizers of that system" (1956: 119). For our purposes, we need to clarify the connection between such a basic concept of *class* as defined by Scott (1997) with the conditions under which *collective* corporate political action can be conceived as *class agency*. We consider class actors to include corporations – as organizations embedded in class-cohesive networks – as well as what Mills referred to as the corporate rich and chief executives.

Two broad conditions underpin corporate class formation in the literature: first, the economic structural conditions that vary historically and by market sector, differentially motivating corporate leaders to organize and act politically to shape business and economic policy; and, two, the social and organizational networks that link corporate leaders together around historical projects. Outside of these two proximate conditions that face corporations are wider societal, governmental, and world historical situations. The differential motivations found among corporate actors arise in part from their specific locations in the larger economy where varying rates of competition/concentration, regulatory frameworks, and labor conditions impact industry-wide business profitability. These, in turn, compel corporate owners and managers to act politically – as companies, industries, or class segments – on markets and the state in pursuit of their perceived economic interests. Though our approach acknowledges these economic structural conditions for class cohesion, the definition developed here also includes an understanding of the *political-organizational* dynamics that make collective identities and collective action possible among corporations and their executives: *class-cohesive* networks work as conduits through which economic motives and ideas are channeled into concrete forms of solidarity or conflict among corporate elite, informing their relations to the state. Coupled with an organizational capacity to act collectively, the dynamic contexts of markets and industries create conditions that motivate owners and managers to engage the state. The variations in economic and political-ideological factors, as well as the dynamics of complex corporate networks in which political action occurs, must be accounted for in a framework for class agency. Thinking about these variations presents a view of class that is contingent on broad historical conjunctures and is conditioned by the social and organizational networks among corporations and their executives.

Let us elaborate further. Because corporations are the hubs for the accumulation of private capital, the twin axes of power and money intersect at the decision-making centers of large corporations. Corporations are one site where economic power takes shape. The interests stemming from this intersection of power and money are not new to the sociological imagination. Mills (1956) establishes an important linkage between the personal and the corporate, where we see a concentration of money and power among wealthy families, top executives, and lawyers associated with the largest corporations. This interconnected group manifests as an economic class of the "corporate rich" (Mills 1956) whose leaders and "chief executives" take part materially as members of a "power elite" in shaping the general contours of the society.[13] Mills offers a relational framework for thinking about the intersection of agency and structure when he argues that "corporations are the organized centers of the private property system" (1956: 119).

Similarly, Domhoff's (2014: 1) "corporate dominance" model explains how corporations, linked through shared ownership and interlocking directorates, achieve "great distributive power" and shape the basic social framework for everyday life. In it, a corporate elite is comprised of people who serve the corporate system. As many scholars in this power structure tradition argue, the corporate rich do not automatically acquire common

---

[13] Mills's conception of the corporate rich is distinct from the power elite. The former are composed of the upper managers and owners of capital, while the latter comprise the leadership segments of each of the top tiers of dominant American institutions (government, corporate, and military).

interests or unified policy positions. The policy process instead involves the cultivation of initiatives that "satisfy as many different members of the corporate community as possible" (Domhoff 2013: 73). In every instance, corporate elite operate in a specific social milieu, responding to social conditions and contending with objections or constraints by other organized social groups. Domhoff's conception of "class dominance" – from our standpoint – involves the exercise of *class agency*, whereby large corporations and the leading members of the corporate rich organize socially and politically through foundations, think tanks, policy groups, and campaign financing to impact governance.

Power elite perspectives generally treat the social and ideological differences among the corporate rich as the basis for factionalization in the corporate community more generally. Burris (1992a, 2008) provides very important empirical justification for this distinction, finding historically and ideologically salient clusters in the networks of leading corporate policy groups over three decades. Among large corporations and their executives, Burris (2001) also shows how the campaign contributions by executives differ from the political donations of the corporations they run. Strategic and ideological factors play a role in these differences. But, importantly, associational dynamics impact both, although in distinct ways. This framework suggests that a concept of class agency, as research in this vein demonstrates, is conditioned by associational and ideological factors. Domhoff's decades-long research trajectory most clearly profiles these factions as "moderate conservatives" and "ultraconservatives" (2013). But power structure and class theories, though implicitly acknowledging important differences among capital in the larger economy, do not typically conceptualize how variations in economic conditions across large segments of capital shape corporate political action or class agency.

As ideological distinctions form the basis for class factions in power structure theories, economic structural divisions among major economic sectors form class segments in the political-economy frameworks, including Marxism. Drawing from the sociological traditions in Weber and Marx, Prechel (2000: 8) explains how "class segments are collectives of social actors that represent the divisions that exist among business segments and conform to the relationship each branch of capital has with the economy." Portrayals of these divisions are often found in the historical division between finance capital and the generally more conservative manufacturing sector, represented by the National Association of Manufacturers (NAM). For Marxist and political economy approaches,

Prechel (2000) acknowledges the contribution that each theoretical per-spective offers. At the macroeconomic level, Prechel argues that "political unity emerges within the capitalist class and class segments" under histor-ical conditions where contradictions or crises in the economy are not readily solved at the corporate or industry level (7).

At the midrange level, institutional and interorganizational ties form the practical context in which class segments ultimately forge unity. At this level, the corporation, including its board and managers, is the site where conceptions of control, the market, and the purpose of a specific business are constructed. Among theorists from these perspectives, we find the argument that, at least in some instances, interorganizational networks are formed as managers attempt to reconcile internal and exter-nal ambiguities in their institutional environments (changes in govern-ment or market conditions) (Fligstein 1990). Of course, as Useem (1984) argued, these interorganizational ties may have the effect of shifting interests from a narrow company to a classwide rationality. Market conditions, as well as internal perceptions and strategies for responding to market conditions, impact capacities for corporate segments to unify politically. Responses by executives and managers may, nonetheless, involve forming board connections with other companies.

Prechel's (1990, 2000) research confirms one of the overarching con-sequences of overlapping board and policy membership – the formation of political coalitions across industries and sectors. Operative at times of economic crisis, these interorganizational networks fuse the particular interests of firms and industries to broader class interests. Scott's (1997) formulation of a capitalist class similarly highlights places of circulation and interaction among owners, families, and executives – places that are based upon and organized around the economic organization of large corporations. Building on this research, we argue that a detailed concept of class agency must explain the many expressions of social and political cohesion among firms that operate in very different economic sectors.

A key gap within prevailing institutional and organizational (atomistic) perspectives on corporate political action, we argue, stems from its inabil-ity to shift between the different scales of analysis discussed above to explain how changing macro-conditions alter the internal motives for networking outside of the firm. Likewise, the power structure approach focuses less on the internal workings of corporations and more on the interconnected spaces where corporate leaders associate socially and poli-tically. But both approaches often ignore the macroeconomic conditions that affect the conditions for intercorporate political alliances and conflicts. For this reason, a macrolevel view on industry sectors is incorporated here, one that contextualizes corporate political action in the variations of the business cycle, but also in longer historical waves of economic expansion and contraction, as with Kondratieff cycles. Prechel (2000) labels his approach an "historical contingency theory" because of the possible ways that these shifting macrolevel economic conditions alter the midlevel dynamics of intercorporate relations as well as the internal organizational structures of firms.[14]

Analytically, these combined arguments inform an important feature of our concept of class agency. As already noted, not all intercorporate connections lead to class cohesion. Similarly, not all corporate political unity is tantamount to class agency. Class agency may involve other noncorporate action. *For our purposes, class agency occurs – and this should be observable – when measurably central network hubs are constructed by leaders among "the corporate rich"* (Mills 1956) *to facilitate sustained political unity across broad economic sectors and guide political action over many years.* This organizational center arises from the agency and network embeddedness of corporate elite, of course, and should empirically conform to a center-periphery system. This capacity to create class cohesion across factions and segments of the corporate rich is a political and organizational imperative expressed within specific historical and macroeconomic conditions. A form of class agency centered on the locus of corporate political action should have an observable network hub around which ideological factions and structurally defined class segments orbit and connect. Empirically, such a network hub would consist of dense corporate affiliations from numerous economic sectors linked by a large hub-spoke structure. The Business Roundtable is an example of such a hub. This conceptualization offers a framework for thinking about the contingent and relational context of class agency, which rests on a conditional capacity by corporate elite to generate cohesion around a political-organizational hub that in turn links factions and segments of corporations and their executives and owners, both of whom are a subset of the corporate rich.

At its base, *class agency* among contemporary corporations is thus understood as a form of collective political action by economic actors

---

[14] Prechel's (2000) research documents how macro conditions intersect to shift internal management of corporations. In particular, his approach explains how the dominant shape of the American corporation went from the Multi-Divisional Corporation to a Multi-Layered Subsidiary Form.

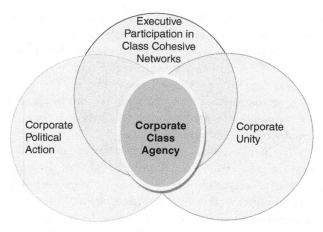

FIGURE 2.1 Simple Venn Diagram of Theoretical Concepts Relating to Capitalist Class, Class Cohesion, and Class Agency

who are (1) constituted in historically situated economic relations, (2) whose participation in formal associations result in sociopolitical cohesion, and (3) whose unity in one setting is reproduced through collective action across other institutions, including corporations, policy planning organizations, and various legislative and policy-making agencies within the state.

Figure 2.1 provides a Venn diagram of the interrelated concepts that form the basis for class agency among corporations and their executives. This framework differentiates corporate class agency from corporate unity and corporate political action. The preceding section in this chapter examined literature that focused largely on the question of *corporate unity* and *class cohesion*. These are important concepts and are necessary preconditions for the conceptualization of class agency developed here. But, as the literature confirms, corporate unity can occur for many reasons, and not all expressions of intercorporate unity have political dimensions. Therefore, specific forms of intercorporate unity are considered, particularly those that have well-understood – or at least reasonably hypothesized – political consequences associated with the *class cohesion* of intercorporate networks. These include board of director interlocks, shared memberships in policy-planning or lobbying organizations, common campaign contributions, and shared membership or participation in government agencies or political parties. Likewise, not all forms of corporate political action take on the significance of class agency. This is because corporate political action can be industry-specific or even company-specific, and it can last for very brief periods. In this way, not all corporate political action depends upon intercorporate unity.

Corporate class agency is therefore defined as collective political action among corporations that is *sustained across major economic sectors* in the economy and drawn together *through class-cohesive networks* in a broad coalition of businesses, leading policy-planning organizations, foundations, and industry associations. These conditions are considered further in subsequent sections. In Figure 2.1, corporate class agency occurs when corporate unity, structured through class-cohesive associations, meaningfully shapes the course of collective political action. Class agency operates in an historically contingent context, where the political-organizational networks among the corporate rich are formed, funded, and staffed to advance the economic, social, and political interests of major owners, families, financial institutions, and large corporations. Corporate political action, under these conditions, is a form of class agency.

In this concept of corporate class agency, we incorporate the decades of research that examines the differential conditions under which corporate and executive networks are formed, sustained, and broken. As discussed earlier, the power structure and class-cohesion perspectives on intercorporate networks allow for such an account. Highly refined methods for measuring and analyzing ties among corporations and their executives have been established, and theoretical expectations about how structural factors of corporate networks facilitate class cohesion have been validated in empirical studies. Hence, when intercorporate unity occurs across major economic sectors and is sustained through a structure of overlapping memberships among corporate owners and executives, *class cohesion* occurs. Some form of class cohesion is a necessary precondition for class agency. The structural perspective on corporations' political and economic action, as outlined in the previous pages, offers this important foundation for a more complete conceptualization of class agency. These theoretical positions are further summarized in Box 2.1.

Once again, we stress that the concept of class agency developed here must account for the ways in which variable economic conditions – such as differential impacts of recession or import competition on an industry – affect intercorporate conflicts and solidarities. Within this framework, two levels of analysis are required for an operational analysis of class agency: one specifying the factors that impact the conditional political unity of executives, owners, and corporations (as found in the corporate unity literature reviewed in the first section of this chapter); and another

BOX 2.1 *Some Theoretical Foundations for Corporate Class Agency*

A capitalist class consists of persons and families who own, control, and manage large corporations and businesses and derive a large share of their income from such activities. A group of corporate elite, corporate rich and chief executives form a leadership group who occupy the top positions of large corporations, foundations, think tanks, and policy groups, and are active in government decisions (Mills 1956; Domhoff 2006).

Corporate political unity can arise for several reasons (Burris 2001, 2005; Mizruchi 1992, 2013).

Threats to business profitability, e.g., labor organizing, new state regulations, withdrawal of state subsidies, broad downturns, or new import competition, are unevenly distributed and can produce motives for corporate owners and managers to initiate corporate political action and struggle politically – as firms, industry, or as class segments. When solutions to crises are not found at the industry level, broader corporate alliances may be sought, and more vigorous action targeting the state is initiated as a more unified class or dominant faction (Poulantzas 1978; Prechel 2000; Scott 1997).

Corporate political unity across major economic sectors, sustained by the associational networks among corporate owners and executives, is the basis for **class cohesion** *(Burris 2005, 2008; Domhoff 1990, 2013; Mizruchi 1992).*
The political-organizational capacity for class cohesion is set in path-dependent historical relations.

State actors may facilitate class cohesion for political and institutional purposes (Dreiling 2000; Martin and Swank 2004; Prechel 2000).

Some form of class cohesion is a precondition for class agency. Corporate political action that emerges from class-cohesive relations and is directed toward a political project is **class agency.**

Corporate class agency *operates in a contingent and relational context, one that rests on a conditional capacity by corporate leaders to generate cohesion around central organizational hubs that in turn link broad market segments of corporations and their executives and owners, both of whom are a subset of the corporate rich.*

---

accounting for macrohistorical conditions that shape varying conditions of accumulation, especially the rates of profit and investment patterns in dominant sectors of the economy, that ultimately motivate large corporations to engage in political action. This study's combination of quantitative network modeling with other historical methodologies allows for such a multilevel analysis. In order to operationalize a concept of class agency in relation to trade policy, we need indicators of corporate cohesion that are consistent with the power structure research discussed above. As we explain in Chapter 3, these indicators of intercorporate cohesion also need to bear on relevant theoretical expectations derived from the trade policy literature. This is something we examine more fully in the next chapter.

CONTINGENT CLASS AND STATE RELATIONS

Corporate elites appeal to the state as the only legitimate "organization with the authority and power to implement the society-wide policies necessary to overcome economic constraints" (Prechel 2000:153). Early models of capitalist-state relations contextualize state policy making as either a reflection of business (capitalist class) domination or of the relative power and autonomy of state actors. The classic debates between Poulantzas and Miliband, for example, are rooted in debates over the extent to which capitalist class dominance is exercised; a privilege that exists regardless of whether business represents a unified "class" in the more traditional Marxist sense (Miliband 1969) or remains a mostly fragmented group with only a generalized common interest in maintaining the capitalist system (Poulantzas [1968] 1973). Later work by theorists such as Skocpol (1979, 1992, 1995) and Block (1977, 1987) granted greater autonomy to the state, arguing that historical conditions (such as economic depression or war) facilitate greater access to state managers for otherwise nondominant groups. At such times, those managers dependent on elections are often more responsive to ideas supported by briefly influential groups, including business and nonbusiness actors.

More recent models of corporate-state relations advance efforts to synthesize the primary concepts developed in earlier work by demonstrating the "historical contingency" of corporate-state relations (Prechel 1990, 2000, 2003; see also Gates 2009; Mintz and Palmer 2000). This approach suggests that factors such as state autonomy, business organization, nonbusiness activism, and other political, economic, and social factors are historically variable and thus their effect or role in policy making will also vary historically. Drawing from Weber ([1921] 1978), Prechel (1990, 2000) argues that the primary theoretical models of capital-state relations are more appropriately characterized as "ideal types" that help describe rather than reflect empirical realities. Prechel (2000) argues that the concepts of state autonomy and corporate class organization are best understood as distinct continuums with "state autonomy" and "class dominance" reflecting opposing sides of one continuum and class cohesion and class fragmentation representing polar ends of another. Researchers must focus on when and to what degree (rather than if) states act autonomously and corporate class interests unify. Of course, for

Prechel, capitalist class unity is most visible during times of economic crises and diminished capital accumulation.

New institutionalist theorists also engage conceptions of corporate-state relations (Martin and Swank 2004). Unlike political theories that cast corporate political interests as derivative of narrow sectoral interests, new institutionalists describe corporate interests as broadly constructed phenomena that arise from social, ideological, and economic relations across a diverse array of organizational settings (Granovetter 1985; Fligstein 1990). Parallel processes are at work in state institutions, too. Like market actors, state actors are embedded in an institutional context, one that impacts their perceptions and courses of action (Galaskiewicz 1991; Martin 1994). Both the historical contingency model and the new institutionalist models agree that opportunities for corporate influence and involvement in the state are not just business-generated. Rather, corporate capacities for influence are *also* state-generated through an increasingly purposeful and deliberate process by state actors (see also Jessop 2007). Consider that political interests inside and outside of the state may benefit more from a struggle to shape the institutional structures of the state than winning a specific policy outcome. Building from both new institutionalist and state-centric perspectives, we argue that state managers themselves also initiate opportunities for business influence and unity. Dreiling and Darves (2011) describe "facilitative state structures" as capacities within states – such as state advisory committees, ad hoc state coalitions, and other state-sponsored forums – forums that not only bring state managers together with business leaders, but allow state managers to collaborate with strategic corporate allies in pursuit of policy objectives. These features of state institution-building reflect the necessarily historical and contingent processes wherein both corporate and state actors create the institutional interfaces that make possible the observed involvement of corporations in trade policy. States do not just act in insulated sociohistorical spaces; they act in relation to other (political, social, economic) actors. The institutional channels that make such actions possible, channels which in part explain our observations of systematic corporate involvement *within* state policy environments, have the effect of making collective, class-oriented action possible. By creating political opportunities for collective access to influential sites of the state, state agents conduct projects by soliciting allies from organized capitalist segments.

Facilitative state structures like these emerge as products of state actors, but they do so, we argue on the bases of our analyses, within a wider political economic context where these strategies intermix with organized business leaders, serving as guides to these very same state agents (who are sometimes former corporate executives) on a quest to build support and legitimacy for complex, long-term political and economic projects. In our narrative account (Chapter 4) of the rise of a neoliberal trade policy system, initiatives by state actors, some of whom are former corporate leaders, fuse ties to influential corporate actors, reproducing their influence and unity. Class organization and the strategic agendas of state actors are thus coupled with an inter-reliant (though contingent) interface, guided by a mutual pursuit of strategic interests and alliances amid important historical conjunctures, usually in the form of major policy or economic events. Structured to facilitate organization and communication with relevant economic actors, facilitative state structures forge a unique institutional interface, one that is often missed in the dualistic conceptualizations of state and economy.

Many of our observations in subsequent chapters support the theoretical argument that government officials collaborate with business allies to bring them on board within the state apparatus. Counter to "strong autonomy" institutionalist assumptions, research on corporate involvement in advisory and non-elected posts in government finds a significant bias for corporate leaders over nonbusiness. This is particularly true in the US trade policy system since 1974. The new directions forged in American trade policy in this era did not arise from an autonomous state. Corporate officials worked alongside state technocrats in American trade policy from conception to execution. The foundations for neoliberal trade policy were crafted in the very spaces where organized corporate leaders met authorities within the trade policy system. As reported in Chapters 5 and 6, this participation of corporate officials is systematic and selectively biased to include firms and their representatives, not from a random pool, but from corporations that disproportionately organize at the center of business policy planning networks. These observations, consistent with claims from power structure, class cohesion, and some institutionalist theorists, pose a direct empirical challenge to strong claims of state autonomy as well as theories where state autonomy operates as a passively expressed (yet highly consequential) feature of the broader model of policy formation.

Throughout this study we integrate several theoretical propositions from the literature above. First, *facilitative state structures* – as contingently organized responses by state actors whose goal is to institutionalize business-state relationships – can promote and encourage the maintenance of business unity for political purposes. Facilitative state structures are part of the state apparatus and are staffed for the purpose of constructing and sustaining political linkages to outside – nonstate – corporate actors. Reflecting observations and analyses, these state structures are constructed by state actors and conceptually define agency within the state apparatus. The creation of advisory bodies to the Office of the US Trade Representative occurred by state actors who were pursuing strategic programs and agendas. Thus, changes in trade policy reflect the impact that a changing political economic context, and the corresponding political action on the part of corporate and state actors, have on structural innovations within the state.

Critics of our approach might be quick to argue that the institutionalist and pluralist concepts of "strategic actors" or "interest groups," respectively, are sufficient to capture the special place that corporate leaders play in American trade politics. Many institutionalist and interest group theories of corporate trade politics present a conceptual framework that locates sustained, multidecade collective action by large corporations and their executives in the same category as gun or environmental advocacy groups. Caution is warranted here. A reductionist view of this sort assumes that all corporate collective action is sufficiently similar and precludes integrating historical analyses of large-scale change with macro- and mid-range approaches that account for variation in forms of corporate collective action. We think this reductionism is unwarranted. Though not always acting in a capacity of class agency according to our definition, corporations and their executives are recognized as a distinct category across the literature in political science and sociology for at least two reasons. First, the concept of interest group does not adequately capture the unique power, resources, and leverage of large corporations in modern political systems. Because of the unparalleled income and wealth possessed by large corporations and their executives, which can easily be converted into valued political resources (campaign contributions, public relations campaigns, lobbyists, and expert viewpoints or testimony), this group exerts incomparable influence over the state's policies and behavior. As the organizational center of capital in modern societies, large corporations generate broad, society-wide points of leverage – points which impact wide swathes of society. Given these perspectives as a starting point, a critical evaluation of the "interest group" concept – in this context – is warranted.

Second, corporate collective action, as many scholars have proposed, does not simply leap forth as "class action." The state is not simply dominated by a class. Dominance, like its softer variant, "influence," is achieved through concerted and sustained mobilizations. Corporations and their executives organize to achieve goals and pursue interests however those might be constructed. Institutionalists are correct to point out the ways that state institutions also shape the actions of businesses. Where these perspectives can fall short is explaining the robust and persistent character of business mobilization and presence throughout the state apparatus. What would be the "interests" of the CEOs of America's largest corporations in joining the Business Roundtable if they were not some kind of shared economic (class) interest? This is an academic question but also, of course, one that frequently boils to the surface of modern politics – as with the corporate finance themes that found resonance in the 2016 presidential campaigns. The belief that corporate interests dominate political life appears to be widely accepted in certain liberal and conservative circles. *How* this dominance occurs, however, can be more difficult to establish – at least in the sound bite format that dominates modern political coverage.

What is clear, at a minimum, is that large US companies, unlike other players, possess resources that far outweigh any other combination of social actors. This is especially true during moments of concerted mobilization by business, as with the NAFTA accord. For this reason, a conceptualization of corporate political action that maintains one possibility as class agency is preferred. This approach acknowledges that firms and class segments with higher levels of participation in interindustry networks – as indicated by high levels of network connectivity to policy-planning organizations and to the boards of other firms – are better poised to *mobilize class agency,* translating the resources of their historically privileged economic position into concrete policy aims. The scope of this influence and the range of its concern – from taxes to trade and environmental policy – render this component of modern life substantively different from what is implied in traditional the category of an interest group.

Expanding on the traditions of power structure and class theory, particularly Prechel's (2000, 2003) model of historical contingency, it was the class power of business, forged in a political mobilization to refit the social and political conditions of accumulation to a shifting world historical context that contributed to the rise of neoliberalism. The two proximate conditions identified by Prechel (2000, 2003) for business influence – business mobilization and state restructuring to advantage capital within the state apparatus – play out in the trade policy arena over the course of decades. State actors morphed the state to facilitate business organization at the same time that corporate elites mobilized to change the conditions for capital accumulation. Certainly struggles occur among factions of business for access to state institutions, as Prechel identifies in his research and is clear in our account on the rise of a neoliberal trade policy network in Chapter 4. The historical transitions facing the US and world economy in the late 1960s and 1970s presented new policy terrain for bureaucratic authorities in the executive branch, while specific leaders of globalizing corporations demanded policy solutions to new profit constraints. These same globalizing corporations also sought to maintain alliances with state actors, pushing the trade policy and legislative agenda toward neoliberal ideals and away from, for instance, the protectionist demands of certain domestic industries or, in the case of labor and environmental groups, demands for fair trade.

In Chapter 4, we discuss the processes wherein postwar economic developments presented new conditions for profitability in the United States. The effect of these conditions was not uniform within every sector of the economy. The steel and textile industries, for example, were especially hard hit by rising import competition in the 1960s. The increased import competition in the steel and textile industries hastened interindustry conflicts over trade policy and began to erode corporate unity after World War II, just as conditions for new conflicts over labor and environmental regulations expanded. These conflicts within business, however, also generated struggles for power over the state's trade policy apparatus. While the threatened industries forged important political allies, they were no match for the globalizers who constructed a powerful corporate alliance around the newly formed Business Roundtable and a cluster of conservative policy groups. The protectionist industries, such as steel and textiles, were defeated. As Burris (2008) points out, the overall density of the policy network increased in the 1970s and 1980s, just as the Business Roundtable took the helm. Linking corporate moderates and corporate conservatives to an emergent neoliberal hegemony, corporate leaders initiated a new direction not just in domestic policy, but in trade policy.

SUMMARY MODEL

Drawing from the structural and atomistic perspectives on corporate political action, these approaches are distilled in Table 2.1 and present a conceptual typology of competing efforts to explain corporate political

TABLE 2.1 *Typology of Corporate Political Action, Atomistic, and Class Perspectives*

Model of Corporate Political Action	Motivations and Political Action	Actors
Atomistic & *Organizational* *Interest* *Theoretical Schools:* Pluralism & Institutionalism Managerialism	*Selective Motives:* Economic- organizational interests define a company or industry rationality *Form of Political Action:* Company or Trade Association	*Interest Organizations:* Strategic actor/interest groups, individual capitalists, corpora- tions, or trade associations
Class Cohesion *Theoretical Schools:* Marxism Political-Economy Power Elite & Class Cohesion	*General Motives:* Interests of dominant corporations and class faction define a classwide rationality, as "what is good for business." *Form of Political Action:* Class Agency	*Class segments:* Broad coalitions of industry groups; inner circle executives, lead- ing corporate owners, and peak corporate organizations like the Business Roundtable

action. The theories in row one are characterized by an assumption that business is not capable of sustaining class cohesion. Corporate unity, when it occurs, is viewed as an ad hoc outcome, not a consequence of sustained interaction in class-cohesive relations. As in organizational and interest group theories, where corporations are typically viewed from an atomistic perspective, firms enter the policy arena pursuing a company-specific rationality. Such corporations are often understood as utility maximizers, whose interests derive from organization or industry-wide economic cir- cumstances (Bauer, Pool, and Dexter 1972; Berry 1999; Dahl 1961, 1985). Mizruchi (1989, 1992) characterizes these positions as theories of business "disunity" where, due to the intense competition of interests and the diverse array of parties involved, political division is the rule. Business unity, if and when it does occur, is derived from the convergence of issue-based organi- zational interests (see Berry 1999, chap. 10).

   In contrast, class cohesion theorists argue that fragmentation is only a partial reality of corporate life, reflecting the disparate conditions facing small- to medium-sized businesses and largely ignoring the more unified character of the most embedded large corporations (Useem 1984; Zeitlin 1974). Domhoff (1978; 2000), Mizruchi (1992), and Useem (1984) argue that the very structure of intercorporate relations, interest group representation, and policy activity generates a structurally embedded milieu that further enables conflict resolution among corporate elite and sometimes the formulation of more general, classwide aims (see Mills 1956). Class formation is thus a consequence of converging concentrations of capital in large corporations and the social overlap of these corporations and their executives in multiple institutional spheres. From a class perspective, an "inner circle" – whose collective outlook is generated from a unique structural locale spanning numerous institutions, corporations, and state agencies – nests within the most interlocked sectors of the most influential corporations (Useem 1984). Following the class cohesion perspective, we depict corporate collective action in a relational manner, where unity stems from the social embeddedness of corporate actors in a wider structure of social class relationships. Corporate class agency is the result.

For political theories that emphasize corporate fragmentation, preferences for collective action emerge from organizationally specific attributes, which in turn shape the ad hoc political strategies corporate actors pursue. This may involve working alone, abstaining from political action if the costs are too high, or mobilizing collectively with similarly interested parties. Class and power structure models, alternatively, emphasize the solidaristic, classwide rationality that drives the collective political behavior of the most densely interlocked corporations and their executives in the United States. Individual motives certainly shape the political behavior of businesses, but for the largest, most central and resourceful firms, the very pursuit of company interests generates a social consequence. A class-embedded milieu transcends individual interests, letting more general classwide interests prevail.

For atomistic models of disunity, the sources of organizational interest emerge from the internal attributes of the firm, whereas it is external and ongoing relationships among corporations that appeal to unity theorists. In the chapter that follows, two operational paths for explaining the political behavior of corporations in trade policy are presented. Within the trade policy and trade globalization literature, we find that the assumptions about corporate influence over trade policy correspond closely with the atomistic and structural, or class cohesion approaches reviewed here. Among the atomistic approaches to trade policy, we find that the transaction cost theories of firm behavior and political participation models of interest group formation possess the common assumption that the *attributes* of corporations explain their preferences and courses of action. These approaches are then contrasted with class cohesion theories of corporate political action, an approach that locates firm political behavior in intercorporate networks.

Based on this theoretical overview, this research expects to show that objective links (unity) among large corporations in the policy and board networks will correlate with their multidecade activism (political unity) in the promotion of neoliberal trade policies. Over the course of twenty years, we contend this activism is best conceptualized as class agency. Class agency is postulated to occur across major industries through the central hubs of the corporate policy network. The conceptual specification presented in this chapter will now be used to review theories of trade policy and help account for the widespread participation of corporations in trade policy making and their sustained political role in promoting a neoliberal global economic order.

3

A Critical Sociology of US Trade Policy

> For the political influence of class and class fractions depends in part on the institutional structure of the state and the effects of state power.
> – Bob Jessop, *State Theory: Putting Capitalist States in Their Place* (1990: 30)

Corporate *political* action directed toward the state's trade policy apparatus is the empirical focus of this book. Thus far, our discussion has established some general connections between corporate organizational theory, models of corporate political behavior, and a framework of corporate class agency. Having considered these issues at a general level in the previous chapter, a more focused examination of the literature on corporate involvement in trade policy and the promotion of neoliberal globalization through trade liberalization is in order. Most of the literature on trade policy and globalization treats multinational corporations as important *economic* forces behind increased international trade and economic globalization. An important gap remains regarding the political character of these corporations in shaping the policy and institutional framework for trade globalization to occur. This gap poses a problem for explaining the pronounced acceleration of economic globalization, especially evident in the GATT and WTO since the NAFTA. Addressing this rift presents a unique opportunity for deepening our theory on the impulse for modern institutions to "go global." How state actors collaborate with corporate and class actors in the construction of transnational market institutions is a tremendously important focal point for social and political investigation. Likewise, the manner in which globalizing capital stimulates states to negotiate transnational regimes certainly requires ongoing study. As demonstrated in this book, testimony to the story of neoliberal globalization must avoid the tendency to relegate the political facilities of multinational corporations to the shadows while their usually more obvious and monumental economic activities remain well lit.

This discussion proceeds, first, through a brief review of US trade policy leading up to and following the landmark Reciprocal Trade Agreements Act (RTAA) of 1934. Several shortcomings are considered in this literature pertaining to its explanation of *corporate involvement* in, and influence over, trade policy formation. Building on this literature review, the final section of this chapter develops several testable hypotheses to explain individual and class-oriented corporate activism in the trade policy arena, suggesting avenues by which corporations – with state actors – can act individually and in concert as *agents of globalization*.

CORPORATIONS AND AMERICAN TRADE POLICY

Nearly all studies of US trade politics consider the 1934 Reciprocal Trade Agreements Act (RTAA) the most important piece of trade legislation ever passed by Congress (Chorev 2007; Cohen, Blecker, and Whitney 2003; Destler 2005; Milner 1988). Because the US Constitution delegates authority over tariffs and other matters of international commerce to Congress, there was, prior to the RTAA, relatively little executive-branch participation in trade policy formation. Whereas other industrialized countries tended to place authority over trade policy under the head of state or various executive-level departments, in the United States, only Congress could enact changes in tariff rates following bilateral or multi-lateral trade negotiations (Cohen et al. 2003:113). This meant that the United States was unable to send a representative with meaningful authority to trade negotiations because any agreed-upon tariff changes required the express approval of Congress.

The delegation of trade policy authority to Congress is widely believed to explain the highly protectionist "beggar-thy-neighbor" policies that predominated prior to the RTAA (Chorev 2007; Destler 2005). Pre-RTAA trade policy contained a host of industry exceptions and tariffs inserted by representatives on behalf of (mostly) domestically oriented US producers (Cohen et al. 2003: 28–33; Frieden 1988). During the eighteenth and nineteenth centuries, the United States' protectionist trade policies were of little concern to its trading partners because the United States accounted for only a small fraction of global production

volume (Frieden 1988: 62). However, beginning in the twentieth century –
and accelerating after World War I – the United States shifted from
economic insignificance to being a major global economic power.
Among the many economic developments during this period, two were
particularly important to trade policy. First, the United States, previously
a net capital recipient, became a major global lender (ibid.). Second, many
firms and industries became more "multinational" through growing
dependence on foreign subsidiary operations, international banking, and
exports to foreign markets (Frieden 1988: 63; Milner 1988).

More internationally dependent firms and sectors possessed a markedly
different foreign economic policy outlook from domestic producers
(Frieden 1988: 67), which led to the emergence of two broadly defined
political blocs: the "internationalists" and "isolationists"[1] (ibid.; Chorev
2007; Woods 2003). The "internationalists" (composed of large financial
and multinational industrial producers) favored lower tariffs, strict monetary policy, and greater foreign investment. The "isolationists," conversely, were not opposed to exports per se but tended to support various
forms of protection from foreign imports (such as tariffs and quotas).
Competition between these political blocs exposed the limitations of the
US trade policy program that grew increasingly erratic as legislators
sought to alternately benefit domestic and internationally oriented
constituents.

For the internationalists, the clarion call of this legislative inefficiency
was the passage of the Smoot–Hawley Tariff Act in June of 1930 that
enacted across-the-board tariff increases to historically unparalleled levels
(often as high as 60 percent of the value of the imported product [Destler
2005: 11]). Intended to shield domestic producers from an escalating
economic crisis, the legislation, unsurprisingly, provoked a slew of hostile
responses from US trading partners and preceded a dramatic decline in
global trading volume.[2] Although the Smoot–Hawley Act was primarily
a response to the Depression, the tariffs it enacted – as well as the trade
war it helped instigate – are widely thought to have deepened and pro-
longed the economic crisis (Cohen et al. 2003; Destler 2005).

In its aftermath, Smoot–Hawley became synonymous with interest
group politics run amuck. This, in turn, augmented political support for

---

[1] Woods (2003) refers to the isolationist bloc as the "nationalists," although, presumably,
the same group of producers is implied.
[2] The trade depressive effects of the tariff increases were, of course, confounded with the
effects of deepening global recession.

the internationalist wing of US capital that favored a radical revision of the US trade program. This desired reform was achieved in 1934 with the passage of the RTAA. While debate remains over the extent to which state and corporate actors shaped the language of the RTAA, there is general agreement that the RTAA constituted (1) a reaction to the perceived failure of protectionist policies (culminating most prominently in Smoot–Hawley); (2) a significant revision of the US trade policy apparatus that established greater executive control; and (3) a victory for internationally oriented US corporations (Cohen et al. 2003; DeBièvre and Dür 2005; Destler 2005; Haggard 1988). In the main, the RTAA shifted authority over trade policy negotiations to the executive branch and granted the president, on a time-limited basis, the authority to enact reciprocal tariff reductions via bilateral and multilateral trade agreements. The RTAA also included *ex ante* controls such as a provision mandating public hearings before engaging in trade negotiations as well as a strict set of guidelines outlining the authority of trade negotiators (DeBièvre and Dür 2005: 1282). These provisions were intended, in part, to secure the backing of import-competing producers who (perhaps correctly) feared that the RTAA would undermine their ability to obtain protection from foreign competition in a weakened Congress.

While in the short run the RTAA was seen as a "victory" for the internationalist wing of capital, institutional theorists also focus on long-run transformations in the domestic trade policy apparatus the policy precipitated – transformations that materialized over the course of years and decades, not months (Chorev 2007; Ikenberry, Lake, and Mastanduno 1988). Among these various transformations, institutionalists highlight two in particular. First, as policy authority was shifted from legislators to various executive agencies, such as the State and Commerce Departments, new organizational interests and centers of expertise were developed within the executive branch (Haggard 1988: 93). A cadre of bureaucratic trade policy experts was assembled who, over time, instituted the forward-looking, "rationalized" trade program that Congress had lacked the competence and, most crucially, the "autonomy" to develop (Chorev 2007; Cohen et al. 2003; Haggard 1988).

Second, the RTAA significantly altered the structure of state–firm relations in trade policy formation. Prior to the RTAA, direct constituent pressures and institutional norms of reciprocity ensured ongoing congressional support for protectionist trade policies (Haggard 1988). The RTAA, however, led to a redefinition of the trade policy issue. Whereas trade policy had previously been viewed as a distributive issue – a mechanism to influence the costs and benefits of trade – it was increasingly defined as a more general regulatory problem (ibid.). As trade negotiations became more open to public scrutiny, cleavages in domestic industry were exposed. Tariff and quota provisions, once buried in a complex host of legislative amendments and riders, were now scrutinized by technocratic officials who were attentive to the broader costs and benefits of trade policy. Because these officials in the State and Commerce Departments were said to be averse to protectionist trade policies, the internationalists found a new and enduring base of institutional support within the executive branch.[3]

While some dispute the extent to which the RTAA signified an expansion of "state autonomy" (Woods 2003), most analysts concede that the RTAA set the major institutional framework for subsequent trade policy conflicts (Chorev 2007; Cohen et al. 2003; Destler 2005; Haggard 1988: 91–93). In point of fact, much, though not all, trade legislation subsequent to the RTAA has affirmed and expanded the central role of the executive branch in trade policy negotiations. It is often said that delegation of authority to the executive is strongly favored by Congress because it allows legislators to use protectionist rhetoric to appease constituents while lacking the political capacity to intervene on their behalf (Cohen et al. 2003; Destler 2005).

Even as the RTAA increased executive authority over trade policy, it is important to note that, as a compromise to secure its passage, the legislation also created new "machinery" for corporate political input and influence (Cohen et al. 2003; DeBièvre and Dür 2005; Haggard 1988: 112–116; Woods and Morris 2007). Under the new system, several mechanisms were designed to ensure ongoing corporate involvement over trade policy in both the executive and legislative branches. First, the president was given trade negotiating authority on a time-limited basis (usually three years). This ensured that industries could mobilize in the legislature and potentially hold hostage congressional renewal of presidential trade authority if it was broadly critical of the US trade program.[4] Second, the Committee for Reciprocity of Information (CRI) was established to hear industry concerns and to ensure that industry

---

[3] Of course, as Domhoff notes of the 1934 RTAA and Chorev (2007) notes of the 1974 Trade Act, this increased support for trade liberalization in the state was the intended outcome of the internationalists.

[4] Haggard (1988) also notes that the renewal provision may have been necessary to ensure the constitutionality of the RTAA, since Congress is constitutionally responsible for the negotiation of treaties (including those pertaining to trade).

interests were reflected in the policy-formation process. This latter development was further modified in 1974 trade legislation, creating the trade advisory committees that greatly expanded business representation in the executive branch. Third, trade representatives were forced to operate within a strict set of legislative guidelines that defined their precise authority and autonomy in trade negotiations (DeBièvre and Dür 2005: 1282). Fourth, and finally, the RTAA mandated that public hearings be held prior to major trade negotiations.[5] Consequently, the RTAA established the politico-institutional conditions for greater executive autonomy in trade policy *and* created specific channels for corporate political engagement in the legislature and the executive in the decades that followed (Chorev 2007; Woods and Morris 2007).

While the new system's mechanisms for industry influence were designed, in part, to ensure ongoing protection for import-competing producers, the legislation was widely seen as supporting the interests of exporters and multinational corporations (MNCs) over those of more protectionist, domestically oriented producers[6] (Haggard 1988: 116). Trade policy hearings and the CRI, for example, exposed the conflicts among different industries and provided an incentive for internationalists to organize, further strengthening their political power (ibid.). Additionally, most of the post-RTAA recourses available to firms adversely affected by trade were primarily "welfare" oriented (e.g., through transfer payments) and tended to support the broader goal of letting international market forces restructure domestic industries. The petition process for trade relief, moreover, proved quite costly, discouraging broad utilization of the system (Lovett, Eckes, and Brinkman 1999: 81).

By making it more difficult and costly for import-competing firms to receive trade relief, the RTAA decreased the political influence of protectionist forces (Haggard 1988). Similarly, the transfer of regulatory authority to State Department officials, who were ostensibly averse to tariffs and other forms of protectionism, may have also increased the political power of the internationalists. It is overly simplistic, however, to attribute coterminous growth in the political power of multinational firms solely to prior actions by the state. While the RTAA changed the institutional context of

---

[5] DeBièvre and Dür (2005: 1282) argue that existence of these various control features is an important counterargument to the view that US legislators have used the RTAA to shield themselves from organized interests.

[6] Some have suggested that this resulted from the political alignment between State Department officials and more international segments of US industry (Haggard 1988).

trade policy formation – and likely emboldened international producers – the political power of MNCs also grew in proportion to their growing share of domestic production (Cohen et al. 2003). Milner (1988: 15), for example, makes a compelling case that US trade policy became less protectionist after World War II because dominant firms and sectors were more integrated within the international economy and not as a result of prior institutional transformations that enhanced executive autonomy.[7] In this view, the United States' growing support for liberal trade was a by-product of the ascendance of MNCs and was not significantly influenced by changes in the locus of policy authority precipitated by the RTAA. Given the arguments and evidence presented by institutionalists (Chorev 2007, for example), however, the transformation of state institutions under the RTAA and the growing economic prominence of multinational corporations seemed to work synchronously to facilitate the expansion of post–World War II trade liberalization.

TRADE POLITICS AFTER THE RTAA

Despite ongoing protectionist undertones in Congress, US trade policy following World War II continued to trend toward further trade liberalization in the wake of the RTAA. The first major trade initiative following the war, the General Agreement on Tariffs and Trade (GATT), was negotiated in Geneva in 1947 and institutionalized the basic provisions governing subsequent international trade negotiations.[8] In the immediate aftermath of World War II, support for trade liberalization through the GATT and other treaties was quite high because many politicians and commentators attributed the outbreak of war to the

---

[7] More specifically, Milner (1988) compares two periods of economic crisis, the 1920s–1930s and the 1960s–1970s, and posits that protectionism prevailed in the former period because domestically oriented producers controlled a larger share of the economy. In the 1960s–1970s, economic crisis also instigated a swell of support for protectionist trade policy; yet these efforts were largely unsuccessful, Milner argues, because the economy's dominant firms were now multinational and/or export dependent. Because Milner observed similar trends in France, she argues that the RTAA has come to assume greater importance in the literature than is warranted.

[8] These provisions, though modified in later rounds of negotiations, persist to this day in the form of the WTO. The general provisions of the GATT included (Canto 1983: 682–683): (1) trade without discrimination (general, most-favored-nation treatment); (2) protection of domestic industries only through tariffs; (3) establishment of a predictable and stable basis for trade; (4) consultation when trade problems arise; (5) waivers and emergency actions that serve as exceptions to the general rules (e.g., escape clauses); and (6) acceptance of regional trading arrangements.

"neo-mercantilist," beggar-thy-neighbor, trade polices prevalent in the 1930s (Canto 1983: 680).

Many years after World War II, however, executive branch and (many) congressional policy makers continued to extol the benefits of free trade while warning against the dangers of isolationism (typically, using Smoot–Hawley as the principal historical justification against tariff and quota increases) (Goldstein 1988: 181). Ongoing (and historically unparalleled) support for trade liberalization occurred, in part, because the post–World War II economic prosperity that coincided with growing exports and diminished tariff barriers were widely thought to be causally related events (Goldstein 1988: 181). The connection between prosperity and trade, over time, gave liberal trade policy an "untouchable" status (ibid.). Belief in the efficacy of free trade became a *prima facie* basis upon which to promote trade policy. It was increasingly unnecessary, therefore, to stake the merits of a proposed policy on the benefits it promised to a specific industry – a purported increase in *aggregate* economic efficiency was sufficient.[9]

Support for lower tariffs continued well into the 1960s, when corporate profitability and trade balances began to decline. The first major trade initiative of the decade, the Trade Expansion Act of 1962, largely affirmed the post-RTAA consensus in favor of liberalized trade relations. The act mainly authorized the Kennedy Round of GATT negotiations to cut tariffs with participating countries by up to 39 percent (Lovett et al. 1999: 81). However, it also, as a compromise to secure its passage, expanded the "escape clause" provision and transferred the State Department's authority over trade negotiations to a new agency, the Office of the Special Trade Representative (later the USTR).[10] The Office was created, among other reasons, in response to criticism that the State Department had not been tough enough in prior rounds of trade negotiations, presumably out of fear that tense trade negotiations would destabilize US foreign relations (Cohen et al. 2003: 37). Despite the creation of this new agency, however,

---

[9] Common in this literature on trade policy history is a view of state actors initiating free trade policies from the executive branch. Corporations are visible as economic actors, or vying interests, but rarely are situated at the center of state policy making. Chapter 4 shows how this approach in the literature misses the important political role played by corporate leaders in policy groups like the CED and the Business Council.

[10] The escape clause provision offers recourse to firms and workers injured by import competition, particularly when harm can be shown to arise from tariff reductions (Destler 2005: 137–138).

the Kennedy Round evoked considerable condemnation by Congress, labor, and import-competing producers (Chorev 2007; Lovett et al. 1999). Many contended that the trade concessions were asymmetric, favoring Japanese producers in particular.

Perhaps unsurprisingly, the relatively neutral 1962 act was followed by the highly protectionist Trade Act of 1970 that proposed quotas on textiles, footwear, and other products. Often compared to the Smoot–Hawley Tariff Act, versions of the 1970 Act passed in both houses of Congress but the congressional session ended before the different versions could be reconciled in committee (Cohen et al. 2003: 39; see Chapter 4 for more details). Shortly after the 1970 act, the AFL–CIO and various import-competing firms and industries assumed an increasingly protectionist stance on trade policy, and their efforts culminated in the Burke–Hartke Act of 1971. Largely written by the AFL–CIO, the 1971 act combined traditional forms of protection, such as tariff increases, with new forms of commercial regulation over foreign investment in the United States (Canto 1983: 683). The legislation, though never passed by both houses, also sought to reduce imports to the average quantity for the period 1965–1969.[11]

The resurgence of support for protectionism had many causes. First, many industries and unions were reacting to a surge of Japanese and German imports that were beginning to undermine the historic trade surplus enjoyed by the United States following World War II. This was especially evident in the trade imbalance with Japan that grew from 17 percent to 50 percent between 1967 and 1977 (Canto 1983: 82). At the aggregate level, the US trade balance also declined throughout the 1970s, rising from a $9.5 billion deficit in 1976 to a deficit of over $25 billion in 1980 (Vogel 1989: 228–229). The United States' deteriorating balance of payments also contributed to its growing inability to support the gold standard (along with a protracted war and budget deficits), which was abandoned in 1971. Even with the massive dollar depreciation instigated by dropping the gold standard, the United States' share of the world market for manufactured goods continued to decline over the decade, falling by 23 percent.

Despite a growing trade deficit, weak US dollar, a recession, and flagging private sector profitability, Congress enacted the Trade Act of 1974 that renewed and expanded the United States' commitment to reduce

[11] Chapter 4 explains how these protectionist initiatives failed in part from the political influence of internationalists in the Senate and Presidency.

tariff and nontariff barriers to trade on a reciprocal basis. Chorev (2007: 102) persuasively argues that the 1974 Trade Act, "just like the one in 1934, was the deliberate creation of internationalists and their supporters in the administration, precisely in order to curb protectionist demands." Like prior agreements, the Trade Act of 1974 included a number of exceptions for politically sensitive products, but reaffirmed the central goal of reducing tariffs on a broader sectoral basis (Cohen et al. 2003: 40; Destler 2005). One of the main innovations of the 1974 Act was the creation of Presidential "Fast Track" authority that forced an up or down vote in Congress on recently concluded trade negotiations.[12] The 1974 Act also created an elaborate system of trade policy advisory committees, composed of industry representatives drawn primarily from MNCs, as well as a small number of union, consumer, and, later, environmental representatives. The influence of these committees grew over time with the trade advisory committees possessing a "de facto veto" over pending trade legislation in recent years (Cohen et al. 2003: 125).

In Chapter 4, the importance of this legislation in transforming the state apparatus is considered further. State actors involved in promoting the 1974 Trade Act are also studied for their roles, which figure prominently in the literature. The historical account that we offer builds from Chorev's (2007) narrative and uniquely examines the close network overlap between those state actors and "internationalist" corporate leaders involved in trade politics at the time. Chorev's (2007) important historical narrative lays groundwork for understanding the strategic actors behind the institutional changes that facilitated the "globalization project: in the United States, this was a tight coalition of top administration officials and the leading associations representing the largest internationally oriented corporations, ranging from banks and computer manufacturers to soft drinks" (102). Moving beyond narrative accounts, the network methodologies employed in the following chapters assess the contours of the corporate collective action, tackling the question of how class agency intersects with state institutional change. As with Chorev (2007), we find that these state transformations were critical to the ability of internationally oriented corporate leaders to accelerate the globalization project and imbue that project with neoliberal ideology.

Following the 1974 Act, tariffs dropped to such low levels that subsequent trade negotiations increasingly centered on nontariff barriers to

---

[12] The main purpose of this provision was to ensure that Congress could not attach amendments to a negotiated trade bill prior to its ratification.

trade (NTBs), such as health and safety standards (ibid.; Lovett et al. 1999). As the subject of trade negotiations began to shift from tariff rates to more politically sensitive issues, such as health, safety, labor, and environmental regulations, the political salience of trade policy quickly expanded with a growing number of interests entering the policy debate.[13] We elaborate on this history in Chapter 4.

WHY THE DECLINE IN PROTECTIONISM IN THE 1970S? THEORETICAL LIMITS OF TRADE POLICY RESEARCH

Most trade policy theories predict that protectionist trade policies are more likely to be enacted during periods of economic decline, particularly when the decline is associated with losses incurred through import competition (Cohen et al. 2003; Destler 2005; McKeown 1984; Milner 1988: 4). This begs an important question: Why did the tumultuous economic conditions of the 1970s and 1980s coincide, not with a return to protectionism, but with *further* liberalization that dropped tariffs to their lowest levels in US history? The answer to this question tends to take either a state autonomy or interest group approach. Our historical-network approach illuminates some different answers to this question, but we first explore prevailing answers. This question is particularly salient given that many interest groups, from unions and environmental groups to domestic industries adversely affected by trade, vociferously opposed the tariff reductions enacted from the 1960s onward.

The institutional changes precipitated by the RTAA and developed in the post–World War II era tend to correspond with subsequent modes of trade policy research, with one track focusing on the policy apparatus in the executive and the other attending to pressure group politics in the legislature.[14] The latter perspective, sometimes termed "interest group" or "society centered," analyzes competition among various domestic

---

[13] The 2000 legislation to enact Permanent Normal Trade Relations with China, for example, evoked opposition from a diverse array of labor, environmental, human rights, and antiabortion organizations.

[14] A third, class-based or "power-structure," approach is also briefly considered in the section to follow (see, for example, Domhoff 1978; Woods and Morris 2007; Shoup and Minter 1977). Some may argue that a fourth perspective on trade policy can be found in the "international relations" literature. However, these studies typically view trade policy as one of several mechanisms used by state actors to pursue broader strategic military and economic objectives. In this view, "government officials are perceived as responding to the particular opportunities and constraints that America's position in the international system creates at any moment in time" (Ikenberry et al. 1988: 7).

interest groups (usually individual firms, industry sector trade associations, and labor unions) in trade policy formation and posits that the content of enacted policies typically reflects the economic interests of dominant social and economic groups (Baldwin 1989; McKeown 1984; Milner and Rosendorff 1996). In this view, trade policy outcomes are a function of the ability of competing firms and sectors to organize and give voice to their interests in the policy process. Congress, and the state more generally, is viewed as an "intermediary" between competing interests that does not exert a significant impact on the decisions that emerge (Baldwin 1986: 176; see also Ikenberry et al. 1988).

In contrast, state-centered and institutionalist perspectives emphasize the effect of state structure on policy struggles. This perspective tends to highlight the unique interests of state actors and their relative autonomy in the policy formation process, particularly since the RTAA and during periods of economic crisis (Ikenberry et al. 1988: 1–7; Prasad 2006; Skocpol and Finegold 1982). While acknowledging the important influence of vying social factions on policy outcomes, this approach rejects the pluralist view of the state as a "weak" actor whose main role is to mediate conflict (Ikenberry et al. 1988). From this perspective, the political impetus for continued trade liberalization arose primarily from *state actors* who possessed considerable autonomy in the policy formation process.

Because of the landmark RTAA, much of the trade policy literature falls into this second mode of inquiry, adopting a "state-centered" or "institutionalist" framework focusing on the authority of trade policy officials to advance – for ideological, juridical, rational-choice, or geostrategic reasons – trade liberalization and resist societal or industry pressures aiming to inhibit the free trade of goods and services[15] (Ehrlich 2008; Feenstra 1998; Lipson 1982; Lovett et al. 1999; Ruggie 1982: 384; see also DeBièvre and Dür 2005). Institutionalists have argued that US trade liberalization stems from "endogenous changes in preferences" resulting from the delegation of trade policy authority to the president that weakened protectionist lobbies in Congress (Ehrlich 2008: 427); although these explanations remain vague as to how and why the

---

[15] Lovett et al. (1999: 86), for example, argue that the Tariff Commission and other federal agencies in charge of trade were "loaded with free trade enthusiasts" who rejected most industry attempts to obtain relief from import competition. Furthermore, they argue that growing business foreign investment in the 1960s–1970s was a response to – and, it would follow, not a cause of – the enactment of tariff reductions, such as those negotiated at the Kennedy round (83).

executive branch *inherently* prefers lowering tariffs.[16] Liberal international relations theory and foreign policy studies adopt a similar perspective, although they emphasize the role of state managers in the executive as
bearers of the "national interest" (Preeg 1998). The fields of political
economy and international relations focus on how *state* actors respond
and react to the amorphous "constraints" imposed by global markets by
promoting trade regimes that protect foreign investment or minimize
international transactions costs (Cameron and Tomlin 2000; Destler
2005; Krueger 1995; Rodrik 1997).

From an institutionalist perspective, trade policy and the construction
of international trade agreements *appear* to emerge almost seamlessly
from the strategic maneuvers of autonomous political elites (Hirst and
Thompson 1999; Shoch 2001). Major trade initiatives, like NAFTA, are
developed by the "calculations of political leaders" (Milner 1997:20).
In Cameron and Tomlin's (2000: 15) account of the NAFTA, for example,
powerful private actors recede into the background of inter- and intra-
state power dynamics, while the "heads of government and their chief
negotiators" take center stage. Given these perspectives' focus on state
actors, corporate involvement in trade policy – as a force for protectionism *or* greater trade liberalization – seems, at least implicitly, somewhat
inconsequential.

Historical institutionalism offers numerous insights into the influence
of strategic corporate actors, such as "internationalists," grounded in
historical methodologies (see Chorev 2007). But with no empirical
exploration of class agency, existing institutional accounts do not adequately theorize collective action of the observed, widespread involvement of large corporations in every corner of trade policy making.
Analytically, the aversion to the concept of class in recent accounts of
neoliberal globalization displays serious shortcomings that too often reify
the economic, state, and ideational processes under scrutiny and reduce
the collective political agency of corporations to interest groups. A healthy
intellectual tension is found in questioning this here, pressing our

---

[16] Chorev (2007) challenges this state-centered institutionalism, arguing that social forces
intentionally target state institutional changes, not just policy. Internationalists were able
to boost their situational power relative to protectionists precisely because of previous
successes in altering the institutional terrain of the state in a direction biased toward
international interests and organization. Building on Chorev's account, Chapter 4 offers
a historical network explanation as to how greater executive authority on trade policy
corresponds to greater integration of corporate authority into the state apparatus on
matters of trade policy since 1974.

epistemological assumptions and disciplinary comfort zones. The absence of rigorous empirical models of corporate involvement in the executive branch, for example, leaves unexamined the notion of state autonomy or restricts research on corporate influence in trade policy to the legislature. Further, explanations that rely on a state-centered or institutional analysis systematically overlook our *observation* of an extensive involvement of large firms throughout the US trade policy process from conception to execution.

The focus on state actors to the exclusion of corporate involvement in the state, including direct influence in the executive branch, follows from the common assumption that business is divided on trade policy issues (Milner 1988, 1997). Among society-centered and interest group perspectives, some historical evidence exists to support this assumption (cf. Bauer, Pool, and Dexter 1972), though much of it is based on a period of intensified shifts in the US and world economy, where greater import competition in the United States, and competition for market share abroad, palpably divided business into "internationalist" and "domestic" producer segments (Chorev 2007; Destler 2005; Woods and Morris 2007). We review this period in Chapter 4. Contemporary production processes are decidedly more complex, making the assumption of a strict divide between domestic versus internationalist interests problematic, especially among large firms. The same firm may simultaneously benefit from and suffer losses from international trade (Gereffi 1995; Milner and Yoffie 1989; Rodrik 1997). This suggests that firm trade preferences may be less clearly defined by product market than in previous eras. Thus, an *a priori* assumption of business political fragmentation would seem to be a problematic starting place for any study of contemporary US trade policy formation, though it is widely assumed in the literature that industry-sector remains the primary dividing line for big business regarding trade policy (Krueger 1995; Milner and Yoffie 1989; Rogowski 1989, 2003).

Even when corporate involvement in trade policy is examined, as in econometric models of corporate lobbying or legislative-choice models, most trade policy analysts focus on rent-seeking industry-sectors or specific lobbyists in the *legislature*, not broader coalitions that include firms from an array of sectors (Destler 2005; Ladewig 2006). Executive branch trade policy dynamics remain largely hidden in this strand of research as scholars search for the determinants of trade policy preferences in firm-level lobbying, corporate support for political campaigns, or district-level factor mobility of industry. More generally, liberal trade theory posits that the aggregate economic inefficiencies imposed on the economy by rent-seeking firms or industry lobbies, as with the tariff concessions secured by the sugar industry at the 1994 "Uruguay Round" of GATT negotiations, follows, in part, from the logic that the gains of protectionism are concentrated while the benefits of trade are (typically) diffuse (McKeown 1984: 218; Murphy, Shleifer, and Vishny 1993). This, ostensibly, makes it easier for protectionist forces to overcome free-rider obstacles and pursue their political interests more readily than free-traders. Morck, Sepanski, and Yeung (2001), for example, model the "occasional and habitual lobbying" of rent-seeking firms in the steel industry. They conclude that the behavior of "habitual lobbyers [for protection] ... is consistent with the presence of economies of scale in rent-seeking and with rent seeking being habit-forming" (2001: 366).

However, Milner argues that this focus on protectionist lobbying, and the firm-specific attributes that yield these preferences, assumes that "important domestic actors ... are solely forces for protection ... [and] fail to consider that some domestic actors may be important sources of anti-protectionist (and pro-liberal) trade pressures" (Milner 1987: 641). Milner (1988, 1997), Milner and Yoffie (1989), and Destler (2005) contributed to an approach in political economy that challenges the focus on protectionist lobbying and accounts for a fuller range of corporate trade demands, though still retaining a focus on industry sector or individual firm behavior. Milner's "multinationality" thesis (1988) argues that corporate trade preferences, though stemming from attributes of individual firms, are situational and strategic, so that exporters and multinational corporations (MNCs) with substantial intrafirm trade flows will be more committed to "resisting protectionism" and supporting free trade. Characteristic of a society-centered perspective, shifts in trade policy toward greater liberalization reflect the structural shifts in the economy and the interests of the dominant, multinational firms. The central actor in this account is the MNC, which, by virtue of its dependence on international trade and investment, resists policy makers' attempts to enact protectionist legislation and instead advocates for free trade (see especially Milner 1988).

Though the hypothesized interests of MNCs shape the context and content of trade policy toward greater liberalization, this literature on trade policy is short on specifics of how corporations act *collectively* across industry sectors in either the executive or legislative sphere to articulate and defend those interests (Chorev 2007; Cohen et al. 2003; Lovett et al. 1999; Milner 1997; Preeg 1998). In a comprehensive review of US trade policy, for example, it is argued that "activism in the private sector affects virtually every decision in US trade policy to some degree" (Cohen et al. 2003: 130). Yet their study minimally addresses the role of prominent business organizations (such as the Business Roundtable) in coordinating and strengthening broad-based corporate political activity, much less what this collective political action might imply for political theory.

For many economists' scholarship on corporations, trade policy, and globalization, we find even further abstraction of corporate interests as aggregated market forces: capital moves through markets, policy makers react. As is commonly the case, we read that policy follows capital flows (Garrett 2000; Rodrik 2000). In these typical economic accounts, expanding investment and trade inspire, *ceteris paribus*, free market policy programs. This line of reasoning also falls short in adequately explaining how and why markets take shape as they do, and, importantly, the role that corporations as political entities – not just state technocrats – play in shaping those markets. For this reason, scholars have pressed the question of how policy frameworks independently shape market liberalization and market governance projects. Thus it is insufficient to explain trade globalization by referring to capital mobility alone. Why and how particular policy paradigms emerge *politically* amid market shifts in investment and trade patterns must also be assessed. Addressing the latter point has produced an interesting array of scholarly efforts to debunk economic determinism and assert "the return of ideas" as causal variables, answering that the substance of policy changes is driven by a convergence of "ideas, interests, and institutions" (Goldstein et al. 2007). Obviously policy paradigms matter (Skocpol and Amenta 1985). Identifying institutional configurations, hierarchies within the state, and broader historical conditions that open avenues for new paradigms to resonate with specific state agencies fills an important analytical gap. As for the conceptual frameworks of neoliberalism – its emergence in neoclassical economics and its adoption in policy environments – this line of research is certainly important to investigate (Fourcade-Gourinchas and Babb 2002; Prasad 2006).

Emphasis on ideational factors is common in the comparative politics literature, where we find the thesis that ideological changes explain broader neoliberal policy shifts (Helleiner 1994; Prasad 2006). More recently, others argue that it is policy making and the institutional changes from that policy that actually facilitate increased trade and investment flows, inverting the standard economic determinist argument (Büthe and

Milner 2008; Goldstein et al. 2007). Prasad's (2006) comparative approach identifies political structures and practices that produce a neoliberal signature in four comparative national cases. In the US case, Prasad (2006) cites instances of business opposition to Reagan's tax policy to suggest a more nuanced approach of the role that business played in the rise of neoliberalism in the United States. Prasad's state-centered approach generalizes from instances of business opposition to Reagan's tax policies to recenter her analysis on politics within parties and the state. It does not follow, however, that because business groups like the Business Roundtable were neutral, or even critical of universal (inclusive of personal income) tax cuts in Reagan's Economic Recovery and Tax Act, that those same corporate groups did not support and help advance the neoliberal turn in general. Broad support for the tax cuts *for businesses* persisted, even though instances exist where business leaders were divided on tax cuts to individual income earners (Mizruchi 2013).

While corporations and corporate elites, undoubtedly, possess varying trade policy preferences, the political cooperation of extremely broad segments of business in support of recent trade initiatives, such as NAFTA, renders the assumption of business political fragmentation over trade policy somewhat suspect, if not highly problematic. This is brought into sharp relief when considering that, in recent decades, large US firms have overwhelmingly supported trade-expanding initiatives and (typically) opposed legislation that increases tariff and nontariff barriers to trade[17] (Cohen et al. 2003: 130; Dreiling 2001; Vogel 1988). While recent trade conflicts, from NAFTA to permanent normalized trade relations (PNTR) with China, have evoked considerable opposition from labor, human rights, and environmental movements, these policy conflicts also proved to be an important catalyst for corporate, proliberal trade policy advocacy. Both of these conflicts, for example, led to the creation of large, temporary corporate political alliances that were funded and operated by the more enduring policy organizations (especially the Business Roundtable and ECAT). These temporary policy organizations, in turn, formed strategic alliances with state actors and pre-existing corporate advocacy organizations to engage in a multipronged trade promotion strategy consisting of advertising, direct lobbying, and targeted campaign

---

[17] The empirical basis for this claim is more fully developed in later chapters through an analysis of *Fortune* 500 Congressional testimony on major trade initiatives between 1994 and 2004. *Fortune* 500 opposition to recent trade initiatives – at least through public congressional testimony – is exceedingly rare.

contributions (Dreiling 2001; Woodall et al. 2000). Despite widespread public and legislative opposition to the NAFTA and PNTR with China (79 percent of Americans opposed PNTR with China, for example), both pieces of trade legislation were eventually ratified by Congress and enacted into law (Woodall et al. 2000).

Together, the combined experience of these recent policy conflicts suggests that corporations, when organized politically, are important political actors promoting ongoing trade liberalization. The structure of corporate collective action remains understudied. Thus, a cogent theory of trade policy and the economic globalization arising in its wake must conceptualize large corporations not only as economic forces, but also as protagonists for further trade liberalization and as political agents of globalization. More recent theoretical debates over trade policy have been subsumed within more enduring debates about neoliberalism and economic globalization. While the term "globalization" has been used to refer to a range of cultural, economic, and political phenomena, in the context of trade policy debates the term is generally inclusive of "international economic integration" or "internationalization" (Woodall et al. 2000).[18] Since the 1980s, these debates over trade policy and globalization have been sharpened by the contention that contemporary trade agreements impinge upon national sovereignty and inhibit the ability of states to regulate multinational corporations. The North American Free Trade Agreement (NAFTA), for example, included the controversial chapter 11 provisions that allow corporations to sue national governments in the NAFTA region if they believe a public regulation or government decision adversely affects their investments. The opening debate for the TransPacific Partnership in 2015 was centered on these same concerns twenty years later. NAFTA and later agreements, such as CAFTA, are also notable for the way they ostensibly equalized, on a regional basis, the trade rights of countries of very different sizes and levels of development (e.g., Mexico and the United States). On the basis of these alignments, some scholars predicted that NAFTA and the subsequently enacted WTO would instigate a global "race to the bottom" (Brecher and Costello 1994).[19] Growing skepticism of the benefits of these regional and global

---

[18] When constrained to refer to economic processes, "globalization" is by no means a recent phenomenon: international trade was also quite high during the gold standard era; see, for example, Destler 2005; Woodall et al. 2000.

[19] Reports claiming success of NAFTA are rare outside of the US Chamber of Commerce and the Institute for International Economics, both of which were strong advocates of the pact. In the twenty years since NAFTA's passage, the most common accounts read in

trade regimes eroded the post–World War II consensus in favor of liberalized US trade relations, as neoliberal globalization has been a harbinger not of growth and prosperity but of increasing inequality and poverty (Krugman 2007; OECD 2011).

TRADE INTERESTS AND CORPORATE POLITICAL ACTIVISM: COMPANY OR CLASS?

In summary, trade policy literature often leans toward one of two extremes. At one extreme, trade policy is a function of the ongoing struggle for influence among nonstate domestic social forces or political groups (McKeown 1984; Schattschneider 1935; see also Baldwin 1989; Lindblom 1977). From this perspective, the state does not assume a significant intervening role in shaping or constraining policy. Power over trade policy rests with domestic actors, whose influence, in turn, is shaped by broader market forces (such as the economic ascension of MNCs and the relative decline of import-competing producers).

At the other extreme, corporate involvement in trade policy is deemed inconsequential, leaving "autonomous" state actors to craft the government's broader trade program. While these state actors make occasional concessions to specific lobbies (as with the sugar industry), their actions, predominantly, are thought to channel some more generalized economic or social "interest" into the development of "structurally imperative" international trade agreements (Destler 2005; Krueger 1995).

While considerable research supports these different perspectives on trade policy, two problems are evident. First, for the society-centered approaches, while corporations are assumed to exert considerable influence over policy makers, the structural mechanisms underlying this influence (e.g., the policy network) are poorly specified. The somewhat limited model of corporate political behavior found in much of the trade policy literature can be traced to the prevalence of atomistic organization theories discussed in Chapter 2. Within an atomistic model, corporations are conceptualized as largely fragmented politically, sometimes forming powerful industry coalitions but rarely achieving broader, intersectoral class political unity. Political disunity ostensibly occurs because firms are

terms of unfulfilled promises. Mexico is more unequal, with more poverty than twenty years ago. Like so many other countries integrated into neoliberal trade pacts, gains from trade have accrued mostly to high-skilled workers, the financial sector, and the highest-income earners (OECD 2011, 2015).

"inward looking," and, consequently, their involvement in policy formation is determined by self-perceived "trade preferences" (Milner 1988).
These trade preferences, in turn, are a function of the attributes of the
corporate unit, not the broader structure of economic and political relations in which the corporation is embedded. To the extent that corporate
involvement in trade policy is a "self-evident" consequence of organizational attributes, the complexity of firm political behavior is artificially
limited.

The limitations of this narrow model of firm interests have long been
noted. For example, in a seminal study of corporate involvement in trade
policy, Bauer et al. (1963 [1972]: 226) argued that:

> the theory of self-interest as a complete and all-embracing explanation of behavior
> breaks down when we realize that self-interest is itself a set of mental images and
> convictions. Whose self-interest does a [business]man see it as his role to serve – his
> own as a physical individual, that of the corporation for which he works, or that of
> some other unit? ... The role businessmen played, the communications that
> impinged on them, their ideology – all influenced their definitions and perceptions
> of self-interest.

Although Bauer et al. correctly identified that executives respond to a
range of factors that originate both within and outside the firm, they
associated "extra-firm" constraints on corporate political behavior with
the vague influence of media, shared norms, and industry trade associations. For example, Bauer et al. (1963[1972]) argued that a central credo
guiding corporate political behavior states that firms should not seek to
"gratuitously" injure one another in order to obtain a competitive advantage. Because extra-firm constraints (such as shared norms or the media)
were thought to be somewhat diffuse – not part of a larger, organized
system of intercorporate relations – they argued that corporate conflict
over tariff policy was indicative of a more general lack of political consensus in the business community.

Bauer et al.'s research naturalized an atomistic assumption of corporate political interests in US trade policy and influenced decades of scholarship on the topic. Subsequent research from the power structure
perspective (cf. Domhoff 1978) demonstrated that "constraints" on corporate political behavior conform to a more definite structure than the
somewhat nebulous effects of media, trade associations, and shared
norms they identified. For example, power structure researchers argued
that the expression of large firms' "economic interests" is itself strongly
patterned by an integrated network of business advocacy organizations
and think tanks (the "policy network"). From this perspective, firm

economic interests do not form in a vacuum, but are shaped and patterned within a broader system that functions to coordinate and enhance the political influence of business. Therefore, any model that conceptualizes corporate involvement in trade policy as a simple distillation of organizational interests (e.g., multinational or domestic) is inadequate, as it fails to consider the broader, integrating function of the policy network.

A second limitation of trade policy literature stems from state-centered approaches that treat government agents as the primary progenitors of trade policy (in particular, liberalizing trade policies), while business is mainly viewed as a force for protectionism – if its political influence is considered at all. The observations of extensive corporate involvement in trade policy – from legislative lobbying to appointments in the executive branch – are poorly understood, if acknowledged at all.

Neither of these perspectives provides a cogent model of *corporate involvement* in US trade policy formation. While corporate trade preferences create opportunities for both conflict and cooperation, they do not, in themselves, explain *how* and *why* corporations politicize their economic interests. To accomplish this, the board interlock and policy networks that provide the ongoing structural basis for business political influence in the trade policy arena must be examined.

Contrasted with the society- and state-centered approaches, power structure and class-based accounts of trade policy emphasize the role of class segments in the policy formation process and their hegemony within the larger business class. Returning to the concept of facilitative state structures presented in the previous chapter, we suggest that the state apparatus can enable corporate leaders to expand their political capacities and reproduce political cohesion across the organizational apparatus of the business sector. While these structures and networks vary over time and across issue networks, a level of durability also persists as both class and state actors attempt to advance interests amid a dynamic and wider political economy. Likewise, these structures enable state actors to energize cooperation with corporate leaders and thereby encourage support and legitimacy for state policy makers and policy outcomes. Borrowing from institutionalists, the form of state institutions can enhance or diminish the situational influence of contending social forces (see Chorev 2007). For these reasons, it is imperative that the preceding actions of state actors to construct (or inhibit) opportunities for corporate leaders while simultaneously contextualizing these opportunities within a framework of latent business class networks be seriously considered. Policy and institutional changes, we argue, are better explained with this historical network model of both corporate political action and state agency.

MODELS OF CORPORATE POLITICAL ACTION
IN TRADE POLICY RESEARCH

Based on the prevailing perspectives on trade policy, efforts to examine corporate collective action in the context of trade policy dwindle to the form of ad hoc interest group alliances. Insofar as interest group theories of trade policy assume that the state is an autonomous broker or a passive arena in which societal interests contest, capitalist class segments remain largely absent from the conceptual framework. Class agency, as summarized in Table 2.1, is not readily conceptualized in this literature. In this regard, conventional political theory leaves vacant the analytical conditions for mediating class political and economic strategy with the development of international trade policy. International trade agreements and trade relations, as well as the corporate engines of international trade and investment, represent important avenues of political-economic globalization, yet their theoretical relationship remains poorly specified.

Over two decades of corporate advocacy for neoliberal trade policies provide an excellent context for assessing the conditions that generate business unity and the competing theoretical frameworks concerning the influence of corporate collective action on state institutions. The broad public opposition *against* the free trade agreements and the near universal, panbusiness efforts, to defend the neoliberal trade agendas reveal a historical moment where state and broad corporate coalitions collaborate toward a larger institutional objective, largely opposed by the public. The corporate mobilizations to create political conditions favorable for the passage of neoliberal trade agreements in the 1990s and 2000s, and the striking success of their collective determination, offer unique empirical instances of broad-based corporate collective action with discernible class signatures.

On the surface, the ad hoc business coalitions that we term "temporary trade policy alliances" behaved as interest groups to promote the various free trade agreements studied in subsequent chapters. These coalitions deployed standard "inside" and "outside" pressure group tactics, retaining highly prestigious public relations firms, law firms, and lobbyists. Leading corporate executives in these coalitions coordinated various media and local-level campaigns designed to employ "grassroots" tactics for mobilizing small business, local Chambers of Commerce, and free-market sympathizers. Each of these coalitions, discussed in greater detail later, served as the principal protagonists for neoliberal trade agreements, from NAFTA to CAFTA. These coalitions, from the USA*NAFTA to USAENGAGE, developed unique names for each major trade policy initiative. Each was well endowed as a conventional pressure group. The corporate free trade coalitions in each case, with assistance from the Clinton and Bush administrations, adeptly managed to turn congressional opposition to NAFTA, the WTO, China free trade, and CAFTA into favorable majorities. However, looking beneath the pressure group form, we find that the leaders of these corporate coalitions shared – over the course of decades – numerous associations, spanning political as well as economic spheres.

We intend to examine the relation between the more enduring corporate policy groups like the Business Roundtable and the *ad hoc* free trade coalitions. To do so, we quickly recap the primary theories of corporate political action identified in Chapter 2 and make some links to the trade policy literature. In the atomistic, organizational perspectives, corporations are conceptualized as largely fragmented politically, sometimes forming powerful industry-level coalitions but rarely achieving sustained, intersectoral or class-oriented political unity. Political fragmentation ostensibly occurs because firms are "inward looking," and, consequently, their involvement in policy formation is determined by self-perceived "trade preferences" (Milner 1988). These trade preferences, in turn, are inferred as a function of the attributes of the corporation and are independent of the broader structure of economic and political relations in which they are embedded. To the extent that corporate involvement in trade policy is a "self-evident" consequence of corporate organizational attributes, the complexity of firm political behavior is artificially limited. However, it would be irresponsible to assume that the organizational attributes of companies do not factor as an element in determining the political and trade policy interests of corporate executives.

Remedying this limitation, the network structural models of business have applicability to accounts of trade policy behavior, despite the limited empirical studies employing this framework on trade politics. As discussed in Chapter 2, corporate interests do not form in a vacuum, but are shaped and patterned within a broader system that functions to coordinate and focus the political interests of and the influence of business in the United States. Therefore, any model that conceptualizes corporate involvement in trade policy as a distillation of organizational interests (e.g., multinational or domestic) is inadequate if it fails to consider the broader, integrating function of the policy and board networks.

Structural approaches thus stand in sharp contrast to organizational interest theories of trade policy, wherein corporations enter the policy arena pursuing a company-specific rationality. Such a view consists of corporations as utility maximizers whose interests derive from organizational or industry-wide economic circumstances (Bauer et al. 1972; Berry 1999; Destler 2005; Milner and Yoffie 1989; Salisbury 1992). Hillman, Keil, and Schuler's (2004) extensive review of corporate political action research found that the bulk of "management scholars emphasize strategic choice and assume that [corporate] managers *choose* to engage in political activity to enhance the value of the firm, and that these choices largely depend upon such firm specific factors" (839, emphasis in original). In the political action literature, as with much of the trade policy literature, the antecedents of corporate political action are rooted in specific firm interests – a "company rationality" as defined by Useem (1984). These perspectives typically emphasize political division among corporations stemming from the intensity of market competition and the vast array of corporate economic interests (whether for trade or protection, regulation or deregulation, or other interests). Corporate political unity is the exception, and when it occurs, it is derived from the convergence of issue-based alliances (see Berry 1999: chap. 10; Vogel 1989).

In contrast, Hillman et al. (2004) identify a group of "institutional explanations for corporate political action" consistent with our structural frameworks described in Chapter 2 and, following Mizruchi (1992), refer to "class unity theories." When applied to trade policy formation, class unity theories accentuate the cohesion of corporations and their executives in the policy network, locating the sources of business political unity over trade policy in the networks linking prominent corporate leaders to government (Domhoff 1990, 2014; Woods and Morris 2007). Domhoff (1990), for example, argues that the 1934 Reciprocal Trade Agreements Act reflected the growing power of the "internationalist" class segment and the contemporaneous declining power of domestic producers who, historically, had wielded significant power over tariff policy through the legislature (see also Frieden 1988; Woods 2003). Likewise, Shoup and Minter's (1977) account of the rise of the postwar trading system emphasizes the role of prominent policy planning organizations, such as the Council on Foreign Relations, in initiating and advancing a foreign economic policy agenda consistent with the interests of an internationalist segment of business. More recent research (Chorev 2007; Woods and

Morris 2007) examines how government trade advisory committees and prominent business organizations were vital to the enactment of contemporary trade agreements from NAFTA to normalized trade relations with China. The most connected firms – not necessarily the largest or most trade dependent – assume a leading role, together with strategically located state actors, in the creation and promotion of regional and global free trade agreements.[20] Within this framework, business political unity is not a "necessary" phenomenon but rather "is socially constructed through negotiation among its leading representatives" (Mizruchi 1992: 22).

The relatively new genre of empirically oriented scholarship on transnational capitalist class networks applies to the class cohesion perspective as well (Carroll 2004, 2010; Kentor and Suk Jang 2004; Sklair 2001, 2002a; Staples 2006). Transnational corporate networks are typically the focus of this research with a principal theoretical objective of testing concepts of class formation at the transnational level. Carroll's (2004) work offers the most extensive application of this research approach to explanations of policy shifts at the national level in Canada. Interest in the "transnational practices" (Sklair 2002a) of corporations and transnational bureaucrats certainly has a place in clarifying accounts of globalization and transnational institution building. For this reason, the parallels that offer contributions to this body of scholarship will be explored. The general focus of this recent scholarship is, however, on interorganizational and institutional networks *beyond* the nation state and steps past the crucial focus of our research *within* US state institutions. Globalizing corporations can penetrate and transform state agendas to advance transnational prerogatives. Empirically, the attention here is on the dynamics within US state institutions responsible for constructing transnational trade governance systems.

We did not measure transnational relations among firms, though no doubt such an approach would be fruitful. The typical orientation of theories of global capitalism focus on transnational and global processes whereas our research brings attention to the active role of both state and class actors at the national level in constructing transnational market institutions. A distinct focus on measuring and testing forms of class cohesion among corporate political actors at the national level characterizes this research. The particular emphasis on measuring state-level

---

[20] The clearest evidence of firm participation in policy formation can be found in the influential trade policy advisory committees within the Department of Commerce and Office of the US Trade Representative.

outcomes for corporate political action also rests on a view that states matter, that transnational environments are suspended, in part, through the actions of states, and that explanations of corporate, class power at the national level can be appreciably improved.

The common assumption behind class cohesion perspectives is that some segments of the business community, despite differing organizational and economic interests, are unified, more or less under different historical circumstances, and that cooperation over trade policy emerges as a *consequence* of the broader, intersectoral interests that stem from their participation in a wide range of corporate and policy networks. More embedded firms use numerous mechanisms of influence, from participation in prominent advisory committees to temporary alliances and congressional testimony, to transmit broader, classwide interests into the state's trade agenda. *These mechanisms of influence, in turn, form the structural basis for enduring business cooperation and influence over trade policy.* Facilitating collective and class-oriented political agency, political theories of class cohesion offer a robust explanatory framework for large corporations as both political and economic engines of neoliberal globalization.

The reviewed literature supports drawing from and building toward – even while incorporating insights from interest group perspectives – a class agency approach to corporate collective action, as explicated in the previous chapter. Specifically in the context of political action, *unified* corporate political action may take on the form of *class agency*, and this need not conflict with institutionalist theories of politics, a historical analysis of neoliberalism, or the dynamics of US trade policy. The analyses that follow offer a concept of class agency that incorporates the uniquely resourceful characteristics of modern corporations but also frames their political capacities in a theory of organizational contingency, conflict, and institutionally specific political action over neoliberal trade policy.

DISCUSSION AND HYPOTHESES

Consistent with the theoretical summary of corporate political action, hypotheses were developed that correspond to expectations in the general literature on corporate political action and on the specific application of those theories to explanations of corporate involvement in trade policy making. In reviewing this literature, the main argument has been that much of the literature on trade policy formation relies on an atomistic model of firm behavior. While nearly all analysts agree that corporations influence trade policy formation to some degree, a remarkable feature of the trade policy literature is the somewhat limited model of corporate political activism frequently employed. Some analysts argue that, because firms are in competition economically, they are unable to form broad intra- and intersectoral alliances in support of or in opposition to pending trade policies. Others assert that corporations influence nearly all aspects of the trade policy formation process, but only marginally consider the structural bases of corporate influence, such as the major business associations (Cohen et al. 2003).

In light of these limitations, one of the central goals of this study is to develop a cogent explanation of firm *involvement* in trade policy formation and the factors that generate corporate *political unity*, particularly factors arising from class-cohesive relations, in support of a neoliberal trade policy agenda.[21] While other issues raised by the trade policy literature are considered – such as the role of state actors in promoting political unity in the private sector – the central question of this study concerns the factors that generate corporate political unity for trade liberalization, individually and collectively, in the policy arenas of the state. Because the research design – fully elaborated in Chapters 4–6 and Appendices 1 and 2 – incorporates measures of corporate political action in both the executive and legislative branches of government, our models identify determinants of corporate political action independent of these varying state structures and across partisan leadership, from President Clinton to President Bush. Accounting for institutional variation in the types of corporate involvement illuminates a puzzling relationship: how state structures impact the tactical form of corporate political action (see Chorev 2007). This methodological test also acknowledges the historical bifurcation of trade policy authority and the varying approaches to trade policy research that mirror these trade policy systems in the United States.

Given the focus of this study and the literature reviewed thus far, it is now possible to develop several testable hypotheses concerning corporate involvement in trade policy to ascertain the character (class or company) of corporate political action for neoliberal trade policy.[22] More fully explained in the appendices, the empirical analyses capture two dimensions

---

[21] As described further in the Chapters 5 and 6, opposition over trade policy among *Fortune* 500 firms is exceptionally rare. Thus, while corporate political opposition is considered at a theoretical level in this chapter, it should be noted that the empirical models presented below do not address corporate opposition to trade liberalization.

[22] Model selection and variable operationalization are described more fully in Appendix 2.

of corporate political behavior: (1) firm-level *participation* in trade policy formation; and (2) the political *unity* of corporate dyads in support of US trade policies. The first dimension, participation, relates to the *individual* firm, specifically, the internal and external factors that influence its involvement in trade policy formation. The second dimension relates to the factors that determine whether all possible pairs (dyads) of firms collectively engage in trade policy, that is, their *political unity*.[23] Because two dimensions of corporate political behavior are examined, each of the hypothesized effects discussed below is considered in terms of its effect on both participation and (dyadic) political unity.

The models developed to explain these different dimensions of corporate political behavior (i.e., participation and unity) contrast two general categories of predictors, "organizational" and "network." Organizational predictors measure the attributes of firms, such as sales or foreign subsidiaries, to explain political behavior. Network variables, conversely, measure the attributes of firm *relations* – for example, through board interlocks or policy group affiliations – to explain policy activism.

Table 3.1 presents the main organizational and network hypotheses as they apply to the questions of participation and unity in this study. Below, each hypothesis is spelled out in relation the relevant literature and the models we will test in later chapters. When the company is the unit of analysis the company-level hypothesis is denoted first as H#a. For models where a pair or dyad of corporations is the unit of analysis, the dyadic hypothesis follows and is denoted as H#b. The distinctions between the types of models are discussed in Chapters 5 and 6. The organizational hypotheses include multinationality, sector, capital intensity, size, geographic proximity, and political donations. The first hypothesized predictor, "multinationality," refers to firm subsidiary operations in foreign countries. According to transaction cost theory, firms with extensive interests or productive facilities overseas will benefit economically from lower tariffs on intrafirm transactions that span national borders and, as such, will be more likely to participate in some aspect of trade politics (Milner 1988: 223; Milner and Yoffie 1989; Yarbrough and Yarbrough 1992). Therefore, it is predicted that:

H1a: As foreign subsidiaries increase, the likelihood of participating in neoliberal trade policy formation and advocacy increases.

---

[23] As with similar previous studies, political unity is measured at the dyadic level. Dyadic political unity refers to whether a pair of companies (a corporate dyad) shares a common political trait (e.g., both dyadic subunits participate in the same temporary political alliance).

TABLE 3.1 *General Hypotheses*

Organizational characteristics	Corporate Political Action Hypotheses
H1: Foreign Subsidiaries	Corporations with more subsidiaries globally, and firm dyads with similarly located subsidiary operations, will tend to participate more in neoliberal trade policy and have more unified political behavior.
H2: Sector	Corporations in the same primary industry will tend to participate more in neoliberal trade policy and have more unified political behavior.
H3: Capital Intensity	More capital-intensive corporations and those firm dyads with similar levels of capital intensity will tend to adopt similar positions and take more unified action on trade liberalization.
H4: Size	Larger corporations and those firm dyads with similar size will exhibit similar and more unified support of trade liberalization.
H5: Political Donations	Corporations with larger PAC expenditures and firm dyads with similar PAC expenditures will display similar and more unified political behavior in support of trade liberalization.
H6: Region	The location of headquarters for corporations will shape their political behavior on trade policy, with similarly located companies having greater political unity in their support of trade liberalization.
Network Characteristics:	
H7: Direct Board Interlocks	Corporations with greater connections to the boards of other companies, and those firm dyads connected by a direct or indirect board interlock, will exhibit greater political unity in their support for trade liberalization.
H8: Business Roundtable Affiliation	Corporate members of the Business Roundtable, and firm dyads sharing CEO membership, will have greater participation in and display greater political unity in their support for trade liberalization.
H9: Policy Network Affiliation	Corporations with more affiliations, and dyads with similar ties to the policy network, will display greater political unity in their support for trade liberalization than corporations with fewer or no shared ties.

Similarly, firms with economic interests in the same foreign markets should have similar trade policy preferences because they are both influenced by tariff and nontariff barriers to trade associated with the given region (Ferguson and Rogers 1986; Mizruchi 1990). Thus, it is expected that:

H1b. Dyads with subsidiary operations in the same region will show greater political unity in their support for neoliberal trade policy than dyads without foreign subsidiaries in the same region.

Firm sector is also frequently cited for its effect on corporate trade preferences (Bauer et al. 1972; Destler 2005; Milner 1988). This is because the effects of trade typically concentrate within certain industrial sectors. For example, firms in tradable-goods sectors, such as large exporters or import-competing producers, have a greater interest in trade policy outcomes and, consequently, are (typically) more active in trade policy formation. This suggests that:

H2a. Firms in tradable goods sectors are more likely to participate in trade policy formation and advocacy than firms in non-tradable goods sectors.

In addition, because firms in the same industries often face similar market constraints (such as those arising from foreign import competition) and investment opportunities (e.g., through the creation of offshore production facilities), firms in the same product market will often support similar trade policies. More generally, firms in the same primary industry share a similar position in the broader market structure and so tend to share similar political and economic concerns (Mizruchi 1992: 80). Thus, it is expected that:

H2b. Dyads in the same primary industry display greater political unity in their support for US trade policies than dyads in different industries.

In addition to the effects of product market, other analysts argue that high fixed-cost, capital-intensive industries generally demonstrate greater support for trade liberalization, since open markets (potentially) increase aggregate demand for their products (Gill 1990: 97; Piore and Sabel 1984). Firms and sectors capable of mass-quantity production will tend to favor open investment and trade with potentially large consumer markets, such as China. Therefore, it is expected that:

H3a. As capital intensity increases, the likelihood of participating in trade policy formation and advocacy increases.

Mizruchi (1992: 83) argues that predictors of firm-level political activism, such as capital intensity, can also be thought of as a grouping characteristic, such that firms with higher levels of a given attribute are expected to display greater levels of political unity. Although the term "grouping" may suggest a spatial metaphor (i.e., where firms are assigned to one of several discrete groups), what is implied here is actually a matter of degree: As firms become more dissimilar along a given organizational attribute, their interests and, hence, their political behavior will increasingly diverge. With respect to capital intensity, this suggests that:

H3b. The more similar the level of capital intensity among dyads, the more similar their political support for neoliberal trade policies.

Like capital intensity, company size is also associated in the literature with higher levels of trade policy activism. The first and most general reason for this association is that large firms possess greater resources to devote to the political process and, hence, are expected to be more politically active. Bauer et al. (1972: 228), for example, found that larger companies devoted greater resources (such as executive time, money, or various public relations efforts) to trade policy advocacy than smaller firms.

A second reason why large firms may be more politically active is that they stand to gain a larger distributive proportion of any favorable trade policy outcome (Mizruchi 1992; Olson 1965). While smaller firms require associations and other collective mechanisms to achieve political influence, for the largest and most resourceful firms, the pursuit of corporate interests often produces a social consequence. As a result, political activism may yield a sufficient economic return even without the assistance of other producers.

Third, Useem (1984) argues that executives representing the largest firms are more politically active because they require a "scan" of the business community that transcends a single product market (most often, because their firms simultaneously operate in several distinct industries). Large firms are thus more likely to establish a host of ties to other firms, policy makers, and advocacy groups in order to "scan" the economic, social, and regulatory conditions facing big business. Taken together, these arguments suggest that:

H4a. As firm size increases, the likelihood of participating in neoliberal trade policy formation and advocacy increases.

In addition, Mizruchi and Koenig (1991: 305) argue that large firms are "well positioned to concern themselves with classwide interests" and, as a result, will tend to exhibit higher levels of political coordination and unity than those seen in smaller firms. Thus, dyads of the *largest* firms should display greater political unity than dyads of comparably sized smaller or midsize firms, or dyads of mixed size (e.g., dyads containing one smaller and one larger firm). Therefore:

H4b. Dyads of larger firms exhibit greater political unity in their support for neoliberal trade policies than dyads of smaller firms or dyads of mixed size.

Aside from direct lobbying efforts, such as testimony before Congress and alliance participation, perhaps the most established mechanism corporations utilize to achieve political influence is campaign contributions through Political Action Committees (PAC) (Domhoff 2006). While research suggests that corporate PAC spending is influenced by a range of ideological (Clawson and Nuestadtl 1989: 751), regulatory (Sorauf 1991: 221), and geographic (Burris 1987, 1992a) factors, overwhelmingly, the evidence suggests that corporate PAC donations are most often made to ensure future access to legislators and/or special favors (Boies 1989; Sorauf 1991). Because most forms of corporate trade policy activism can be generally described as an effort to achieve political influence, it is probable that higher levels of political spending via PACs will correspond to higher levels of political participation. Thus, it is expected that:

H5a. Firms with larger PAC donations are more likely to participate in trade policy formation and advocacy than firms with smaller PAC donations.

Likewise, several studies suggest that firms that coordinate their lobbying activities in the trade policy arena also make greater than average PAC contributions (Darves and Dreiling 2002; Woodall et al. 2000). While it is conceivable that firms with larger than average PAC donations could also oppose one another on trade policy, recent research suggests that firms with larger PAC donations are more likely to be active in the major sites of business political coordination, such as the Business Roundtable (Darves and Dreiling 2002). Thus, firms with the largest PAC expenditures can be expected to display higher levels of political unity in their support for US trade policies. Therefore, it is expected that:

H5b. Dyads with larger combined PAC expenditures exhibit greater political unity in their support for neoliberal trade policy than dyads with smaller PAC expenditures or dyads with expenditures of mixed size.[24]

---

[24] Dyads where one subunit possesses large a PAC expenditure value and the other a relatively smaller value is an example.

Although most studies of corporate political networks find that they are generally national in scope (i.e., include firms from a range of geographic regions), some research finds evidence that corporate political activism and unity is clustered by region[25] (Mizruchi 1992; see also Burris 1987). Mizruchi (1992: 81), for example, argues that firms with headquarters in the same state will often face similar political issues and constraints and, for this reason, are more likely exhibit higher levels of political unity. Thus, it is expected that:

H6b. Dyads with headquarters in the same region will exhibit greater unity in their support for neoliberal trade policy than dyads with headquarters in different regions.

CLASS-COHESION SOURCES OF CORPORATE POLITICAL ACTIVISM

Another set of hypotheses, drawn from Chapter 2 and the previous sections of this chapter, suggests that class-cohesive networks may also influence corporate political behavior. For example, several studies demonstrate that companies with two or more shared directors are more likely to forge alliances with outside firms and have higher levels of involvement in state advisory committees (Mintz and Schwartz 1985; Useem 1984). Likewise, firms with "indirect" board interlocks through a third company are also more likely to display similar political behavior (Jacobs 1999; Mizruchi 1992). While board interlocks are only a proxy for class unity and do not measure actual communication, a large body of research suggests that executive interaction through shared directorships facilitates a number of processes that generate political cohesion, such as information exchange, persuasion, deference, and conformity with group norms[26] (Burris 2005: 273; Mizruchi 1996; Sonquist and Koenig 1975: 198; Useem 1984).

---

[25] Although not theoretically motivated, controls for firm geographic region were also introduced to the firm-level participation models presented in Chapter 5. However, because they did not significantly improve model fit, region controls were omitted from the firm-level models. For this reason, only the hypothesized effect of region (specifically, geographic proximity) on dyadic political unity is discussed in this section.

[26] When describing the effect of interlocks on corporate political behavior, it is important to note, as Burris (2005: 253) explains, that the structural properties of a network of firms linked by directors may differ from the network of executives linked by firms (i.e., the interfirm network and its dual). In this study, the interest is mainly with the *organizational* consequences of interlocks, although it should be noted that the ties in interfirm and executive networks are not directly analogous and may produce different social consequences (Burris 2005).

Research on trade policy in particular has found that higher levels of interlocking positively relate to trade policy activism (Dreiling 2000; Dreiling and Darves 2011). Therefore, it is expected that:

H7a. As direct board interlocks increase, the likelihood of participating in neoliberal trade policy formation and advocacy will increase.

Other studies of corporate political behavior (Mizruchi 1992; Mizruchi and Koenig 1991) have also found that direct and indirect board interlocks[27] positively relate to political unity. Thus, it is expected that:

H7b. Dyads that are connected by a direct board interlock will exhibit greater unity in their support for neoliberal trade policy than dyads without a direct interlock.

H7c. Dyads that are connected by an indirect board interlock exhibit greater unity in their support for neoliberal trade policy than dyads without an indirect interlock.

In addition to board interlocks, several researchers note the unique and central role of the Business Roundtable (BR) in coordinating the political activities of large corporations (Burris 1987; Dreiling 2000; Mizruchi 1992). The restriction of BR membership to CEOs of the largest US corporations renders the organization qualitatively different in its political influence from other business interest groups. As a site of political coordination for a range of policy issues (including those pertaining to international trade), its members are more politically active than comparable nonmember firms. Thus, it is expected that:

H8a. Firms in the Business Roundtable are more likely to participate in neoliberal trade policy formation and advocacy.

Similarly, because the Business Roundtable functions as a central site of political coordination for large US corporations, its members generally exhibit higher levels of political unity than nonmembers (Mizruchi and Koenig 1991: 304). Therefore, it is expected that:

H8b. Dyads with common membership in the Business Roundtable will display greater unity in their support for neoliberal trade policies than dyads without common membership.

---

[27] As further explained, firm-level studies of corporate political behavior (e.g., Dreiling 2000) typically operationalize board interlocks as a frequency measuring the number of board interlocks the firm possesses to the entire population (e.g., the *Fortune* 500). For studies of political unity, interlocks are typically measured between the unit of analysis (e.g., a corporate dyad) and will typically include both direct ties and indirect ties through a third company.

In addition to the Business Roundtable, a host of related policy organizations assume a crucial role in the ongoing coordination of corporate political activity. The most important of such organizations in the area of trade policy include the Business Council, Conference Board, Emergency Committee on Trade, National Association of Manufacturers, Council of the Americas, Trilateral Commission, and United States Council for International Business.[28] Prior research suggests that firm affiliation with these organizations – part of the larger "policy network" – positively correlates with a range of political behavior, from campaign spending to participation in temporary issue alliances (Boies 1989; Burris 1992b; Dreiling 2000; Useem 1984). Thus, it is expected that:

H9a. Firms with more ties to the policy network are more active in neoliberal trade policy formation and advocacy than firms with fewer ties to the policy network.

Similarly, because these associations function as a site of ongoing business political coordination, their members can be expected to exhibit higher levels of political unity. Therefore, it is expected that:

H9b. Dyads with more shared ties to the policy network will display greater political unity in their support of neoliberal trade policies than dyads with fewer shared ties.

These hypotheses are tested in Chapters 5 and 6. In Chapter 4, a historical presentation develops a narrative around the question of class agency and the historical transition to neoliberal trade and globalization. A strictly "instrumentalist" view of corporate, class agency is found unwarranted, as the series of transformations in American trade policy from the early 1970s to 2013 are understood through an account of class and state collaboration, contingent on historically structured state institutional changes and the conditional efficacy of class-oriented collective action. The prevalent view in the institutionalist literature, however, is also challenged in the historical analysis. Agency is apparent in the institutional settings of both the state and the dominant corporate policy planning organizations. The common parlance in institutionalism does not consider the sustained, collective action of corporations over decades as class agency. The network centrality of the Business Roundtable, ECAT, and several corporate leaders over several decades of trade policy reflect what Chorev (2007) declares to be "intentionally designed" agency

---

[28] See Dreiling (2001) for a detailed discussion of the political activities of each of these organizations.

among internationalists, linked through organizational hubs of a larger, cohesive corporate political coalition. The sustained nature of this corporate unity warrants a rejection of the "interest group" nomenclature in this case. This sustained network provides structural links across major industries and unites moderate and conservative ideological factions of corporate elites. These historical and network accounts of the corporate policy organizations involved in promoting trade liberalization provide the first empirical, network examination of corporate actors working concertedly over several major trade agreements.

In Chapter 5, the results of several firm-level statistical models of the role of corporations and key corporate policy planning organizations in promoting trade liberalization is further explored and formally tested. In Chapter 6, dyadic regression techniques model the determinants of corporate *political unity* in support of US trade policies. Briefly, the results indicate that corporate activism and political unity among corporations are strongly influenced by both organizational and network factors, suggesting that a productive theoretical synthesis is possible between the organizational and networks factors described above.

4

Forging a Neoliberal Trade Policy Network, 1967–1994

Thanks to the new institutional arrangements, protectionist measures, when taken, did not threaten the emerging project of globalization.
  – Nitsan Chorev *Remaking US Trade Policy* (2007:148)

Neoliberal priorities shaped US trade policy positions in global trade talks throughout the 1980–1990s (Chorev 2007). Nearly synonymous with much of the discourse about globalization, these neoliberal trade initiatives sparked worldwide transformations in markets as well as conflicts within and between nations. Much like Polanyi's (1944[2001]) account of "the road to the free market," trade liberalization in Europe, China, or across North America was paved by extensive *state* intervention. But, as we argue below, the notion that the state acted on its own – as conceived in much of the trade policy literature – is problematic.

An alternative view is presented here using a historical approach to argue that it is necessary to conceptualize agency on the part of *both* class and state actors to grasp the wave of trade liberalization policies examined in later chapters. Conceptually, it is necessary to examine how neoliberal trade policy relied on the development and expansion of a political-organizational network in the United States, linking ascendant corporate policy-planning networks (particularly the Business Roundtable and the Emergency Committee for American Trade) to nascent state structures committed to building a cooperative interface with large, globalizing corporations. First, the historical overview explains how disputes among business leaders over trade policy contributed to a restructured political coalition among US corporate leaders in the 1960s and early 1970s. Second, both state and corporate actors urged substantive and structural changes to trade policy-making institutions. Beginning with the 1974 Trade Act, new state capacities emerged to bridge interindustry interests on trade policy, enabling corporate actors and state institutions to interact and co-evolve in a strategic organizational and institutional milieu. This chapter's analytic approach substantively highlights the relational elements in the narrative, particularly the brokering role played by specific policy-planning organizations in a concerted historic drive to transform institutions governing global markets and finance.

HISTORICAL CONJUNCTURE, INSTITUTIONAL CHANGE, AND CLASS AGENCY

Illuminating the rise and passage of recent international trade deals, the narrative in this chapter sets the stage for the rigorous quantitative analyses of corporate trade-policy activism in later chapters. Building toward these careful assessments of corporate political action in US trade policy in the 1990s and 2000s, this historical discussion casts a picture where state *and* corporate actors intersect on new terrain created by institutional changes arising from the 1974 Trade Act. Those state transformations in the 1970s, as Chorev (2007) and Panitch and Gindin (2013) document, facilitated a more assertive role for the president and greater access for globalizing corporations to press for the expansion of neoliberal markets from the 1980s and onward. Consistent with the theoretical propositions in the previous two chapters, a narrative on the origins of neoliberal globalization that fails to account for extensive corporate involvement in its promotion is too limited. Instead, and unlike most of the literature on trade policy, our framework identifies key corporate leaders and policy organizations that established a clear intention to move American trade policy – and the state's institutional authority on trade – in a new direction even before US government officials promoted such changes. The motives to shape the US trade agenda in this way emerged in a context imbued with interindustry disputes – between Chorev's "protectionists" and "internationalists" – which were triggered by a confluence of world economic transformations and conflicts that squeezed the profitability of several US industries. Those same world economic transformations simultaneously expanded opportunities for globalizing industries, some of which took on important new leadership roles in the promotion of neoliberal markets domestically and globally.

Did those corporate leaders – and the policy organizations they led – shape the institutional changes in the 1970s and emerge as a class force to advance neoliberal trade in the decades that followed? The political role of key business leaders and policy organizations in the late 1960s and early 1970s forms the center of our answer to this question. The quantitative analyses in the next two chapters confirm the importance of the ECAT and BRT to later trade policy initiatives. But how is their activism forty years earlier relevant to the turn toward neoliberal globalization? The historical narrative lays a foundation for assessing this question and for considering the significance that specific groups play in the quantitative analyses in later chapters. Exploring the historical conditions that gave rise to the business organizations that pushed an expansive trade agenda is necessary to grasp the class-imbued character of corporate political action in the decades that followed.

Rather than focus exclusively on the policy process, or a single trade policy event, as is common in many trade policy studies, we view the rise of free trade agreements in the United States as constitutive parts within the much larger historical process generally referred to as neoliberal globalization. Each of these path-dependent parts was expressed in the context of specific political struggles yet also reveals something about the world-historical patterns of neoliberal globalization. Our quantitative analyses of corporate support for these specific trade liberalization policies are thus nested within a larger historical argument. Analytically, we draw from historical sociology and, in particular, McMichael (1990: 392), who views "comparable social phenomena as differentiated outcomes or moments of an historically integrated process," as opposed to conventional comparisons, which often "treat such social phenomena as parallel cases."

The development of the US free trade program has been sporadic and uneven. The confluence of world-historical events in the 1960s created an opportunity for a change of course. The corrections that emerged did not just end the embedded liberal model of selective free trade, but ushered an end to the Bretton Woods monetary arrangements more generally, freeing the system of pegged exchange rates by creating a floating, free market system. The politics that brought this about corresponded to the re-ordering and expansion of international trade associated with America's globalization after World War II, and was deeply guided by the multinational corporations (MNCs) that gained influence during that that period. Initiatives aimed at freeing financial markets from the Bretton Woods institutions were tangled up with the same globalizing forces that sought liberalization of trade through multilateral institutions. Each trade policy initiative, or the particular moment of corporate advocacy on trade, is not seen here as a discrete instance that is otherwise disconnected from previous initiatives. A focus on concrete forms of political action and institutional change offers a view that zooms-in on particular moments of policy making while our historical approach simultaneously illuminates "a world-historical perspective [that] conceptualizes 'instances' as distinct mutually-conditioning moments of a singular phenomenon posited as a self-forming whole" (McMichael 1990: 391). This "emergent whole" or "totality" is an imminent rather than a *prima facie* property in which the whole is discovered through analysis of the mutual conditioning of parts. Institutional developments in the state and markets are conditioned by previous courses of change. Neoliberal globalization, and the political institutions that embed its economic processes, emerge as a series of path-dependent actions, orchestrated by both state and class actors. Our methodological pivot from the historical sociological "incorporated comparison" (McMichael 1990) to our quantitatively measured actions of corporations acting on state agencies allows us to simultaneously engage theory about the role of large corporations in American trade policy as well as make better sense of the class political agency at one particularly important historical conjuncture.

McMichael (2005: 588) approaches neoliberal globalization in two analytical steps: first by scrutinizing globalization as a general condition of capitalism "particularizing its contemporary form; and second, demystifying globalization's phenomenal, or empirical forms by examining it" through the politics set in its wake. Analytically, this approach allows one to consider the active construction of neoliberal globalization as well as the resistances and institutional changes that are simultaneously pressed upon states and societies. In the first step, the dramatic shift in the global economic system that began in the 1960s is explored, with particular focus on the rise of fiscal deficits, US balance of payments problems, surpluses of foreign-held dollars, rising import competition, and the profitability crises common among nonfinancial US corporations (Dumenil and Levy 2004, 2011; Foster and Magdoff 2009). Together, these broad historical conditions conspired to dissolve the international systems regulating finance capital and propelled state actors and corporate managers to pursue alternative market frameworks. At stake in the 1960s and 1970s, we posit, were the terms of those market frameworks.

Applying the second step of McMichael's reasoning to our analysis of the rise of neoliberal markets, we examines how the *politics* of liberating markets from the postwar system took shape alongside historically specific efforts to expand the force of financial capital amid a crisis in profitability for nonfinancial capital in the United States (Dumenil and Levy 2011; Foster and McChesney 2012) all while resisting protectionist interests in labor and some industries. These broad economic conditions set a backdrop against which business, as abstract interests, institutionally and politically reacted to changing conditions of profitability on historically specific institutional terrain. Politically, this involved well-documented interindustry struggles over the direction of American trade policy, together with strategic initiatives to alter the institutional form of the state policy-making apparatus. As Chorev (2007) documents, both substantive policy changes as well as more general institutional changes arising from the 1974 Trade Act, reflected these struggles.

At the same time, an ideological struggle among corporate leaders also unfolded. Within the United States, this was characterized by the re-articulation and deepening resonance of economic liberalism among corporate conservatives, who mounted a serious campaign (backed by a conservative wing of the corporate rich) to affect a rightward tilt in the political orientation of key corporate policy organizations (Domhoff 2013). A key and recurring feature of this conservative package of economic goals was the general rationale to unhinge markets from the state. Although these goals were not met without conflict within the business community, the general logic of "unhinged" markets resonated with internationalists sponsoring the fight for free trade against protectionists. At the same time, broader macroeconomic changes during this period supported the mobilization of a new political-organizational apparatus among corporate leaders, including the Business Roundtable and numerous other conservative corporate policy organizations. In the process, a class coalition of advocates for deregulation, free trade, and monetarism emerged, favoring a broad societal turn to a vision paralleling Polanyi's (1944 [2001]) account of *haute finance* and the utopia of a "self-regulating market." Corporate elite shifted this new coalition of business to the right, politically. The strident defense of free markets internationally offered an ideological upper hand to more conservative economic voices domestically. Conservative business leaders moved from more marginal positions in the policy network of corporate organizations to newer and more important ones of the era, bringing with them the emerging ideology of neoliberalism (Mizruchi 2013). Together, free trade abroad and free markets at home *fused in a new conservative economic ideology and a politics of domestic deregulation and neoliberal globalization.*

While this general aspect of the historical interpretation is not entirely new, our specification of these relationships clarifies the historical location of trade policy within the emergence of neoliberal globalization. Further, this historical argument identifies the linkage between political initiatives to liberalize trade over the course of many decades and key moments of corporate collective action where class agency was a guiding force.

To summarize, a number of important economic and political transformations occurred between the mid-1960s and early 1970s. Important new corporate policy organizations emerged during this period, as did macroeconomic fluctuations propitious to radical transformation of the American trade policy process. This conjuncture had political and economic dimensions that ultimately shifted the relative power center and ideology of the leaders of large manufacturing and financial corporations in the United States decidedly rightward, creating space for resonance with the emergent framework of neoliberalism and supplyside economics. We also argue that the Emergency Committee for American Trade (ECAT) – which was founded during this same era – can be viewed as a focal point for this historical narrative on the rise of neoliberal trade policy. The general coherence of this corporate group's agenda and its effective policy activism across time are inconsistent with much conventional trade policy literature that portrays political disarray among corporate elite, forcing government leaders to become the primary progenitors of neoliberal trade policy. In contrast, the historical presentation below shows that corporate leaders acted assertively and creatively through a political-organizational apparatus that brought both corporate leaders and their vision into the Johnson, Nixon, and Ford administrations, collaboratively advancing the 1974 Trade Act. The tone and the institutional precedents were set for a new era of neoliberal globalization, one that comes fully to the fore in the North American Free Trade Agreement (NAFTA).

GLOBAL INSTITUTIONS AND AMERICAN TRADE POLICY: THE CUSP OF A NEW ECONOMIC ERA

Accounts of the postwar (1945–1970) transformation in international institutions and global capitalism abound (cf. Evans 1995; Ruggie 1998). Generally, scholars agree on numerous key developments within that period. In the twenty-five years after World War II, for example, scholars often highlight the importance of: the militarization of the United States and USSR during the Cold War, the collapse of the formal colonial system and subsequent decolonization, the expansion (in both size and operational scope) of US multinational corporations, and the buttressing of American economic and political power through international institutions. Collectively, these diffuse transformations contributed to a deep restructuring of the world system wherein the United States emerged as a world superpower. Key to the growing political power of the United States was the success of its multinational firms in the areas of finance, manufacturing, advanced technology, and energy; in many cases, the growth of these corporations was fueled by the successful globalization of their operations, which included both foreign production and entry into non-US consumer markets. In tandem with these changes, a new international division of labor closely linked to the colonial system quickly took shape in the postcolonial order. With infinite local derivations, the political conflicts associated with decolonization and other postcolonial conflicts became tightly fused with Cold War politics. This drew local struggles for autonomy into the highly politicized economic development strategies associated with the two global powers. The geopolitics, foreign policy, and military interventions of the United States often reflected its interest in shaping and preserving a global "free enterprise system" (Arrighi 1994). The historical conditions were set for a new era of globalization.

Within this broader context, state *and* corporate leaders in the United States worked closely together during the war while hosting the United Nations, sponsoring negotiations for founding the Bretton Woods institutions and, later, successfully founding the General Agreement on Tariffs and Trade (GATT) (see Domhoff 2013). While state actors often feature prominently in historical accounts of the important developments, Chorev (2007) argues the Bretton Woods and GATT institutions were not *just* the product of political leaders. Instead, corporate leaders in the Business Council, the Committee for Economic Development (CED), the Council on Foreign Relations (CFR), and US delegates to the International Chamber of Commerce (ICC) were all instrumental in the development of the GATT and the Bretton Wood institutions. These same organizations and their leaders worked closely in the decades that followed to open the world trading system and, later, to reform the international monetary system. Expanding global economic power and market opportunities were thus driven not only by state elite but also by corporate elite who worked closely with the state during and after World War II.[1]

---

[1] See Panitch and Gindin (2013, chaps. 3–5) for a full account of the Bretton Woods institutions. See also Ruggie (1998), McMichael (2012), and Evans (1995).

Well-documented historical accounts shed light on the importance of corporate leaders who worked closely with state leaders to provide the specific policy and institutional formulae, ensuring that business interests matched or exceeded other political priorities. During and after World War II, for example, Domhoff (2013) explains how corporate internationalists in the Committee for Economic Development (CED) led the effort to expand the international trade and monetary system. Shoup and Minter (1977) provide detail on how the Council on Foreign Relations (CFR) worked behind the scenes to establish a framework for postwar US economic dominance. Domhoff (2014: 10) cites the CFR's Economic and Financial Group, which "concluded that the full productivity of the American Economy ... could only be realized if corporations were able to invest, purchase raw materials, and sell products in ... Western Europe, South America and the British Empire." International economic interests were formulated by corporate elite and channeled through the policy discussion circles to government officials, resulting in a concerted push to expand international trade and investment and boost American corporate interests.

What became known as the "Grand Area" strategy in elite foreign policy circles included major US foreign policy projects, including expanding influence in Southeast Asia and Japan, and the establishment of international financial and trade institutions (Domhoff 2013). The CFR and CED, which was formed in 1942, began to work closely together. Domhoff (2013, 2014) summarizes the convergence of corporate moderates in the CED and the CFR during and immediately following the war. Once the Bretton Woods negotiations began, the trustees for the CED were well positioned as corporate and financial leaders who were able to assuage the conference negotiators who openly fretted about the possibility that an IMF would usher in programs favorable to more labor-friendly interests and Keynesian liberals (ibid.). Once the CED stepped in and published its official statement, *The Bretton Woods Proposals* (1945), the Committee "received considerable acclaim in the media" (Domhoff 2013: 50).

A few years later, the General Agreement on Tariffs and Trade (GATT), negotiated in Geneva in 1947, set the terms for international trade with a strong bias favoring "the preferences of the internationalists" (Chorev 2007: 54). Chorev (2007: 52) cites the rationale for rejecting the earlier proposal for an International Trade Organization (ITO) by the US Executive Committee for the US Council of the International Chamber of Commerce (later renamed the US Council for International Business).

Their statement on the ITO read: "It is a dangerous document . . . because it jeopardizes the free enterprise system by giving priority to centralized national governmental planning of foreign trade . . . and in effect commits all members of the ITO to state planning for full employment" (ibid.). As Chorev (2007: 53) concludes, with the rejection of the ITO Charter in the United States, "all that remained was the General Agreement on Tariffs and Trade." Though weaker in jurisdiction than the proposed ITO, the GATT paved the path for an international trading system focused on international openness with "very little consideration of domestic concerns" (ibid.: 54). In the decades that followed, the GATT proved an effective means for committing nations to substantial tariff reduction while assuring that the size and scope of the US market would give US policy makers substantial leverage in *selectively* implementing GATT agreements.

Promoting free trade is not unique to the neoliberal era. After World War II, for example, the ideology of free trade permeated US foreign economic projects even though, in practice, the articulation of these ideas within actual policy remained limited. On this point, many US officials as well as the leaders of the largest banks and exporting corporations advocated for international institutions to match *selective* free trade priorities (Chorev 2007). Overall, their efforts succeeded. By the end of the 1960s, tariffs dropped globally, and export processing zones grew in Latin America, the Caribbean, and Asia. The postwar institutions and policies expanded markets for globalizing US corporations and fueled a rapid re-industrialization of Europe, Japan, and several emerging, or newly industrializing countries (NICs). Ruggie (1998) explains how embedded liberalism set a framework for trade policy that encouraged relatively open trade while acknowledging how these trade practices were "embedded" in a postwar social accord that assured some protection to citizens from the costly dislocations that can stem from the international trading system. Chorev (2007) discusses how the sources of "selective" protectionism stemmed less from an international agreement inspired by norms of embedded liberalism and more from the constraints imposed by domestic political institutions and practices in the United States. The key point for our discussion is that the postwar system advanced free trade, but did so in a way that was circumscribed by both domestic coalitions and international economic developments.

Domestic politics about trade, economic growth, and governance were of course impacted by the emergent postwar position of the United States as a superpower, domestically and internationally. Cold War anticommunism interacted with liberal democratic politics that first arose in the New Deal. Conveniently, anticommunism rhetoric provided ideological fuel for both the backlash against organized labor domestically as well as the articulation of US geopolitical interests abroad.[2] Notably, the same domestic and international constraints played out ideologically among top business leaders. As Domhoff (2013) and Mizruchi (2013) argue from slightly different stances, corporate political preferences were constrained on the left by organized labor and liberal constituencies and on the right by social and religious conservatives, anticommunists, and a faction of *laissez-faire*–minded corporate leaders and owners. Following the war, American business leaders engaged in recurring ideological disputes concerning the role of the government in the economy, as they had done during the decades prior.

The broad span of business leadership shared a general disdain for organized labor, although certain conservative organizations, such as the National Association of Manufacturers (NAM), were particularly aggressive in their attempt to dismantle labor protections through targeted congressional lobbying (Domhoff 2013). For the CED, goals for full employment along with protections for labor were deemed practical, and if applied modestly, served as a way to stave off revolutionary impulses in the workforce. CED co-founder, Paul Hoffman of Studebaker Automobile Company, for example, warned conservative business leaders that socialism and collectivism could indeed come to the United States, not by "design on the part of the revolutionaries" but because of "business leaders' failure to protect against mass unemployment through economic planning" (Fones-Wolf 1994: 23). Former CED employee Karl Schriftgiesser (1967) explained how tensions among the elite played out between an "old guard" – for whom Hayek's "*Road to Serfdom* was then the Bible" – and moderate corporate leaders. According to CED advisor John Clark of Columbia University, Keynes was "the antithesis to orthodoxy" for the moderates in the CED (Schriftgiesser 1967: 15 quoting Clark). Again citing Clark, Schriftgiesser explained how a postwar pragmatism ruled among moderates, as Keynes would be needed "to 'break through the crust of outworn ideas' and to 'fashion a synthesis in both theory and in policy'" (ibid.). In practice, Keynesian theory ruled for pragmatic, not ideological reasons. Thus, while the influence of Hayek's neoliberal economic philosophy did not disappear in the course of postwar history, it did take a backseat

---

[2] Silencing communism in the ranks of labor movements and steering center-left politics toward a "labor-capital" compromise was pivotal to the domestic constraints alluded to here. Domhoff (2014) spells these out in detail.

and even fell to the margins for some time, only to be picked up and put on the front burner of another important corporate-backed think tank: the American Enterprise Association (Domhoff 2013).

Free market and libertarian ideologies were frequently expressed within the group Domhoff describes as the "corporate conservatives." A key member of this group was the American Enterprise Association (later renamed the American Enterprise Institute (AEI)), which was founded in 1943 by Lewis H. Brown, head of the Johns-Manville Corporation. Like other free-market conservatives, Brown reacted strongly to the New Deal and feared that the entire foundation of American capitalism was threatened by government incursions on the profit motive (Fones-Wolf 1994). In the postwar period, AEI developed a board of trustees with support from a wide range of corporate leaders. The organization, influenced heavily by the works of Hayek and von Mises, connected a group of ultraconservative business leaders around an ideology built in opposition to Communism, Keynesian economics, and New Deal politics. While disputes among the corporate elite persisted in the postwar era, none would force a major ideological shift among the dominant corporate coalitions until the early 1970s, when conservative reactions to the New Left reached a fever pitch. By the late 1960s and early 1970s, the AEI and other conservative groups successfully organized a series of decidedly right-leaning corporate coalitions that fused conservative social agendas with a deregulatory, neoliberal turn in national economic policy. This will be explored further below.

MOBILIZING TO LIBERATE TRADE AND FINANCE: THE EMERGENCY COMMITTEE FOR AMERICAN TRADE

Responding in the early 1960s to growing political challenges at home and abroad, rising import competition, and growing tensions with the dollar, new pressures mounted among globalizing American corporations to protect the free trade program in the United States. By no means was business unified at this time. Some industries facing heavy foreign competition, such as steel and textiles, escalated their demands for trade protection. The AFL-CIO joined in calls for protection of basic industries as import competition rose. Tensions escalated between import-competing industries and more internationally oriented industries; in part, these conflicts were actually the *result* of the internationalists' earlier success in reducing tariffs worldwide. With President Kennedy promoting further tariff cuts, battle lines sharpened. The Trade Expansion Act (TEA) of 1962, which was a precursor to the opening of the GATT Kennedy

Rounds, sought to expand the authority of the president to unilaterally reduce tariffs over a five-year period, in concert with the GATT negotiations (Chorev 2007; Domhoff 2013). Anticipating the political challenges facing the TEA, the Committee for Economic Development (CED) mobilized to help ensure its passage.

As the legislative effort began, the CED published a report outlining the rationale for continued trade expansion and liberalization (Domhoff 2013). The report raised fears that the United States would encounter closed doors to the European Common Market and that developing countries would find affinity with the Soviet bloc if "they cannot find markets in the Free World" (Domhoff 2013: 107). Attempting to appease the textile sector, President Kennedy's special trade advisor – and former CED trustee and banker – Howard Peterson negotiated arrangements to enact special tariffs on textiles and subsidize cotton growers, assuring the industry's support for the bill (ibid.). Once passed, the initiative granted new authorities to the president in trade negotiations and established the Office of Special Trade Representative (STR) (Bauer, Pool, and Dexter 1972). This new position created a brokering capacity for the president, given that this executive appointee would now serve as a principal exchange between foreign governments, other government agencies, and Congress (Destler 1995: 107).

After the passage of the TEA, William M. Roth was appointed as the Special Trade Representative to the President. Mr. Roth, also a CED trustee, led the United States in opening the GATT negotiations (Domhoff 2013). The TEA also opened new avenues for the president to sway protectionist industries with the expanded authority to offer trade-related adjustment assistance. Though these remedies would be nominal, this particular institutional avenue would offer successive administrations new negotiating power with industries that otherwise sought relief through congressional lobbying for tariffs. Consequently, in advance of opening the GATT Kennedy Round (1963–1967), and with the authority of the new STR to directly affect trade remedies, the administration constrained the avenues available to industries getting punished by growing import competition (Destler 2005). In this way, the TEA helped set the stage for a strategic repositioning of protectionist demands directed at Congress (Chorev 2007). Because, as Destler (2005) and O'Halloran (1994) document, Congress proved more responsive to industry appeals for trade remedies, the political stage was set for a series of protectionist measures in Congress and a struggle over the contours of trade policy making in the United States (Chorev 2007).

By this time, the political strategy of moderate internationalists in the CED and the USCIB had focused on extending agreements between business leaders in the largest economies and on transforming the authority of the president to shape trade policy (Domhoff 2013). A 1965 CED annual report, written with a Ford Foundation four-year grant, explained their goal of promoting a unified trade strategy among business leaders in Japan, the United States, and Europe, just as negotiations unfolded between governments for a new round of the GATT (Domhoff 2013). Domhoff (2013: 106) reported that the CED-led negotiations among international corporate leaders amid the GATT Kennedy Round "were a very crucial step in the internationalization of the economy that corporate moderates had been advocating for over twenty years."[3] In 1967, the CED issued another report, prepared in association with their counterparts in Europe, Japan, Britain, and Sweden, outlining a strategy for "trade policy toward low-income countries" (CED 1967: 7), stating that: "The next order of business ... should be to liberalize the policies of the high-income countries with respect to their trade with the low-income countries."

The successful completion of the GATT Kennedy Rounds resulted in across-the-board tariff reductions. This pushed import-competitive industries into crisis mode as imports surged. Facing the pinch ideologically, textile industry leaders denied that their "proposed legislation to establish quantitative controls on textile imports" was protectionist (Wilcke 1967b: 79). At this time in 1967, lobbying by the steel and iron industries pressed for new import restrictions, that President Johnson opposed, and interindustry squabbles reached a new pitch. How might these tensions be resolved? Efforts within the CED and the Johnson administration pointed to a goal that was crystallizing: to simultaneously open markets globally but rely on the use of "adjustment assistance" to weaken protectionist political influence in the Congress. Further, the CED and the International Chamber of Commerce (ICC) were identifying nontariff barriers to trade, a term that would not enter fully into the trade policy lexicon of the Organisation for Economic

---

[3] The CED, as with the International Chamber of Commerce and Business Council, helped institutionalize corporate policy organizations in Europe and Japan in the postwar era. These international partners emulated the CED and Business Council in important respects, not the least of which were the names of these corporate organizations. The Japan Committee for Economic Development, the European Committee for Economic and Social Progress, and Britain's Political and Economic Planning organization all adopted the CED framework for uniting scholars, business leaders, and former political leaders in their advocacy structure.

Co-operation and Development (OECD) countries until a few years later. But the outlines for the next several years were emerging.

Mr. Arthur Watson, son of the IBM founder and vice chairman of the corporation, delivered a speech to an annual forum of world business leaders in Montreal in May of 1967 (Jones 1967). As incoming president to the International Chamber of Commerce[4] and chairman of the US delegation, Mr. Watson possessed a strikingly direct sense of the interdependence between the world financial system and world trade. A long-time member of leading business organizations, like the US Council for International Business, Mr. Watson shared with IBM executives and the leaders of other globalizing firms a view that international markets were buckling. Their solution, unlike the protectionists, required unfettered movement of capital, goods, and services globally – a reliance on market mechanisms. Like their economic conservative counterparts, they perceived the need to let markets work and this meant restructuring the Bretton Woods monetary arrangements and a transformation of national economic agendas rooted in Keynesianism. These leaders increasingly sought a multilateral market framework unbound from such national prerogatives.

Unlike protectionist leaders, the positions among business leaders at the ICC were bolstered by the recent conclusion of the latest GATT tariff reductions worldwide. International business leaders praised those major reductions in tariffs – averaging a 40 percent reduction among industrial nations' manufactured goods – but viewed the end of the GATT Kennedy round as an opportunity to further reduce obstacles for international business (Jackson 1997). The global monetary system was viewed as one of those obstacles to unfettered capital mobility. Mr. Watson explained to the gathering:

It matters little to free world industry whether the monetary system is ultimately based on gold, paper or sea shells. It matters a great deal that we have a system that will allow fairly wide swings in debt and credit. Trade is expanding and it must have an international monetary system that expands with it (quoted in Jones 1967: F43).

Though not significantly different from the views of his peers, Mr. Watson's prescriptions for changing the world monetary system

---

[4] The International Chamber of Commerce (ICC) was formed in 1919. In 1945, the US delegation to the ICC adopted a new organization, now known as the US Council for International Business. Mr. Arthur Watson was the first president of the ICC who father (Thomas J. Watson, founder of IBM) was also a president of the group.

were linked to his perception of an urgent need for a more robust system of multilateral trade liberalization.

For many corporate leaders whose business operations expanded internationally after World War II, the international monetary system posed growing challenges to those firms active in international markets. Bankers were particularly motivated to change the Bretton Woods system of pegged currency valuations to a floating system. David Rockefeller of Chase Manhattan Bank warned Congress in 1961 that the "build-up in U.S. short-term liabilities, which has supplied a massive dose of needed international liquidity, now poses problems to the United States. The dollar is no longer invulnerable to any and all circumstances" (Rockefeller 1963: 151). While Mr. Rockefeller understood the benefits that accrued to the United States with the gold-backed fixed exchange system, in 1961 he laid out the steps for abandoning the dollar's link to gold: "remove the requirement that gold be held against the note and deposit liabilities of the Federal Reserve Banks" (Rockefeller 1963: 153). Because, Rockefeller continued, New York's large banks are a "major part of the financing of our exports and imports of goods and services" the "United States must exercise a role of leadership in international financial matters. This is a part – an important part – of our role in contributing to the defense and development of the free world" (Rockefeller 1963: 158). This meant decoupling the international monetary system from postwar institutions.

The "dollar crisis" in 1960 had raised concerns among bankers as well as foreign finance ministers, especially in Europe, that the dollar could not match the demands on private speculation for gold (Panitch and Gindin 2013). As speculation drove gold up, the crisis forced President Kennedy to pledge to fix the value of the dollar at $35 an ounce (ibid.). This currency "fix" was deemed temporary and was premised on a combination of promoting US export competitiveness through Keynesian stimulus and trade liberalization with the TEA and GATT. Opening European capital markets to US finance was part of this fix in the early 1960s, something pushed through with the OECD's 1961 Code of Liberalization of Capital Movements (ibid.). Additional attempts with voluntary capital controls proceeded into the mid- and late-1960s. Growing balance of payments problems and the pressure they put on the dollar were creating macroeconomic incentives for policy makers, including President Johnson, to restrict imports and curb outward flows of capital stock in manufacturing investments. This condition was unacceptable to globalizing industries in finance, technology, and diversified manufacturing. Indeed, as much as these efforts helped internationalize and stabilize financial markets, administering fixed exchange rates became increasingly onerous "in the face of huge amounts of private foreign debt and volatile short-term capital movements" (Panitch and Gindin 2013: 130). Increasingly, the free play of the market would be seen as the antidote to the challenges of administering a pegged currency system. Resolving the burden of administering the fixed exchange rates would come – tenuously – when Nixon's Treasury (with Paul Volcker as undersecretary) abandoned the dollar's link to gold in 1971. But a political fight over trade came first.

In mid-1967, government and business free traders publicly announced their interest in the formation of a new coalition to push back against the protectionists (Chorev 2007). While several existing corporate organizations had long advocated the principle of free trade, the tone was shifting. The successful tariff reductions from the GATT Kennedy Round were in jeopardy. Activists were needed. At the largest annual gathering of business leaders, policy makers, and foreign leaders sponsored by the National Foreign Trade Council (NFTC), the urgency for doubling down on free trade was voiced. Senator Jacob K. Javits (R-NY) joined the Johnson Administration's chief trade negotiator, William M. Roth, to urge business to form an "emergency coalition" (Wilcke 1967a: 63). Their speeches were delivered to nearly 2,000 business executives attending the trade conference hosted by the NFTC at the Waldorf-Astoria Hotel. Ringing the alarm for an emergency coalition, they called for more than simply defeating protectionist impulses and aggressively urged moving the US trade agenda to new heights. Senator Javits reported that: "Except for the international anti-dumping code, the Kennedy round scarcely touched the vital area of non-tariff barriers. Yet these are the real inhibitors of expanded and liberalized world trade" (ibid.). Mr. Roth, the Special Trade Representative (STR) for the Johnson Administration and a trustee on leave from the CED, rallied the business leaders: "These are not the run-of-the-mill protectionist bills that crowd the Congressional hoppers every year and perish at the end of the session. They add up to a coordinated, concerted campaign," further citing that textile, steel, and chemical industry calls for mandatory import quotas would win out should longer term agreements fail to be reached with US trading partners (Wilcke 1967a: 67). If enacted, these bills, he argued, would "menace" the entire economy (ibid.). Of course, this sharp rhetoric also helped the STR do his job of negotiating the 1968 Voluntary Restraint Agreements for steel and textile imports from Japan and Europe. But it did more.

At the Waldorf-Astoria, a political strategy was brewing, one for bridging the divide between protectionists and internationalists, even as tensions climaxed. Senator Javits called on Congress to facilitate a solution by expanding the authority of the president to offer "trade adjustment assistance" to industries threatened by imports and to offer retraining assistance to workers dislocated from heightened trade (ibid.). This policy – when expanded in later years as Chorev (2007) argues – turned the attention of protectionists away from demands on Congress for protectionist measures and toward seeking adjustment assistance through the institutional channels of the executive branch. This strategic pivot arose as corporate leaders mobilized to overcome divisions within their ranks and institute changes in trade policy. Following the fifty-fourth annual convention of the National Foreign Trade Council, the group authored a thirty-page declaration urging the president to expand adjustment assistance to industries negatively impacted by surging imports. At the same time, the group's declaration – adopted by approximately 2,000 participants including business leaders and foreign diplomats – called for an end to the Interest Equalization Tax and the Voluntary Foreign Credit Restraint Program,[5] "without further restrictive controls" (Wilcke 1967a: 67). Trade and financial liberalization were explicitly linked.

A reporter covering the event for the *New York Times* wrote that "the formation of a business committee might be close to realization" (Wilcke 1967b: 71). It was also reported that a message from President Johnson read at the event called on "all of us" to preserve the "constructive trade policy built over 30 years" (ibid.). Just over a week later, Wilcke reported that an executive with the American Importers Association, who met with "about a dozen organizations" and Senator Javits had helped form a "blue ribbon committee" that would initiate a national campaign to promote the merits of free trade (Wilcke 1967c: F71). Others in that meeting spoke of the need to shift the agenda in Congress. A coordinated campaign was underway, with written requests for support "sent to about 1200 business executives across the country" (Wilcke 1967c: F75, Col 5). Less than a week later, and just two weeks after the conference at the Waldorf-Astoria Hotel, the new "emergency coalition" was formed. The Emergency Committee for American Trade (ECAT) arose following these meetings of several US "business leaders ... concerned that a new worldwide trade war was in the making" (ECAT 2008). Concerned that new demands to restrict trade were passing through Congress and that

---

[5] A government program initiated in 1963 to limit US capital outflows for foreign investment (see Diebold 1971; Williams Commission 1971: 80).

retaliatory trade threats were being made between nations, these corporate leaders voiced an agenda for an open, multilateral trading system, and began a national public relations campaign on the merits of free trade and the menace of protectionism.

Alongside the older organizations associated with the promotion of free trade, especially the National Foreign Trade Council and the US Council for International Business(USCIB), ECAT organized and educated corporate leaders about foreign markets and current policy developments at annual conventions. Officially, the USCIB also served for decades as the official conduit between globally oriented corporate leaders in the United States and the International Chamber of Commerce (ICC). But ECAT was different, and the mandate was strategic and activist. Table 4.1 lists the corporate founders of ECAT in 1967. Eighteen of the twenty-two co-founders were involved in the CED while they led some of the largest corporations in America; many were also first- and second-generation heirs to the great corporate estates of America's corporate elite. Headed by Arthur Watson of IBM, son of IBM's founder, ECAT launched an immediate public relations campaign with ads in major newspapers warning of the consequences of protectionism. David Rockefeller, grandson and heir of John D. Rockefeller and president of Chase Manhattan Bank, served as cofounder, along with George S. Moore of First National City Bank. David Packard, chairman of Hewlett-Packard, Henry Ford, II, chairman of Ford Motor Co., H. J. Heinz, II, of H. J. Heinz, and several other notable corporate leaders joined as cofounders of ECAT (Jones 1968: F10). Without delay, this group swung into action, impacting subsequent trade policy disputes in the United States.

Strategically, ECAT formed a visibly public face over the next few years. Of the twenty-two group cofounders, all but four were either trustees of the CED or had CED members on their corporate boards. ECAT's leadership maintained robust connections to the central business organizations of the period, and many were appointed to positions in government to help overhaul American trade institutions under Nixon, Ford, and Carter.

In 1970 ECAT worked alongside the Nixon administration's STR and former CED trustee, William Eberle, showing how it would conduct free trade advocacy in the years ahead.[6] Beyond the public media campaigns and meetings with government officials, ECAT assumed an important intermediary role during major international trade negotiations. Led by

---

[6] See Chorev (2007), chapter 4 for a full account of the dispute over textiles.

TABLE 4.1 *Founding Corporate Executive Members of the Emergency Committee for American Trade, 1967*

ECAT FOUNDER	CORP	Title	CED
Rockefeller, David	Chase Manhattan Bank	President	
Watson, Arthur	IBM	Chairman	CED
Moore, George S.	First National City Bank	Chairman	CED
Hewitt, William A.	Deere & Co	Chairman	CED
Ingersoll, Robert S.	Borg-Warner Corp	Chairman	
Linen, James	Time, Inc	President	CED
Packard, David	Hewlett-Packard Co	Chairman	CED
Peterson, Peter G.	Bell & Howell Co	President	CED
Peterson, Rudolph A.	Bank of America	President	CED
Powers, Jr., John J.	Chas. Pfizer & Co. Inc	President	CED
Roche, James M.	General Motors Corp	Chairman	CED
Taylor, A. Thomas	International Packers, Ltd.	Chairman	CED
Thornton, Charles B	Litton Industries, Inc	Chairman	CED
Wilson, Joseph C.	Xerox Corp.	Chairman	CED
Allen, William M.	Boeing	President	CED
Ball, George W.	Lehman Brothers International	Chairman	CED
Blackey, William	Caterpillar Tractor Co	Chairman	CED
Dean, R. Hal	Ralston Purina Co.	President	
Ford, II, Henry	Ford Motor Co	Chairman	CED
Grace, J. Peter	W.R. Grace and Co	President	
Haggerty, Patrick E	Texas Instruments Inc.	Chairman	CED

(*Source:* Gerd Wilcke, "Watson of I.B.M. Heads Group Opposing Import Quota Moves," *New York Times*. November 16, 1967d: 69)

Kendall, CEO of PepsiCo and a long-time confidant of President Nixon, ECAT formed an entourage of executives to meet with the chief industrialists in Japan. Alongside the PepsiCo chairman were the CEOs of several large corporations, including Chrysler, General Motors, Caterpillar, and, representing Chase Manhattan, David Rockefeller (Jones 1970: 128).

Instead of offering support for domestic protectionists, the ECAT leaders delivered the message that the "Japanese will have to accept some kind of voluntary quotas. We in ECAT are not in favor of quotas, but so long as they are voluntary, they can be changed" (Jones, March 9, 1970: 56). According to an interview with Kendall reported in the *New York Times*, the ECAT delegation argued that Japan could no longer proceed with a "leisurely liberalization"; dramatic steps to open imports and investment rules would be needed if Japan were to retain the benefit of accessing US markets (ibid.). In addition to meeting directly with Japanese premier Eisaku Sato, Rockefeller and other members of the ECAT delegation met with Japanese business leaders of San-Ken, led by the president of Tokyo Electric Power Company. Executives from Mitsubishi, Mitsui, and Sumitomo were part of ECAT's Japanese counterpart coordinated by the Japan Committee for Economic Development (ibid.). ECAT's strategy was clear: accelerate liberalization and voluntarily limit textile exports or face the consequences of protectionist forces in the United States. Observers of trade policy disputes at the time acknowledged that large Japanese companies supported increased trade and investment liberalization, but smaller businesses in Japan resisted such moves. Mr. Kendall, however, reported optimism: "I think it is well known that Japanese business and Government are noted for walking down the same track together" (ibid.).

In the days that followed, headlines reported fears of a "textile war" with Japan. Nixon's chairman to the Council of Economic Advisers, Paul McCracken, stated: "It is not overly alarmist to say that ... we may be on the verge of a trade war with Europe and Japan" (quoted in Chorev 2007: 79). These reports echoed in the halls of Congress and were taken up within the Ways and Means Committee. Despite growing tensions in the United States, Tokashi Oka, reporting from Tokyo, summarized a plan by business leaders to end the "impasse" (Oka 1970: 49). The plan involved an agreement crafted by the two business groups, ECAT and San-Ken. While the Kendall/ECAT agreement was lauded as a step toward ending an impasse, it was also acknowledged as "only a private suggestion" that would not necessarily "deter Congress from enacting restrictive legislation" (Oka 1970: 51).

For the next six months, as a major trade bill in Congress prompted speculation of a return to Smoot-Hawley and an end to thirty years of freer trade, ECAT and other corporate leaders continued to press on with private meetings with government officials in Japan and Europe. Creative agency on the part of corporate leaders was evident in their visibly strategic pivots from publicly voicing threats of American protectionism to foreign leaders and, while at home, warning the public and elected officials about lost exports and jobs if US trading partners retaliated against any protectionist legislation from Congress. Though the textile bill passed in the House, the bill never reached a vote as a result of "some very effective behind-the-scene lobbying ... carried on by members of ECAT" (quoted in Chorev 2007: 81). The conflict over this bill, Chorev (2007: 81) argues, exposed a deeper clash "because the division of responsibility between Congress, which had control over unilateral protectionist measures, and the administration, which was responsible for bilateral negotiations and agreements, made it difficult to reach a compromise between protectionist and internationalist interests." Exposing this institutional chasm prepared internationalist corporate leaders in ECAT and the Nixon administration to develop a path beyond the policy system that offered protectionists a path to success not only in a single industry but across a range of sectors. As Chorev (2007: 69) explains,

In a counterattack, internationalists managed to block the textile bill that the protectionists had promoted. More fundamentally, internationalists established a second institutional transformation: the Trade Act of 1974 delegated further authority from the unreliable Congress to the executive branch, thereby weakening protectionists' political influence and curbing future protectionist threats.

A revision of trade policy *institutions* was now on the table.

INTERNATIONALISTS TAKE STRIDE: SETTING THE TRADE AGENDA AND LIBERATING THE DOLLAR

US policy leaders viewed trade liberalization as an American project, integrated with broader US foreign policy objectives. Nixon's Williams Commission's first report in 1971, *United States Trade and Investment Policy in an Interdependent World*, attributed the peace in Europe – no longer the "world tinderbox" – to the "economic prosperity and the closer economic integration of the continent brought about by a sharp reduction in barriers to trade and investment" (Williams 1971: 6). Created to guide the Nixon administration on international economic policy, the Williams Commission gathered business leaders, academics, and two union presidents in a forum to craft a broad foreign economic policy agenda. The Williams Commission developed a framework for rethinking multilateral trading systems in the context of heightened pressures from protectionist interests in the steel, textile, and chemical industries. Disputes over trade policy were relatively clear-cut in the corporate community, and the avenues to resolve them were already in the making. Indeed, the Williams Commission was designed with this aim. But other conflicts within the corporate community were becoming apparent in the late 1960s, and these would spill over into the factional battles within the CED. Even as the CED continued to author influential reports that would guide Nixon's domestic policy, some of the leadership in the CED moved in a more liberal direction (Domhoff 2013). Conservative trustees would become increasingly vocal in their criticisms of CED staff, even as more conservative members found sway within the Nixon administration.

By the time the Williams Commission was formed, a group of conservative business leaders, which included ECAT co-founders, assumed an important role in Nixon's administration. On the Commission were nine CED member corporations and several CED trustees, including Williams himself. The president of the CED, Alfred C. Neal, was also appointed to the Commission. Two ECAT co-founders were also appointed to the Commission. Another ECAT co-founder and conservative CED trustee, Pete G. Peterson (former chairman and CEO of Bell & Howell)[7], was appointed by Nixon in 1971 to be the Assistant to the President for International Economic Affairs (and chair of the Council of International Economic Policy). In 1972 he was named secretary of commerce and, as such, was the chief executive branch authority presiding over the STR. Most accounts of US trade policy, including Chorev's, fail to mention that Mr. Peterson was also a co-founder of ECAT. Instead, they presume that the administration advanced the trade agenda forged in the Williams Commission, with some help from business, but fail to acknowledge that some of the authors of the 1974 bill were also the founders of ECAT and active in the CED. The fact that Nixon's secretary of commerce was a co-founder of ECAT ensured that the voice of globalizing corporations would be heard in future action on trade. In fact, as lobbying for the 1974 Trade Act began, Mr. Peterson proved vital. With his ties to ECAT, the CED, and the Council on Foreign Relations, he and others "advocated the amendments exactly to limit the congressional role in trade policy formulation" (Chorev 2007: 70).

Nixon also appointed as his first Special Trade Representative (STR) the former chair of the CED's research committee on trade and currency,

---

[7] Mr. Peterson became a major force in the rightward drift in economic ideology in the 1970s and 1980s. A market-centered, neoliberal vision of economic policy runs through his career. Before founding The Blackstone Group, he served as chairman and CEO of Lehman Brothers and sat on numerous corporate boards. He is chairman emeritus of the Council on Foreign Relations, served on the Conference Board, and many other policy groups. From 2000 to 2004, he was chairman of the Federal Reserve Bank of New York. He has contributed millions of dollars to both moderate leaning and conservative policy organizations, from the Heritage Foundation to the Committee for Economic Development. As a recent trustee for the CED, he has committed over $1,000,000 to advocacy for Social Security privatization. His contributions to the Peter G. Peterson Foundation helped found the "Fix the Debt" group where his son Michael Peterson, COO of the PGP Foundation, serves on the steering committee. See http://pgpf.org/board/peter-g-peterson; http://bridge project.com/?organization&id=291870; http://www.fixthedebt.org/who-we-are, accessed November 7, 2013.

William Eberle. As STR, Mr. Eberle collaborated with Mr. Kendall of ECAT in their "private" negotiations with business leaders in Japan and Europe. Of note, and as part of the trade policy program that the Nixon administration would advance, Nixon appointed CED trustee David M. Kennedy of Continental Illinois Bank in Chicago as his first treasury secretary (Domhoff 2013). Nixon would continue to rely on CED trustees for this position, appointing George P. Schultz, CED advisor and former dean of the University of Chicago Business School, to the Treasury in 1972 (ibid.). Domhoff (2013) identifies several other CED appointments of note within the Nixon Administration. But importantly, the decisions in Treasury proved vital to Nixon's unfolding foreign economic policy, and the CED proved to be the brainchild for those developments.

On matters of trade policy, delicate negotiations over market access and import controls were ongoing as the world economic situation entered into general stagflation. Ongoing problems in international trade, and domestic inflation in mid-1969, prompted the Nixon administration to consider the lead of the Treasury, as it developed a strategy to decouple the dollar from gold, if needed. That strategy was advanced a year later by the Williams Commission, as advisers wrestled with the question of how to support the competitiveness of US exports when the dollar was propped so high, artificially. The problem extended to imports as an overvalued dollar made foreign products more attractive, compromising profits for US businesses and jobs for American workers. To deal with domestic economic problems, an international agenda was needed. For Nixon's advisors, the "central policy dilemma ... became how to maintain the system of fixed exchange rates that revolved around the dollar without jeopardizing both economic growth and the momentum towards liberalized trade and capital flows" (Panitch and Gindin 2013: 123). For years, Eberle, as STR, would work alongside the Secretary of Treasury to negotiate a resolution to both trade issues and the system of currency exchange. International monetary and trade policy were inextricably linked. And the further liberalization of both was at hand.

By late 1970, these same advisors in the Williams Commission urged an end to the 1962, 1965, and 1968 voluntary restrictions on capital outflows (VFCRs). This occurred despite the drop in tariff barriers that was presumed to be the reason for US corporate investments in Europe – to move production closer to the intended markets and avoid import tariffs in Europe. Now with tariff rates dropping and the lack of evidence that these capital outflow restraints solved any problems with current reserves, one advisor for the Commission asked: "Why not allow free play to these market forces and let banking funds move freely into other countries?" (Pizer quoted in Williams 1971: 90). Though the question had been asked many times before, and even suggested a decade earlier by David Rockefeller, the problem was not with the United States, but "because of the difficulties for foreign monetary authorities." Pizer continued, "viewed as a measure to bridge the gap until such broad evolutionary changes can take place, the present method of restraint seems impractical. The VFCR tends to freeze existing patterns of US banks' foreign activity, and to lack flexibility as markets and institutions change" (quoted in Williams 1971: 92). The question of when to "close the gold window" produced a constant wavering in Treasury, leading some observers to wonder if Undersecretary of Treasury Paul Volcker would push the dial forward (Domhoff 2013). The answer came, as the "Nixon Shock" to the world, on August 15, 1971, when the United States withdrew its pledge to convert dollars into gold (Destler 2005: 57). Two years later, by early 1973, amid a spate of reports of a "jittery Europe" and following years of negotiations, the resulting fiat currency began to float against other major currencies. As Destler sums up, "American exports benefited; import competition eased somewhat; and the management of trade-restrictive pressures was somewhat less of a burden" (ibid.: 57). Just as the program for the liberalization of currency markets unwound, a resolution to the dilemmas for trade policy came forth. The birth of neoliberal globalization as a distinct shift in trajectory had begun.

TRANSFORMING THE STATE: LOBBYING FOR THE 1974 TRADE ACT

Freeing the monetary system of pegged exchange rates and instituting a floating exchange rate system corresponded to the re-ordering of US international trade priorities, particularly among the leaders of the MNCs that came to dominate elite class networks at the time. By the early 1970s, a number of public speeches matched the policy urgings of the ICC, the ECAT, and USCIB. Well documented in Barnet and Muller (1974a), statements by corporate managers revealed a conscious and deliberative understanding of the role that globalizing corporations should play as a new force in history. "For business purposes," said Maissenrouge (president of IBM World Trade Corporation), "the boundaries that separate one nation from another are no more real than the equator ... The world outside the home country is no longer viewed as series of disconnected customers and prospects for its products, but as an extension of a single market" (quoted from Barnet and Muller 1974a: 14–15). These were not pronouncements of a global humanism, but reflected a sharpened understanding of new constraints and challenges in the US economy that demanded new corporate and policy initiatives.

IBM, Motorola, General Electric, and many other corporate leaders embraced a one-world market vision. The postwar boom had consolidated interests among the leaders of America's largest corporations, organized into a leadership network well documented by Domhoff (2013) and Mizruchi (2013). Many of these same leaders came of age in an era where Keynesianism, while successful in national development objectives, introduced several restrictions to the corporate vision of a *global* free market. This emerging utopian vision helped define a new course for American corporate leaders, even as disputes among corporate conservatives and moderates choked the postwar status quo and set the stage for the birth of a series of rightward-leaning business organizations that would supplant the CED as the corporate network's center of gravity. Indeed, as economic pressures mounted transformations in the US and world economy had set the stage for a conflict among business leaders over free markets and the role of the state. Forging a uniform, national trade policy agenda would require diminishing the influence of those sectors whose interests demanded heightened trade protection while simultaneously elevating those sectors advancing more a liberalized vision of trade, such as finance, technology, and services. The promises of free trade, moreover, resonated with the *laissez-faire*–minded corporate leaders who decried growing government regulations and the political power of the New Left.[8]

With the introduction in 1973 of the Trade Reform Act, US leaders leveraged support for their international trade and monetary negotiations taking place in March (when finance ministers agreed to drop any further discussion of returning to a fixed system of currency exchanges) (Domhoff 2013). The introduction of the trade bill was designed to empower the president's position at those negotiations, both domestically and internationally. As Chorev (2007: 83) argues, the draft bill's "unilateral measure, which faithfully followed ECAT's suggestion, asked Congress for presidential authority to retaliate against any country" that implemented tariffs or other restrictions deemed unreasonable to the United States.

---

[8] The passage of the Occupational Safety and Health Act, the National Environmental Protection Act, and other environmental protection measures raised the ire of corporate conservatives and inspired a movement by business leaders to rally against excessive regulations as an attack on free enterprise (Domhoff 2014).

This portion of the bill would come to be known as Section 301. The other substantive development in the bill sought to expand the negotiating authority of the president in multilateral talks. But this authority, like the constitutional challenge its predecessor in the 1934 RTAA encountered, ran up against the division of powers within the US Constitution, which prohibits the president from implementing international treaties or agreements that require changes to domestic law. The STR agreed to a solution, however, known as "fast track," which would effectively submit trade agreements to Congress for an up or down vote, without amendment and within a limited timeframe (Destler 2005).

Many observers of US trade policy note that this was a major transformation in the authority granted to the president. Chorev (2007: 84) argues that the move was "as revolutionary as the delegation of authority over tariffs in 1934, for it strengthened the credibility of the US administration at the international realm, at the expense of Congress's ability to unilaterally defy compromises made during international trade negotiations."

Strategically, the draft bill included recommendations coming out of the Williams Commission that would not only increase the odds of the bill's passage in Congress but also enhance the powers of the president to pursue strong negotiating tactics internationally. Robert Norris, president of the National Foreign Trade Council, stated it was clear that the new bill reflected a "coordinated development of the proposed legislation which is designed to take fully into account the inter-relationships of our trade policy and our foreign economic policy with domestic economic policy" (Jones 1973: 75). Mr. Kendall, Nixon's personal friend and leader of the ECAT, remarked that the bill was a "clear-cut mandate from the people," and lauded the president's call for more authority on trade matters as "reasonable and right" (ibid.: 75). The deputy STR under Nixon at the time, William Pearce, was also a member of the Williams Commission and a former vice-president for Cargill.[9] Chorev (2007: 85) cites a memo from Pearce that explained how support for the bill would be crafted: "Extensive consultations will be required to develop a dependable core of private backing around which major support can be mobilized." Even as Nixon was engulfed in the Watergate scandal, supporters for the bill – including ECAT – organized a vigorous lobbying campaign. Because other trade initiatives allayed concerns of the textile and steel sectors, and because the bill expanded adjustment assistance, protectionist opponents were weakened. Passage of this legislation, first in the House in 1973 and

---

[9] See Williams (1971) for the full text of the report.

then in the Senate in 1974, dramatically expanded the institutional authority of the executive branch in trade policy negotiations; among other changes, it formalized avenues for business participation in trade policy while simultaneously diluting the authority of Congress.[10]

Chorev's (2007: 102) astute analysis concludes that the institutional shift in the 1974 Trade Act "allows us to identify the actors who were behind the globalization project: in the United States, this was a tight coalition of top administration officials and the leading associations representing the largest internationally oriented corporations" whose "goal was ... to allow those protectionist measures that do not disturb the project as a whole." The Nixon administration, stacked with leaders from the CED and ECAT, created opportunities for a strategic dialogue about trade in a changing global economy. The goal of these corporate leaders was not simply to influence legislation, but to transform the structure of the state itself. In doing so, an institutional environment more conducive to the pursuit of the globalization project was developed. Shifting trade policy away from Congress and toward the executive branch reflected a political strategy by internationalists to thwart protectionist opponents and consolidate a new form of strategic power within the state (Chorev 2007).[11]

For the purposes of this study, a key component of the new institutional context arising from the Trade Act of 1974 was the creation of a three-tier system of federal trade policy advisory committees serving in the newly formed Office of the US Trade Representative (USTR). These advisory committees allowed industry representatives to provide policy input and recommendations to US trade negotiators. This elaborate system of "private sector advisory committees" was established "to ensure that US trade policy and trade negotiation objectives adequately reflect US commercial and economic interests" (Office of the US Trade Representative 1994: 114). Revised under trade legislation three times since 1974, this advisory system has been greatly expanded to "provide information and advice on U.S. negotiating objectives and bargaining positions before entering into trade agreements, on the operation of any trade agreement once entered into, and on other matters arising in connection with the development,

---

[10] See Chorev (2007: 85–101) for a review of the major substantive developments in the 1974 Trade Act and how the policy shift was "the deliberate creation of internationalists and their supporters in the administration."

[11] Barnet and Muller (1974b) wrote a scathing Op-Ed in the *New York Times*, naming the ECAT as a primary antagonist in the gross exit of manufacturing jobs from the United States.

implementation, and administration of U.S. trade policy" (Office of the US Trade Representative 1994: 114).

Corporate leaders are appointed to these advisory committees by the president and the US Trade Representative. These appointed positions enable corporate executives to engage in an ongoing dialogue between diverse groups of corporate leaders, trade associations, and various cabinet-level officials under the president. Under the "fast track"[12] rules established by the Trade Act of 1974, the executive branch must submit pending trade legislation to the Trade Advisory Committees (TACs), which evaluate whether the pending trade legislation is "consistent" with US producer interests. Because it is exceedingly rare for Congress to support trade legislation that is opposed by one or more of the various advisory committees, they possess a de facto veto over pending trade legislation (Cohen et al. 2003: 125). In addition to their evaluative function, TACs provide direct input into active US trade negotiations. While information regarding the specific activities of TACs is not disclosed, their organizational self-description explains: "The Department of Commerce (DOC), Office of the U.S. Trade Representative (USTR), and other agencies work side by side with business leaders [TAC members] who serve as advisors to the Government" (DOC 2000: 3). These TACs function as a facilitative state structure, drawing business leaders into the state apparatus for focused dialogue and negotiations over the future of American trade policy. As the chapters ahead address in greater detail, these institutional frameworks offer an opportunity for organized corporate leaders to exercise class agency in the making of US trade policy.

RISE OF THE ROUNDTABLE: MODERATES ON THE ROPES

A discussion of this period would not be complete without a review of the political realignment of the corporate network in a new policy-planning system that elevated the Business Roundtable to the center by1976. Mizruchi (2013) charts the decline of moderate leaders in the CED, while Domhoff (2013) offers evidence that the decline of the CED and rise of the Business Roundtable reflected a departure of conservative corporate leaders, who had always pressed for limitations on labor and

---

[12] Fast Track allows the Executive Branch to submit a recently concluded trade negotiation to Congress for an up-or-down vote, without the possibility for the inclusion of amendments. These rules were modified in 1998 and are now referred to as Trade Promotion Authority (TPA) for the President.

New Deal projects. Their detailed analyses are drawn on heavily in the account that follows. In addition, an overview is needed as many existing analyses do not explain how the rightward turn of corporate leaders during this time helped fuse insurgent free market conservatives with the more established free trade internationalists – a nexus that ultimately forged a new class coalition uniting the ascendant banners of conservativism, free trade, and deregulation.

As the Nixon administration was advancing its economic plan, including the previously discussed trade policy initiative, political momentum for conservative corporate leaders was building. These leaders sponsored new think tanks, foundations, and policy-planning organizations – all with the aim of shifting the corporate and national political ideology to the right. The AEI, the Heritage Foundation, the American Legislative Exchange Council, and others were the main benefactors of this renewed fight by corporate conservatives; other benefactors included "an alternative group of foundations with strongly conservative views ... the most prominent of which were the ... Olin, Scaife, and Smith Richardson foundations" (Mizruchi 2013:152). Combined with huge sums of private money and growing corporate contributions, corporate conservatives raised the profile of free market ideology just as a number of moderate corporate leaders were finding new reasons to rethink their support for the middle-of-the-road policy agenda that took hold in the postwar years. On this point, an important debate among corporate leaders had begun over the state's role in economic policy, and support was tilting away from Keynesian prescriptions and toward monetarist and supply-side solutions. Notably, this shift occurred just as increased import competition met rising costs in raw materials, labor, and environmental and workplace regulations. These conditions produced what economists Bowles, Gordon, and Weiskopff (1990) refer to as the "profit squeeze" on American business that began in the late 1960s. Flagging profits intersected with the growing momentum of right-leaning business groups, creating an opportune moment for business leaders to focalize and advance a new, more market-friendly agenda. As these debates over the direction of the US economy unfolded, opportunities were created for more conservative free market factions to align with the free trade internationalists. A paradigm shift for national economic policy was close at hand. The fights against import quotas and for free trade proved critical to this shift, as ECAT allied with conservative corporate leaders in NAM and the Chamber of Commerce, as well as other internationalists in the USCIB, to advance the 1974 trade bill.

The conservative factions' real influence took hold in the early 1970s as the system of "embedded liberalism" began to unravel. Stoked by the liberal-left movements of the period, conservative elites offered a program to aggressively defend "the free enterprise system." The infamous Powell memo, mentioned in the Introduction, inspired many corporate leaders in the conservative movement. Phillips-Fein (2009) notes how John M. Olin, leader of the chemical manufacturing giant Olin Industries, was moved by the Powell directive. In a letter to the head of the AEI, which Olin would contribute to generously, he explained how he found inspiration "for a well-organized effort to re-establish the validity and importance of the American free enterprise system" (quoted in Philips-Fein 2009: 162). It should be noted, however, that the Powell memo merely reflected a groundswell of conservativism that was already well underway with right-leaning business leaders. For example, executives of large manufacturing firms, including Business Council members, NAM members, and CED trustees, had already hatched two efforts, the Labor Law Study Group to weaken labor law (1965) and the Construction Users Anti-Inflation Roundtable (1969), to press against rising labor costs (Domhoff 2013; Mizruchi 2013). These efforts outside of the CED would eventually overtake the organization as an exodus in members and funding took root after 1972.

The eventual disputes among CED leaders reflected wider conflicts among business leaders at the time. Amid growing contention among CED leaders following a speech by liberal-leaning chair of the Research and Policy Committee, Domhoff (2013: 195) quotes one CED member who asked "whether CED should continue to be a proponent of Keynesianism doctrine." Domhoff notes that this member and others were leaning toward the works of Friedrich Hayek, the 1974 Nobel Laureate in economics.[13] Hayek, who offered lectures to AEI audiences, helped seal the intellectual turn toward neoliberalism among corporate-backed policy groups. Domhoff (2013.: 197) cites another memo among CED leaders from September 24, 1975, which suggested that the CED "should use more American Enterprise Institute people."

The sentiment was contagious. Even though AEI had expanded its influence in the 1960s, managing to attract large contributions from

---

[13] Hayek's *The Road to Serfdom* (1944) proselytized on the promise of free markets and the tyranny of state planning and helped establish neoliberal economics, first promoted in Europe through the Mont Pelerin Society, and later, with the help of conservative business leaders, in the United States (Mirowski and Plehwe 2009).

corporations that also "had representatives who served as trustees of the CED," its influence paled in comparison to the CED at that time (Mizruchi 2013: 149). Yet by the mid-1970s AEI's membership and funding exploded. In 1980, as Mizruchi (2013: 149) documents, "AEI had a budget larger than the venerable Brookings Institution ... and included an eminent group of corporate leaders as fundraisers." In fact, by the end of the 1970s the CED would be seeking ways to work with the AEI and other business policy groups. The AEI's conservative platform found resonance among business leaders both in and out of the CED who sought a policy framework to push back on wage growth, labor unions, and new workplace and environmental regulations.

Internal schisms in the CED, as well as growing disinterest in Keynesianism by key trustees, led to a gradual shift in domestic economic policy. Efforts to curtail labor costs, particularly in the construction trades, led to the formation of the Construction Users Anti-Inflation Roundtable in 1969, a key organization that supported a larger, empirically unfounded campaign to pin inflation on labor costs alone (Domhoff 2013). The growing distance from Keynesianism by corporate moderates was met with answers from an expanding chorus of neoliberals – from Mont Pelerin to the American Enterprise Institute – who tirelessly echoed the mantra that markets are self-regulating.[14] Libertarians and neoliberals in the Nixon administration embraced this view, of course, with Alan Greenspan, appointed to Nixon's Council of Economic Advisers (CEA) and later to the chair of President Ford's CEA, being perhaps the most recognizable among them.

The CED, as Domhoff (2013) reports, faced more conflicts over economic policy at this time. The Keynesians were losing, particularly those friendly to labor who sought to control inflation by rolling back corporate subsidies and tax breaks (Domhoff 2014:19). As a number of corporate elite began to shift their ideological positions toward those advocated by the AEI, leadership in the CED became so worried that an internal study of the organization was commissioned in 1973 to assess the impact of declining membership dues on the organization's long-term sustainability (ibid.). This surge of interest in neoliberal economics occurred just as business conflicts over the efficacy of Keynesian prescriptions for inflation

[14] Harvey (2005) is among many scholars who attribute the spread of neoliberal economics to the Mont Pelerin Society (MPS). The society adopted the name based on the Swiss resort where the group was formed in 1947, led by Friedrich Hayek. Milton Friedman was an American notable at the founding of the group and later became president of the MPS.

were challenged and market forces were determined to be the solution to persistent balance of payment problems and an overvalued dollar. Conservative corporate leaders in the CED, the Business Council, and the NAM aligned with (and often financed) this growing neoliberal chorus. All of this occurred as domestic challenges by business leaders to government regulation aligned with the internationalists' heightened campaign for trade liberalization. A new consensus and faith in markets was emerging, one that would come together in the newly formed Business Roundtable.

In March of 1972, the CEOs of several large firms, including antiunion, conservative CED trustee John Harper of Alcoa, and another conservative CED trustee, Fred Borch of General Electric, met with Treasury Secretary Connally and Federal Reserve Chairman Arthur Burns to help launch a new kind of business organization (Mizruchi 2013). The group that emerged was identified as the March Group and eventually linked together with other corporate CEOs in the Labor Law Study Group and the Construction Users Anti-Inflation Roundtable, eventually forming the Business Roundtable in late 1972. Domhoff (2013) spells out the specific steps that forged the group and how its initial leadership was structured. By mid-1973, the BRT was putting together its administrative structure, expanding its initial membership, and devising a program. Domhoff (2013: 186–187) notes that the BRT's thirty-five founders "spanned the breadth of the corporate community," noting that twenty-two "were members of the Business Council … twelve were trustees of the CED, and four were trustees of NAM." This new group's "inclusion of trustees from both the CED and NAM" and the CED's movement "to a secondary position in the policy planning network" serve as evidence of "greater unity in the corporate community" (ibid.: 214–215). Mizruchi (2013: 157) explains how the BRT "quickly became a part of the conservative resurgence, backing organizations such as the AEI and committing itself to the primary conservative goals of the period: reducing government regulation of business, limiting the power of unions, and reforming the corporate tax code." By 1976, Domhoff (2013: 214) argues, "the Business Roundtable was clearly at the center of the corporate financed policy planning network in terms of interlocking directors."

The Roundtable responded to the nation's economic malaise by advocating for supply side economic policy and attempting, publicly, to build support for the idea that labor costs were the root of inflation. This focus on supply side, or "cost push inflation," as the Roundtable's opening declaration asserted, was a policy solution that would attack government protections on wages, beginning with the repeal of prevailing wage rules and limiting future hikes in the minimum wage (Domhoff 2013: 188). Burns, the Federal Reserve Chairman who was quoted in the Roundtable's founding statement of purpose, explained the inflationary debacle as one rooted in "runaway unit labor costs" that make "a limited recovery from low profit margins" conditional on business raising prices (quoted in Domhoff 2013: 188). Other publications from the Roundtable reiterated this sentiment. Hostility to labor unions and regulations were found in their 1974 report on the construction trades (Business Roundtable 1974). Their 1979 multivolume report on the *Cost of Government Regulation Study*, produced by their accounting firm Arthur Andersen & Co., detailed every major "regulatory burden" facing their member companies in 1977 (Arthur Anderson & Co. 1979). The agenda was now clear: weaken labor unions and promote major forms of deregulation that ease business operating costs. This framework resonated deeply with many corporate leaders, especially conservative leaders in NAM and the COC. Even as Roundtable executives maintained their close ties to the Business Council and CED, its leadership group expanded to include more conservative leaders from the National Association of Manufacturers. Business was highly unified.

By the 1980s, the unabashedly supply-side focus of the BRT and its vigorous advocacy for domestic deregulation, corporate tax cuts, and global free trade signaled a class realignment of historic proportions, one unquestionably inflected with neoliberal ideology. Pouring resources into Reagan's victory in 1980, the CEOs in the BRT led the conservative economic reforms of the era, abandoning Keynesian economics and New Deal policy priorities while aggressively attacking "labor unions, federal social welfare programs, and government regulation of the economy" (Phillips-Fein 2009: xi). Reagan appointed scores of AEI and Heritage Foundation members to his administration. With the AEI rising to prominence among think tanks, the BRT retained its central place in the larger corporate network. By the end of the 1980s, the BRT and its member-CEOs would also emerge at the center of a trade policy network geared toward challenging trade restrictions in the United States and abroad.

CONSOLIDATING A NEOLIBERAL TRADE POLICY NETWORK, 1983–1994

With the completion of the GATT Tokyo Rounds in 1979, US trade policy made several sharp turns, shifts that are particularly evident in the different agendas facing the Tokyo (1976) and Uruguay Rounds, which opened in 1986. As early as 1981, intentions were solidified within the US Trade

Representative for a new round of GATT (Chorev 2007; Cohen et al. 2003). US officials began to urge new rounds at both official and unofficial gatherings, and, despite reluctance by the GATT Secretariat, European leaders, and numerous developing nations, a GATT Ministerial meeting was convened to draw up draft recommendations and an agenda (Raghavan 1990). While the Tokyo Rounds advanced dispute settlement options for sensitive nontariff barriers to trade, the Uruguay Rounds expanded attention to nontariff barriers while also introducing a series of new concerns. These new themes included an unprecedented emphasis on Trade in Services, Trade-Related Intellectual Property Rights (TRIPs), and Trade-related Investment Measures (TRIMs).[15]

Following the Caribbean Basin Initiative in 1982, and just as the Uruguay Rounds of GATT began, other transformative trade liberalization projects emerged. Beginning with the Canada-United States Free Trade Agreement and culminating with the passage of the 2005 CAFTA, these trade policy negotiations established a policy bulwark for the broader neoliberal agenda in North and Central America. In the early 1980s, ECAT – pursuing the broader project for trade liberalization, particularly in services and investments – coordinated a small but powerful alliance under the banner of the Multilateral Trade Negotiation coalition to support free trade policies in the US Congress. Members of this group were highly active in the President's Advisory Committee on Trade Policy and Negotiations (ACTPN) during the early 1980s.[16] Participation in the MTN required a $200,000 initial contribution, followed by annual dues (*Inside US Trade* 1990). Consequently, even with the membership of several corporate lobbying groups, such as the Business Roundtable and ECAT, the MTN remained a very small group with a deliberate focus on trade policy. Following the successful negotiation and implementation of the United States–Canada Free Trade Agreement, interest grew for a bilateral free trade agreement with Mexico that could also serve as a model for trade relations throughout the hemisphere. This initiative, pursued in the USTR and among senior economic advisors to President George H. W. Bush, eventually morphed into the North American Free Trade Agreement.

By the late 1980s, a well-practiced strategy founded on the MTN experience emerged among corporate leaders advocating for further

---

[15] See Destler (2005), Chorev (2007), and Cohen et al. (2003) for a fuller discussion of the GATT priorities at this time.

[16] Determined with reference to the memberships of the Advisory Committee on Trade Policy Negotiations, US Trade Representatives' Office, 1982 and 1992.

trade liberalization. Leveraging the resources of the BRT, ECAT, NAM, the COC, and the USCIB, business collaborated to form public ad hoc organizations to assure congressional approval of "fast track" negotiating authority and passage of trade agreements. This strategy was realized in the effort to pass the NAFTA in the United States, which faced growing challenges from a broad coalition of labor, environmental, and other groups (Dreiling 2001). The leadership of the corporate campaigns to pass NAFTA and ratify the Uruguay GATT agreement arose not only from the central policy planning organizations but also from active leaders in the administration, revealing how the TACs created by the 1974 Trade Act facilitated class agency in defense of neoliberal trade policy.

A NEOLIBERAL TRADE POLICY NETWORK: DEFENDING THE NORTH AMERICAN FREE TRADE AGREEMENT

On January 1, 1994, the North American Free Trade Agreement (NAFTA) was implemented. Many viewed this event as a major policy victory for the architects of neoliberal trade. The NAFTA, like its close relative and successor, the 1995 World Trade Organization (WTO), departed significantly from previous multilateral trade initiatives in that trade in agricultural goods, as well as enforceable protections in intellectual property and foreign investment, were set for liberalization and institutionalization (Chorev 2005). Consequently, the mechanics of NAFTA and the WTO came to represent components of a much larger process of neoliberal globalization – a vision for a global, market-governed society with globally enforced investor rights (Wallach and Sforza 1999). The NAFTA architects, recognizing the plan's broad opposition as a threat to the planned trade zone, helped form a powerful business lobby that initiated an extraordinary campaign through the ad hoc USA*NAFTA coalition. Though not without considerable political conflict, the treaty's opponents were defeated, and the NAFTA was signed into law. The US Council for International Business triumphantly served international leadership awards to corporate executives for their role in "the business community's successful effort to pass NAFTA."[17] Upon the bill's passage in the United States, the Heritage Foundation declared

---

[17] US Council for International Business monthly newsletter, October 1994, p. 7. The USCIB is the formal representative of US business to the OECD. The OECD, or Organization for Economic Cooperation and Development, is a forum for the leadership of the largest economies of the world.

that "Ronald Reagan's vision [is] realized."[18] The Council of the Americas – founded in 1965 by David Rockefeller – described the NAFTA victory as a "realization ... of David Rockefeller's original vision when founding the Council" (Council of the Americas 1994: 5).

Political unity among the NAFTA's defenders came swiftly. Large corporations poured enormous sums of money, donated personnel, and contributed their leadership to a counter-movement aimed at protecting the NAFTA and the neoliberal agenda represented therein. A wide range of US businesses from many economic sectors participated in the lobbying, coalition building, and public opinion campaigns. Established business associations used their networks and communication infrastructures to reach out to their membership and advocate industry-wide support. As a whole, big business in the United States embarked on an unprecedented campaign to ensure both the NAFTA's passage and the completion of the Uruguay Rounds of the General Agreement on Tariffs and Trade (GATT), which created the World Trade Organization (WTO).

The case of business advocacy for the North American Free Trade Agreement (NAFTA) provides an excellent context for assessing the consolidation of a corporate, neoliberal trade policy network. The 1974 federal advisory system provided corporate members appointed to the trade advisory committees (TACs) long-term channels for sustained influence. As reported extensively elsewhere (Ayers 1998; Dreiling 2001), the conflict over NAFTA mobilized very broad segments of US society *against* the agreement, stimulating a major corporate effort to defend the agreement. At the same time, a substantial proportion of the public remained opposed to the ratification of the NAFTA and, later (1995), the GATT Uruguay Rounds.[19] The corporate mobilization to create political conditions favorable for the passage of NAFTA, and the striking success of their

---

[18] Michael G. Wilson. 1993. "The North American Free Trade Agreement: Ronald Reagan's Vision Realized," Executive Memorandum. Washington, DC: The Heritage Foundation.

[19] Proponents and opponents alike argued that the NAFTA received the widest corporate support of any preceding policy objective, only superseded by the much larger list of business supporters for the Uruguay Round of the GATT less than one year after the passage of the NAFTA. The list of individual businesses in the "GATT-NOW" coalition exceeded 10,000, including nearly every major business and industry association in the United States. This, we believe, can be attributed not to the resounding enthusiasm for GATT and the newly constructed World Trade Organization, but to the collective momentum that followed the mobilization for the NAFTA.

collective efforts, also offer a unique window into the selection processes that shape instances of broad, class-oriented collective action.[20]

On the surface, the corporate mobilization to defend the NAFTA behaved as an interest group. That is, the coalition deployed standard "inside" and "outside" pressure group tactics, and retained highly prestigious public relations firms, law firms, and lobbyists.[21] The so-called State Captain corporations, in addition to national coalition activity, assumed the task of creating state-level, quasi-independent pro-NAFTA coalitions designed to employ grassroots tactics for mobilizing small business, local Chambers of Commerce, and other free-market sympathizers. These State Captain corporations, with the resources and commitments of upper management backing the corporate action, became important protagonists in the NAFTA defense. Their leadership of the larger USA*NAFTA coalition, as well as their pro-NAFTA activism in local and state-level political environments, was decisive in the overall corporate mobilization. Together, the leading corporate State Captains and the corporate members of the USA*NAFTA coalition were well endowed as a conventional pressure group. The coalition, with assistance from the Mexican government and the Clinton administration, also adeptly managed to convert the congressional majority opposing NAFTA in the summer of 1993 into a favorable majority by November 1993 (Newport 1993).[22] However, looking beyond the pressure group tactics, we discover that the leaders of this important political defensive shared numerous private and public associations, spanning political as well as economic spheres.

---

[20] It is beyond the scope of our discussion to assess whether the USA*NAFTA defense of the NAFTA was, in the last instance, the source of the NAFTA's passage. Yet, it would be hard to imagine congressional support for the agreement without USA*NAFTA's media campaign (which sponsored press conferences of all living, former presidents, as well as the infamous Gore-Perot debate), nationally coordinated pressure-group tactics in their home districts as well as on Capitol Hill, and persistent lobbying and committee testimonies by the most prestigious corporate executives, business associations, and economists. An estimated $30–50 million was spent by proponents of the NAFTA, making it among the most expensive foreign policy campaigns in US history (Center for Public Integrity 1993; Lewis and Ebrahim 1993).

[21] See Walker (1991) for a comprehensive analysis and discussion of the process of interest group mobilization, including the role of tactics, organizational forms, and incentive structures.

[22] The earliest poll on the NAFTA, in March 1991, found that 72 percent of Americans believed that its impact would be "mostly good" for the United States. By September 1992, when candidate-Clinton announced his position on the NAFTA, only 55 percent of respondents were NAFTA-favorable. One year later, September 1993, public opinion had shifted in favor of opposing the NAFTA by a slight majority (Newport 1993).

THE STATE CAPTAIN INTERCORPORATE NETWORK

To illuminate how defenders of the NAFTA arose from a neoliberal trade policy network, we used a sample of 228 corporations from the USA*NAFTA coalition, all of whom were pro-NAFTA. Yet, not all corporations participated equally in this coalition. The self-proclaimed leadership of the coalition – the State Captain corporations – took responsibility for a series of exceptionally intense efforts to mobilize broader business support for the bill. These State Captains spanned diverse economic sectors, from retail to finance, and represented every major region of the country. These corporate Captains exhibited an intense and sustained expression of business unity. We measure the cohesiveness of each subgraph with a measure of its connectedness, which provides a weighted proportion of the pairs that reach each other via a network path of any length. These subgraphs capture a very cohesive network that is also well connected to the major policy-planning organizations. Of the thirty-five State Captains in our sample, it is notable that fifteen were ECAT members, twenty-eight were members of the BRT, and all but one, NationsBank, had a representative on one of the USTR's advisory committees.[23]

State Captains were central to overcoming the collective action problem (Olson 1965). Leaders in a wide range of collective actions perform such a role. Their interests and motivations are more intense, their vision of the problem more comprehensive, and, generally, they are better connected to communities targeted for mobilization.

While the actions on the part of government officials in the Bush and Clinton administrations in the negotiation of the NAFTA were obvious, less apparent was the role of sustained and coordinated corporate action in the development of the NAFTA. In the next two figures, we briefly probe the interpenetration of corporations and state policy-making activity during the NAFTA negotiations. This graph-analytic approach identifies networks among the thirty-five State Captains that cut across the Advisory Committees within the executive branch and private sector ties to corporate boards and policy-planning associations. We argue that this close coupling of advisory appointments and corporate leaders was made possible by the 1974 Trade Act, a bill that in turn reflects the historical confluence of increasingly probusiness facilitative state structures and the growing network of globalizing corporations (particularly those in ECAT and the Business Roundtable). As discussed earlier, the formation of these

---

[23] See Appendix 1 for details on the pro-NAFTA State Captains and the data we utilize here.

TACs and the emerging corporate policy groups (such as the ECAT and Business Roundtable) established a new political space, one defined by the simultaneous mobilization of corporate networks aimed at advancing a new economic consensus *and* state actors who harnessed new authorities to galvanize policy responses to a changing global political and economic environment.

Examining this group of thirty-five core firms reveals their social proximity, both within the state apparatus (as advisory committee members) as well as outside of the state in their shared memberships on boards and in policy groups. In Figures 4.1 through 4.3, the network formed by these firms is plotted graphically; in effect, this network visually portrays the dense network of communication and cooperation that exists among politically active US corporations. Coordinates derived from a multidimensional scaling (MDS) are utilized to plot the nodes, capturing "similarities" between all pairs of organizations.[24] Among social network methodologists, MDS is considered a useful technique for visualizing network-structural characteristics, such as centrality and core-periphery relations (Wasserman and Faust 1994). These relationships are designated as interactions across three social networks: board of director interlocks; co-membership in the corporate policy-planning network, including the Business Roundtable; and co-membership in the TACs. Each of these graphs illustrates a high level of connectivity among the State Captain corporations, both in the nongovernment networks of the policy groups and board interlocks as well as in the state apparatus of the TACs.

Figure 4.1 plots eight major policy-planning organizations that were active on trade policy issues between 1990 and 1994, the period of the NAFTA's negotiation and implementation. Membership in NAM was broken down by appointments to their four major leadership committees. The arcs between these policy organizations are formed as a result of membership overlap among the sample of thirty-five State Captains. Note that all of these influential business groups are linked together by the common membership ties of only thirty-five corporations (each of these groups has more than thirty-five members). The subgraph has a connectedness score of 1.0, a compactness score of 0.985, with an average

---

[24] Pearson correlation coefficients were used as indicators of the spatial similarity shared between each pair of corporations in relation to all other potential relationships among the remaining twenty-nine corporations. A high value between two firms will draw them closer together in the plot.

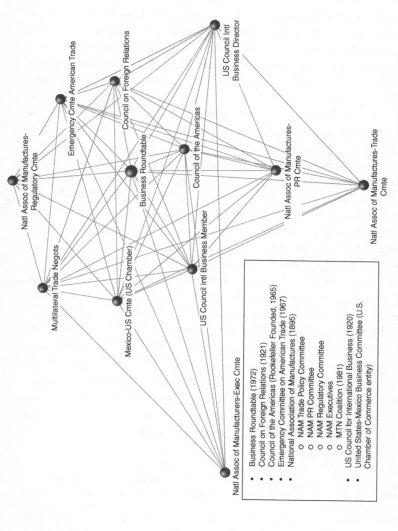

FIGURE 4.1 Overlapping Policy-Planning Organizations Resulting from Membership of Thirty-Five Corporations Plotted using MDS coordinates. *Connectedness, 1.0; Compactness, 0.992; Density 0.985.*

Nodes (labels in figure):

Natl Assoc of Manufactures-Regulatory Cmte

Emergency Cmte American Trade

Council on Foreign Relations

US Council Intl Business Director

Business Roundtable

Council of the Americas

Natl Assoc of Manufactures-PR Cmte

Multilateral Trade Negots

Mexico-US Cmte (US Chamber)

US Council Intl Business Member

Natl Assoc of Manufactures-Trade Cmte

Natl Assoc of Manufacturers-Exec Cmte

Legend:

• Business Roundtable (1972)
• Council on Foreign Relations (1921)
• Council of the Americas (Rockefeller Founded, 1965)
• Emergency Committee on American Trade (1967)
• National Association of Manufactures (1895)
  ○ NAM Trade Policy Committee
  ○ NAM PR Committee
  ○ NAM Regulatory Committee
  ○ NAM Executives
  ○ MTN Coalition (1981)
• US Council for International Business (1920)
• United States-Mexico Business Committee (U.S.
  Chamber of Commerce entity)

distance of 1.015 and a density of 0.985.[25] To put the matter succinctly: this is a very tight network. In effect, this policy-planning network brings corporate leaders together into larger, cohesive interorganizational space that gives *structure* to corporate political activism.

Figure 4.1 is plotted with coordinates from a nonmetric MDS. The eight organizations and their founding dates are presented below the figure. Here, it is evident that relationships among the corporations overlap considerably. While this figure captures only eight such groups, all of these organizations were important NAFTA-advocacy organizations in their own right, in addition to possessing the influence of their respective corporate members. In terms of organizational prominence within this network, there is little doubt that the Roundtable plays a central role. First, the Roundtable is (quantitatively) the most central organization in this network. Second, the leadership role that the Roundtable played and the significance of its political strategy are widely documented and recognized among political sociologists (Burris 1992a, 2008; Domhoff 2006; Dreiling 2001; Mizruchi 1992; Useem 1984; Vogel 1989). Finally, the CEOs of Roundtable-affiliated corporations make deep personal commitments to participate in political matters of concern to big business in the United States (Domhoff 2013).

It is not surprising, given the history of the organization, that the BRT played a leading role in the mobilization to defend the NAFTA. The strategy that became so characteristic of the Roundtable was also used by its many members who supported the USA*NAFTA coalition: congressional testimony, press releases, and frequent lobbying.[26] Even the *Wall Street Journal* announced that "the USA*NAFTA" group was one "set up by ... members of the Business Roundtable" (Davis 1993: A20). As one prominent insider stated, "the business community felt, as a whole that these agreements [NAFTA and GATT] would just go through ... So we had to convince our members to get more passion."[27] Groups closely affiliated with the Roundtable, such as the Emergency Committee on

---

[25] Each of these measures of cohesion indicate a very well connected network. Density, the simplest of the measures, is the proportion of ties in the network to the total possible number of ties [n(n-1)/2].

[26] The Wexler Group and Arthur Anderson & Co. were retained by the USA*NAFTA. Each has a history of providing regular accounting and public relations services to the Business Roundtable.

[27] Author interview, October 20, 1994, with Arthur Simonetti, lobbyist with the National Foreign Trade Council, who personally lobbied for the NAFTA alongside "General Motors' chief lobbyist ... nearly 150 times."

American Trade and the National Foreign Trade Council, testified regularly before Congress and organized hundreds of lobbying sessions involving the CEOs of companies as influential as General Motors and AT&T.[28] Meeting directly with President Clinton for "regular" briefings by White House officials, BRT members of USA*NAFTA worked closely to select Lee Iacocca (former Chrysler CEO) as the president's "NAFTA Czar."[29] These frequent associations with prominent decision makers stem from the unique structural location afforded to inner circle corporate leaders.

In Figure 4.2, these same companies are plotted by their direct board interlock ties to one another during this period. Their relative placement is plotted by coordinates derived from multidimensional scaling (MDS). A multidimensional scaling of the "similarities" of connections among corporations places each one closer or further apart based on those scores.[30] Through the MDS plot, we are able to glimpse into the structure and organization of corporate political communication. Here, each node depicts a corporation, and an arc between two nodes indicates a shared seat by one executive in the two companies. Nodes with more links that are also more spatially centered are considered more central, as is clear in the case of Citicorp. Firms closer in proximity to each other share a similar position across the totality of measured affiliations. The subgraph has a connectedness score of 0.890, a compactness score of 0.367, with an average distance between nodes at 3.030 and a density of 0.092. Certainly less dense than the previous graph, Figure 4.2 depicts a modestly close knit community of corporate leaders with a notable core-periphery structure. Still, only two firms – Warnaco and Nike – were isolated from all other boards. In 1992, both of those corporations barely made the Fortune 500 list.

For Useem (1984), the defining characteristic of inner circle actors is their frequent interaction across several corporate boards. Consistent with this thesis, State Captains maintain an average of nearly eleven interlocks with the other companies in the larger sample – about five more connections per firm than the mean frequency. Among multiple-interlocked executives and

---

[28] Author interview, Arthur Simonetti, lobbyist with the National Foreign Trade Council, October 20, 1994.

[29] Author interview with Leslie Touma, director of the Michigan International Trade Coalition, July 17, 1993.

[30] Pearson correlation coefficients were used as indicators of the spatial similarity shared between each pair of corporations in relation to all other potential relationships among the remaining thirty-four corporations. A high value between two firms will draw them closer together in the MDS plot.

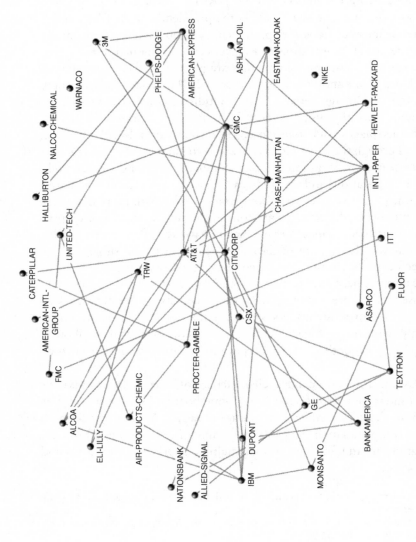

FIGURE 4.2 Board of Director Ties among Thirty-Five State Captain Corporations, 1992

Plotted using MDS layout, adjusted for visibility. *Connectedness, 0.890; Compactness, 0.367; Density 0.092.*

boards, a class-wide orientation is stimulated and narrow interests discharged as their capacity to scan the breadth of business concerns improves. Stated quite clearly by the Business Roundtable in a widely distributed statement, the CEO in particular "is the agent and collaborator of the board, as public spokesman for not only his own enterprise but also for the larger corporate community, in defending the essential elements of the American private enterprise system and in promoting the political conditions essential for its effective operation" (Business Roundtable 1980: 24). State Captains were stationed within this interlock network in a way that greatly enhanced their visibility and responsiveness to classwide concerns. Prominent political and corporate leaders promoting the NAFTA could then rely on these networks to further their goals.

The following example illustrates what was reportedly a widespread phenomenon. President Clinton and US Trade Representative Mickey Kantor, "with assistance from the corporate-sponsored USA*NAFTA," were able to secure a reversal in NAFTA-votes by "identifying a number of corporations in Mr. Wheat's Kansas City–area district – including J.C. Penney, AT&T, Hallmark Cards Inc., and Allied Signal – [and] ask[ing] the business officials to pressure the lawmaker" (Frisby and Davis 1993: A24). AT&T was quite central in the board interlock network. With 19 direct interlocks to the other 227 corporations in the sample, including J.C. Penney (a USA*NAFTA member, but not a Captain), AT&T was well positioned to deliver leverage within the political community and, as a State Captain, in the wider business community. Intercorporate ties through boards and policy associations facilitated this type of political strategy in addition to elevating the visibility of particular corporate leaders.

Figure 4.3 plots the same thirty-five corporations by the connections formed through common membership in a Trade Advisory Committee. Affiliation with the TACs created an array of opportunities for articulating concerns within "government circles" and, perhaps more significantly, provided a forum for sharing diverse economic interests with the aim of creating a consensus on trade policy. The significance of membership in a TAC, in which several companies had multiple seats, becomes more apparent when we consider that State Captains were more than twice as likely as non-Captains to sit on a committee under the USTR. The rate of membership within the President's Advisory Committee on Trade Policy Negotiations (ACTPN) is 3.5 times the average in the sample. The president's ACTPN sits at the apex of the trade advisory system. Its advisors are appointed directly by the president. Perhaps the best overall indicators

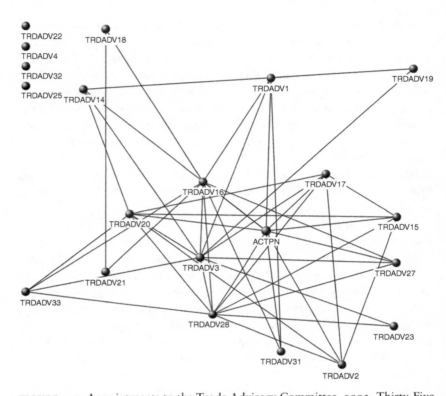

FIGURE 4.3 Appointments to the Trade Advisory Committee, 1992, Thirty-Five Corporations
Plotted with MDS layout, adjusted for visibility of nodes. **Connectedness, 0.589; Compactness, 0.379; Density 0.195.**

of political activism among inner circle corporate actors, the advisory committees of the federal government, and in this case, the TACs, bring together diverse segments of business to formulate more generalized policy. The subgraph has a connectedness score of 0.589, a compactness score of 0.379, an average distance of 1.801, and a density of 0.195. TAC memberships thus exemplify the cohesive and strategic properties of policy-oriented interactions among corporate leaders, and, as this study illustrates, these committees form an important site from which an informed and motivated leadership can be selected to protect the broader policy project.[31]

---

[31] A logistic regression of the sample corporations on appointment to a TAC revealed that membership in the BRT increased the chances that a corporation would be appointed to

It is notable that, early on, the NAFTA did not have sufficient House and Senate votes for ratification (Dreiling 2000; Woodall, Wallach, Roach, and Burnham 2000). As discussed earlier, the DOC and its associated trade advisory committees strongly supported NAFTA, but the House and Senate must also ratify bilateral and multilateral trade agreements. For this reason, corporations must assert their interests around trade policy in the legislature, and as was the case with NAFTA, with public audiences, too.

The nongovernment network ties in the board and policy planning network, as depicted above, capture elements of class association. The way in which these ties among the same firms are mirrored within the trade policy apparatus of the government (the TACs) illustrates the close coupling of corporate actors and facilitative state structures. As Dreiling (2000) observed, a strong legislative and public opinion defense of the NAFTA was mounted by many of the same corporations involved in shaping the agreement. In this way, corporate political agency strategically engaged the political structures of the state, intricately connecting action in the executive branch tacs, efforts to shape public opinion, and the votes in the Legislature. It is for this reason more generally that corporate promotion of trade policy centers on *both* the executive and legislative branches of government. The implementation of the NAFTA and subsequent trade liberalization projects relied on coordinated corporate political support across these institutional domains.

CHINA PNTR AND BEYOND

"Trade globally, prosper locally!" This was the slogan for the corporate campaign to extend trade promotion authority to the president in 1999. Raising the banner to globalize trade, the group "America Leads on Trade" (A LOT) was applying tools learned five years earlier during the NAFTA conflict. Faced with growing popular concern about "globalization," however, the "Battle in Seattle" (November 29 to December 1, 1999) abruptly stalled efforts to extend trade promotion authority (TPA) for the president (in effect, Clinton's reformulation of "fast track" authority). The stage was already set for a wave of post-NAFTA contention over free trade, and TPA was just one point of contention. Despite these

---

a TAC by over 250%, while companies sharing a board member would see an increase in their chance of appointment to a TAC by 6% for each additional shared director in the network.

challenges, negotiations for new free trade agreements continued, including plans to expand the NAFTA to Central America and South America, the bill to permanently normalize trade relations with China[32] (PNTR), and the bilateral agreement with Doha. These initiatives, and most significantly the passage of China PNTR, concluded a decade of contentious politics over international trade policy, highlighting the mounting controversy over trade politics and neoliberal globalization.

DISCUSSION: THE CORPORATE NEOLIBERAL POLICY NETWORK

An important historical shift unfolded in the late 1960s and early 1970s. As outlined above, the confluence of events, processes, and actors that featured prominently in this era conspired to shift the ideological center of the leaders of large US manufacturing and financial corporations decidedly rightward; these actors, in turn, leveraged emerging strands of neoliberalism and supply-side economics to form an enduring and effective platform for probusiness policy activism. The Emergency Committee for American Trade effectively joined with government officials to change permanently the dominant institutions of US trade policy. These corporate leaders acted assertively and creatively through a political-organizational apparatus that brought corporate leaders and their vision deep within the Nixon and Ford administrations, collaboratively advancing the 1974 Trade Act. The tone and institutional precedents of this time brought about a new era in neoliberal globalization that was, in many ways, most fully realized in the North American Free Trade Agreement (NAFTA).

Two important conclusions can be drawn from these diverse events. First, the pathway to the 1974 Trade Act relied on concerted political action from the leaders of globalizing corporations. These firms made huge strides in the postwar economy, gaining near monopoly power in some domestic sectors while also reaching global market prominence. While conflict among firms was evident, it is a mistake to assume that these disputes reflected irreconcilable differences and divisions among the corporate elite. While it is certainly true that import-competitive industries pursued protectionist trade policy goals at odds with the state leaders of the period, those differences did not preclude a high level of unity

---

[32] In the span of a little over one year, a sweeping pancorporate alliance spent over $113 million to pass the legislation, making it the most expensive policy campaign in US history (Woodall, Wallach, Roach, and Burnham 2000).

among the most embedded (and influential) corporate advocates of trade liberalization. Perhaps most problematic is the common assumption that trade policy goals reflected strategic maneuvers on the part of political leaders who acted mostly independent of corporate elites. Like its predecessors, the Nixon Administration did not advance the trade policy agenda only to let business react. Evidence of sustained, though sometimes uneven, corporate leadership on trade makes it impossible to see the origins of the 1974 Trade Act as *sui generis* to Nixon; instead we see that corporate leaders staffed the offices recommending the policy, formed the groups that lobbied for it, and provided the expertise, resources, and legitimacy to pass it. A more appropriate historical interpretation, then, accounts for the role of corporate leaders in advancing an American trade policy in concert with state leaders. A theory of class and state agency is thus needed. The very corporate leaders involved in the creation of ECAT, and later the Business Roundtable, publicly presented a case for institutional change that would materialize in the 1974 Trade Act. In the intervening years, these same corporate leaders played a pivotal role in the Nixon Administration's campaign to curtail protectionist interests and wrest authority from Congress as a means to advance the emerging globalization project. In hindsight, the new corporate groups emerging at this time became important actors in the development and implementation of a free trade project that would truly culminate in a system of transnational market governance two decades later. Our account above brings corporate, class-oriented actors to this historical stage.

Second, the institutional transformations under the 1974 Trade Act, particularly the creation of the trade advisory system, offered new avenues for corporate leadership on neoliberal trade policy to emerge in the decades that followed. Participating directly in the trade policy process, the corporate leaders who mobilized to defend the NAFTA drew from their associations both in and outside of the state. Two decades after the passage of the 1974 Trade Act, these institutional settings offered a strategic pathway for corporate, class agency to be exercised on US economic policy.

Too often, the story of neoliberalism misses the conflicts and realignment among corporate leaders that linked free trade internationalists and domestic deregulation proponents around an intraclass coalition committed to a new economic agenda. Rooted in conflicts over the role of the state in the economy, the adoption of neoliberalism as a political-economic ideology provided a framework for corporate unity in an era of global economic transformation, one that would shift the focus and priorities of corporate elite for decades. Consequently, the Business Roundtable is widely cited as a new source of unity for corporate leaders in the United States. Further, its role in pressing domestic deregulation and global free trade is well documented. But its origins stem from the conflicts sparked by transformations in global capitalism in the 1960s as well as the capacity of business leaders to author the political and organizational apparatus to resolve the disputes that inevitably emerge among large companies. This historical account highlights the avenues through which the creative action of corporate leaders was geared toward a reformulation of class cohesion, a reformulation that necessitated the mobilization of new organizational and discursive tools in a quest to alter the form of state and market institutions.

5

Inside the State: Corporate Participation in Trade Policy

> If neoliberalization has been a vehicle for the restoration of class power, then we should be able to identify the class forces behind it.
> – David Harvey, *A Brief History of Neoliberalism* (2005: 31)

From the historical and network analyses presented in the preceding chapter, it is evident that corporate promotion of trade policy centers on *both* the executive and legislative branches of government. In the *legislature*, corporations advance trade initiatives such as NAFTA and China PNTR through temporary trade policy and lobbying alliances, which, in turn, are formed by the more enduring policy organizations, such as the Business Roundtable and the Emergency Committee for American Trade. As depicted in the preceding pages, these relationships are explicit in the stated objectives of these organizations and evident in their overlapping networks across major trade policy settings spanning many years.

Within the executive branch, a deeper form of corporate influence is apparent. Under the banner of industry consultation programs, state actors work in concert with strategic business allies to form the policy objectives and broader trade programs ultimately advanced by the Department of Commerce and the president of the United States. These "trade advisory" officials are unelected, and attempts to determine specific rationales for their selection, through interviews for example, produced only more ambiguity.[1] The actual criteria that the state employs for

---

[1] A phone interview with Angela Cazada at the US Trade Representative's Office revealed that there are no explicit or publicly disclosed procedures for selecting advisors for these committees (October 4, 2005).

admittance to a Trade Advisory Committee (TAC) are unclear, although the Department of Commerce (DOC) claims "the primary factor for consideration [of an application] is the company or association that a nominee will represent" (DOC 2000: 2). Scholarly literature and the actual characteristics of the trade advisory system indicate that product market undoubtedly plays an important role in selection, since each sub-committee focuses on a specific domain of trade policy, such as international finance or trade in services. Unsurprisingly, banks are heavily represented in the finance advisory committee, service firms in the service sector advisory committee, and so on. Less clear, however, is what determines the participation of firms within the same industry. As documented in the preceding chapter, the influence of the trade policy committees has expanded since their creation in 1974. Under the Fast Track[2] rules established by the Trade Act of 1974, the executive branch must submit pending trade legislation to the TACs, which evaluate whether the pending trade legislation is "consistent" with US producer interests. In addition to their evaluative function, TACs also provide direct input into active US trade negotiations. It is common, for example, for TAC members to communicate directly with US officials during active trade negotiations to provide input on the language of a treatise or to make other requests.[3]

The overlapping dynamics within the executive and legislative branches result in significantly different abilities to shape trade policy under distinct conditions within the polity. On one hand, the executive branch, essentially captured by industry interests in *this* policy domain, offers preordained support for trade expansion initiatives. On the other, trade policy outcomes in the legislature are more contested, given the greater number of social actors competing for influence in Congress, especially since the hotly debated NAFTA.

It was observed that these dual patterns of corporate participation in American trade policy stemmed from underlying patterns of participation in corporate policy planning groups, such as the Business Roundtable and the Emergency Committee for American Trade (ECAT). In the executive branch advisory committees, we argued that these "facilitative state structures" – state structures that enable active corporate involvement in

---

[2] To reiterate, Fast Track allows the executive branch to submit a recently concluded trade negotiation to Congress for an up-or-down vote, without the possibility for the inclusion of amendments.

[3] Information obtained in a 10/4/2005 interview with Angela Cazada, a Department of Commerce official who oversees the trade policy committees.

policy formation – interact with organized corporate organizations to create and promote hemispheric and global trade regimes, often despite broad opposition in the public sphere (Dreiling 2000). Facilitative state structures promote business unity for political purposes. However, business unity is not simply a function of state coordination, as institutionalists have suggested. Equally (or more) important are the mechanisms of corporate class networks that channel business elite toward sites of influence within the executive branch (as policy advisors) and the legislature (via temporary political/lobbying alliances). In this way, extant, cohesive networks among top executives, corporations, and across industries serve as a source of political leverage.

Based on the reasoning in the historical narrative in Chapter 4, the analyses now turn to a series of models that explore and test statistical the factors that drive corporate participation in trade politics in both the executive and legislative branches of government. To systematically examine the role of several corporate policy organizations in advancing a neoliberal trade policy program, we operationalize corporate participation in the policy networks among those organizations and present the results. Corporate leaders in these networks pressed forward with free trade institutions in the Caribbean, with Canada, with NAFTA, with the creation of the World Trade Organization at the end of the GATT Uruguay Round, and liberalized trade with China. It was also clear that the corporate support for the advance of these free trade programs did not begin and end with individual executives. As geopolitical and global market conditions changed, so did the particular policy initiatives. However, the thrust toward trade liberalization pressed on, and our historical and network analyses revealed a consistent partnership between state actors and leaders in the neoliberal corporate policy network. What factors best explain the active role of corporations in these trade policy-making institutions in the executive and legislative branches of the US government?

FORTUNE AND FORBES 500 (FF500) COMPANY-LEVEL ANALYSES

The seven hypotheses of firm participation in trade policy formation and advocacy described at the end of Chapter 3 were developed from theoretical assumptions in the literature on trade policy. The first set of hypotheses is tested using data that measures company-level characteristics. See Appendix 2 for details on the data sources and operationalization of the variables. The sampling universe consists of publicly traded (i.e., non–privately owned) corporations listed in the 1998 and 2003 *Fortune* and *Forbes* 500 directories (FF500). Because the *Fortune* and *Forbes* lists overlap considerably, the combined firm directories typically contain about 560 public and private companies in a given year. After dropping privately held firms, the sample size for each wave of data is approximately 484. Privately held companies are dropped from the sample because they (typically) do not produce financial statements analogous to the Securities and Exchange Commission 10k filings incumbent on publicly traded firms, which confounds cross-sectional comparison.[4] Table 5.1 summarizes those hypotheses, our variables, and data sources. The data sources are discussed more fully in Appendix 2. Of principal interest is the impact of network position on the odds of corporate participation in three domains of trade policy advocacy: Trade Advisory Committees, temporary trade policy alliances, and testimony before Congress at trade policy hearings.

The first dependent variable, which measures involvement in a Trade Advisory Committee, is a proxy for corporate trade policy activism in the executive branch. The second dependent variable, which measures the frequency of corporate testimony at congressional trade policy hearings, is a proxy for direct corporate lobbying of the legislature. The third dependent variable, trade policy alliance participation, measures individual involvement in nonstate advocacy groups lobbying Congress and conducting public relation campaigns for specific trade policy outcomes.

Trade Advisory Committees

The Trade Act of 1974 created a three-tiered system of federal trade policy advisory committees that allow industry representatives to provide policy

---

[4] The firms under study approximate a population. Given that the firms were not selected on the basis of a random sample, some may take issue with the employment of statistical significance tests. While several have analyzed the political activities of the Fortune 500, issues pertaining to the interpretability of the population's parameters have received little attention in the literature (Boies 1989; Clawson and Neustadtl 1989; Domhoff 2006). Boies (1989) examined the PAC contributions of the entire Fortune 500 but did not offer justification for his employment of statistical significance tests. With little consensus in the literature, Gold's perspective on sampling is adopted here: "A test of significance can be viewed as an indication of the probability that an observed association could be generated in a given set of data by a random process model, without respect to sampling considerations" ([1970] 2006: 174). The coefficients and *p*-values are interpreted heuristically, as a proxy for both the direction of association and the "effect size" of the predictors on the three dependent variables.

TABLE 5.1 *Summary of Variables, Measures, and Hypotheses*

Variable	Units and Coding	Source	Predicted Effect
ISAC Participation	Count of total memberships in ACTPN and/or ISACs.	US Department of Commerce, 1998, 2003.	–
Size	Principal factor of sales, assets, and employees.	1998/2003 *Compustat Industrial Annual.*	+
PAC Contributions	Combined PAC expenditures in two preceding election cycles (for the 1998 firms, 1996 and 1998 election cycles; for the 2003 firms, the 2000, and 2002 election cycles).	US Federal Elections Commission.	+
Foreign Subsidiaries	Log of the count of firm subsidiary operations in foreign countries.	Uniworld Business Publications, *Directory of American Firms Operating in Foreign Countries.*	+
Product Market	Two-digit Standard Industrial Classification (SIC).	1998/2003 *Compustat Industrial Annual.*	Variable[a]
Capital Intensity	Log of the quotient of assets divided by number of employees.	1998/2003 *Compustat Industrial Annual.*	+
Board Interlocks	Dummy variable for number of board interlocks. Firms with five or more interlocks are coded 1. Interlocks are calculated using the Freeman Degree Centrality score for a firm-by-firm matrix of board of director affiliations.	Proxy statement, *Disclosure* (for 1998 firms), *IRRC* director database (for 2003 firms).	+
Policy Network Affiliation	Count of total memberships ties to the Business Council, Conference Board,	Public and requested membership rosters.	+

(continued)

TABLE 5.1 *(continued)*

Variable	Units and Coding	Source	Predicted Effect
	National Association of Manufacturers, Council of the Americas, Trilateral Commission, and the United States Council for International Business.		
Business Roundtable Participation	Dummy indicator of Business Roundtable membership.	Publicly available membership roster.	+
Temporary Trade Policy Alliances	Count of participation in temporary trade policy alliances (for 1998 firms, membership in America Leads on Trade and/or USA Engage; for 2003 firms, membership in the Business Coalition for US-Central America Trade and/or the US Trade Coalition).	Public membership rosters.	+

[a] Product market is modeled as a level-2 grouping variable such that firms within each two-digit SIC code are assigned a unique mean rate of TAC participation (intercept).

input and recommendations to US trade negotiators. The bottom tier of this program consists of seventeen Industrial Sector Advisory Committees and three Industry Function Advisory Committees. These committees evaluate the impact of US trade negotiations on specific US commercial sectors, such as aerospace or high technology. At the second tier, six committees consider general issues pertaining to trade, such as labor and the environment. At the apex of the advisory committee structure is the Advisory Committee to the President on Trade Policy and Negotiations (ACTPN). Unlike TAC participants, who apply for a committee membership through the Department of Commerce, ACTPN participations are appointed directly by the president of the United States.

While information regarding the specific activities of TACs is not disclosed, their organizational self-description explains: "The Department of Commerce, Office of the U.S. Trade Representative, and other agencies work side by side with business leaders [TAC members] who serve as advisors to the Government" (DOC 2000). Analysis of several speeches delivered during TAC sessions indicates that the committees are highly committed to the expansion of international commerce through trade agreements such as NAFTA and CAFTA. During an earlier speech delivered to TAC members on May 6, 1998, Secretary Daley also referenced the need for public support for free trade policies, claiming, "We need to build a consensus in our country, and around the globe, that trade is good" (Daley 2000). These comments, together with other committee materials and interviews with TAC staff, suggest that the committees are proponents of trade-expanding initiatives, such as NAFTA, and oppose tariff and nontariff barriers to trade.

For the firm-level models, TAC participation is measured as a *count* of the total number of trade advisory committee memberships. In the class cohesion dyadic models (Chapter 6), TAC participation is measured as a count of the number of *shared* committee memberships within the corporate dyad.

Testimony Before Congress

FF500 congressional testimony at US trade policy hearings is measured for the period 1993–2004.[5] Similar to Mizruchi's (1992) study, testimony is measured across several years because, in any given year, there are insufficient instances of FF500 congressional testimony to permit statistical modeling. The testimony data were collected by compiling a list of major trade policy initiatives (such as NAFTA, FTAA, and CAFTA) during the period under investigation and analyzing the invited testimony of FF500 corporate representatives. For each trade policy initiative, a variable measuring firm support or opposition was created.[6] Next, the testimony of each FF500 firm that appeared at the congressional hearing was coded as being in support or opposition to the pending legislation. Each instance of testimony was coded by two researchers to augment inter-rater-reliability. Overwhelmingly, FF500 firms professed unambiguous support

---

[5] Specifically, testimony for the period 1999–2004 were measured for the 2003 wave of companies, while testimony for the period 1993–1998 were measured for the 1998 wave.
[6] Mizruchi's (1992) research on corporate congressional testimony (on any policy, not simply trade related) employed an "unrelated" category to describe some instances of shared testimony. However, this was deemed unnecessary in the present study, because nearly all recorded instances of FF500 testimony were either clearly supportive or clearly opposed to the pending trade legislation, making a third category unnecessary.

for pending trade initiatives (nearly all which sought to further liberalize US trade relations),[7] which simplified the coding process.

For the firm-level models, congressional testimony is measured as a *count* of the number of company appearances before Congress in support of trade-expanding policy initiatives (e.g., NAFTA or PNTR with China). We limit the analysis to testimony at trade-*expanding* policy hearings because, quite simply, very few firms in the FF500 appear at trade hearings to request increased tariffs or other barriers to trade. While smaller firms (in particular, those in the agricultural sector) may lobby for various forms of protection, such requests are exceedingly rare from FF500 firms. Where it did occur, FF500 opposition to trade expansion took one of two forms: testimony *against* a trade-expanding initiative (e.g., at the NAFTA hearings) or testimony in *support* of trade restrictions of some form (e.g., at the February 1999 congressional hearing to evaluate steel producer requests for temporary tariffs on foreign steel imports). Because support for protection is somewhat distinct from support for trade expansion, these two forms of testimony were not combined in the firm-level models. Additionally, because so few FF500 firms opposed trade-expanding initiatives, and because those that did were almost exclusively drawn from a single sector (steel), we determined that a separate "opposition" model would yield little useful information. In other words, given that opposition is almost perfectly predicted by firm sector, a multivariate regression model of opposition is unnecessary.

Temporary Alliance Participation

The third dependent variable, trade policy alliance (TPA) participation, measures corporate involvement in four prominent political alliances that lobbied Congress in support of Fast Track Renewal, PNTR with China, the Free Trade Area of the Americas, and the Central American Free Trade Agreement. The first coalition, America Leads on Trade (ALOT), was formed in 1997 by the Business Roundtable and several other protrade business coalitions to lobby Congress to renew President Clinton's Fast Track negotiating authority (Neil 1997). By the end of its campaign, ALOT had spent over $2 million on ad-buys and lobbyists in support of the legislation and organized a "grass-roots" corporate campaign in multiple states. The second coalition, USA Engage, was formed by several

---

[7] Steel firms were the only major exception to this, as they tended to oppose certain tariff and non-tariff barrier reductions.

prominent corporations to lobby the legislature and build public support for congressional ratification of permanently normalized trade relations with China. The third coalition, the Business Coalition for US-Central America Trade, was an intersectoral coalition of US companies and associations that lobbied Congress to enact a free trade agreement (modeled after NAFTA) with the governments of Costa Rica, the Dominican Republic, El Salvador, Guatemala, Honduras, and Nicaragua. This agreement was later passed by Congress as the "DR-CAFTA" bill, and implemented in 2006. The final organization, USTrade, was formed by approximately 250 large corporations to lobby congress in support of the (NAFTA-like) Free Trade Area of the Americas.

In the firm level models, TPA participation is operationalized as a dummy indicator of whether a firm participated in a temporary trade policy alliance. For the 1998 wave, alliance participation is measured by firm involvement in America Leads on Trade and/or USA Engage, while for the 2003 wave alliance participation is measured by firm involvement in the Business Coalition for US-Central America Trade and/or USTrade.[8]

STATISTICAL METHODS: FIRM-LEVEL MODELS

The models presented below use multivariate regression to analyze firm level and dyadic involvement in three domains of trade policy formation and advocacy: temporary political alliances, testimony before Congress, and TACs. The first dependent variable, trade policy alliance participation, is dichotomous, indicating that binary logistic regression would provide a suitable method for the purpose of statistical modeling (Long 1997). The other dependent variables, congressional testimony and TAC participation, are Poisson-distributed ordered counts. While some researchers use Ordinary Least Squares regression to analyze count data, such an approach is likely to violate the model's assumptions that the error terms are homoscedastic and normally distributed (ibid.). Thus, in the models of TAC participation and congressional testimony we utilize Poisson regression, which better models the error structure produced by count data.[9]

---

[8] As this variable could only assume one of three values (0, 1, 2) it was dichotomized to simplify interpretation. Re-estimation of the model using a technique for ordered counts (e.g., Poisson) did not change the substantive interpretation of the findings.

[9] Because the models displayed evidence of overdispersion, estimates were made using SAS's overdispersion correction in the PROC GLIMMIX macro.

A final issue to consider concerns the operationalization of firm product market in the participation models. One way to operationalize product market is to create a dummy indicator for whether a firm produces in a tradable goods sector. Generally, this would include any firm whose one-digit Standard Industrial Classification code is one, two, or three. While this would provide a rough control for firm sector, the information contained in the second SIC digit is unnecessarily discarded. Because it is generally preferable to retain statistical information when possible, other modeling strategies are more appropriate.

A second way to control for the effects of product market is through the incorporation of k-1 dummy variables for each two-digit SIC grouping (i.e., a "fixed effect" model). However, given that there are 58 two-digit SIC groupings extant within the 1998/2003 FF500, this approach, while unbiased, would yield inefficient estimates (Kennedy 2003).

Still a third approach to control for the effects of product market is to utilize hierarchical non-linear models (HNLMs), where firms are nested within two-digit sector groupings. Using this approach, the intercept is allowed to vary as a random effect across two-digit product markets, such that the conditional odds of the outcome for firms in the jth sector are a function of both the grand mean across all sectors and the unique increment to the intercept associated with sector j (Raudenbush and Bryk 2002)[10]. Because HNLM provides a more *efficient* estimate of intersectoral variability than the fixed effects model, it is utilized for the three models of firm level participation. Using HNLM, the general form of the participation models is:

Level 1 Model

$$Trade\ Policy\ Participation = \beta_{0j} + \beta_{1j}(Subsidiaries) + \beta_{2j}(Cap.\ Inten.) + \beta_{3j}(Size)$$
$$+ \beta_{4j}(PAC) + \beta_{5j}(Brd.\ Interlocks) + \beta_{6j}(Pol.\ Network)$$
$$+ \beta_{7j}(Bus.\ Roundtable) + \beta_{8j}(Year) + r_{ij}$$

Level 2 Model

$$\beta_{0j} = \gamma_{00} + u_{0j}$$
$$\beta_{1j} = \gamma_{10}, \beta_{2j} = \gamma_{20}, \beta_{3j} = \gamma_{30} \cdots \beta_{7j} = \gamma_{70}$$

---

[10] A fixed-effects model of the three dependent measures was examined as well. Because both modeling strategies supported similar substantive conclusions, we opted to estimate the models using HNLM, which controls for the effect of sector with greater efficiency than the fixed-effect model.

Combined Model

$$Trade\ Policy\ Participation = \beta_{0j} + \beta_{1j}(Subsidiaries) + \beta_{2j}(Cap.\ Inten.) + \beta_{3j}(Size)$$
$$+ \beta_{4j}(PAC) + \beta_{5j}(Brd.\ Interlocks) + \beta_{6j}(Pol.\ Network)$$
$$+ \beta_{7j}(Bus.\ Roundtable) + \beta_{8j}(Year) + u_{0j} + r_{ij}$$

As discussed in Chapter 3, most trade policy analysts emphasize the effect of organizational attributes (e.g., primary product market) on firm trade preferences and political advocacy (Baldwin 1989; Cohen et al. 2003; Destler 1995; Milner 1988). In other words, these studies suggest that corporate political behavior in trade policy is a function of their pursuit of specific company or industry interests. Consequently, few of these studies move beyond organizational factors to examine whether the types of network positions examined via our narrative and graph heuristics in the preceding chapter – for example, board interlock and policy networks – influence firm participation in US trade politics. More, what is the relative magnitude of influence of company economic interests and ties to various corporate networks?

Our central problem, then, is to account for patterns of variability in corporate participation in trade policy formation. If the predictions of interest-centered trade policy analysts are correct, then the prevailing cause of corporate political activism – firms with greater economic interests in freer trade, such as those with multiple foreign subsidiary operations – will be the *most active* in trade policy formation. Conversely, if the perspectives emerging from the class cohesion perspective are relevant to the study of corporate involvement in US trade politics, we expect firms in class cohesive networks, particularly where top executives and the CEO form multiple connections to outside corporate policy organizations, to be most active in trade policy formation.

PARTICIPATION IN TRADE ADVISORY COMMITTEES

Table 5.2 presents an inter-correlation matrix for the dependent and independent measures of firm participation. None of the zero order correlations exceeds .6 and the variance inflation factor for each parameter in the three participation models is less than three. Table 5.3 presents a cross-tabulation of advisory committee participation by one-digit SIC code. As predicted by hypothesis 2a (Chapter 3), mean TAC affiliation varies significantly across one-digit product market groupings. Firms in tradable goods sectors (one-digit SICs 1, 2, and 3) have the highest levels of TAC

TABLE 5.2 *Correlations for All Variables (N = 966)*

	1	2	3	4	5	6	7	8
1: TAC Total								
2: Capital Intensity	-0.0357							
3: Subsidiaries	0.2948	-0.1030						
4: Size	0.3262	0.1554	0.2684					
5: PAC Expenditures	0.2636	0.1633	0.1774	0.5106				
6: Interlocks	0.2833	0.0039	0.3732	0.4976	0.2966			
7: Policy Network	0.4882	0.0717	0.4708	0.5207	0.3832	0.4420		
8: Bus. Roundtable	0.3916	0.0034	0.3718	0.3877	0.3320	0.3989	0.5512	
9: Temp. T.P. Alliances	0.4905	-0.0339	0.4362	0.3565	0.2719	0.3529	0.5602	0.4631

TABLE 5.3 *TAC Affiliation by*
One-Digit Sector Grouping (N = 966)

One Digit SIC	Mean Affiliation
1	22%
2	39%
3	49%
4	12%
5	4%
6	8%
7	18%
Average	23%

X^2 = 118.109 (Pr. < .001)

participation (22%, 39%, and 49%, respectively), while the next highest participation rate is 18% (SIC 7). Consistent with expectations, service industries such as retail (SIC 4) and banking/insurance (SIC 6) possessed the lowest rates of participation (4% and 8%, respectively).

This intersectoral variability across two-digit sector groupings is modeled in Equation 1 of Table 5.4, which presents the results of a one-way ANOVA with random effects. The one-way ANOVA model (eq. 1) yields variance component estimates of the intercept and level-1 residual structure that combine in the intraclass correlation coefficient (ICC) to estimate the between- and within-sector variance in TAC participation. The ICC is given by (Raudenbush and Bryk 2002: 71):

$$\hat{\rho} = \frac{\hat{\tau}_{00}}{(\hat{\tau}_{00} + \hat{\sigma}^2)} = \frac{.9937}{(.9937 + .6477)} = .605$$

indicating that approximately 60% of the unconditional variance in TAC participation is *between* sectors. Analyses of separate years of TAC participation yielded a similar finding: 60.3% in 1998 and 57% in 2003 of the unconditional variance in TAC participation is *between* sectors. Together, these results suggest that TAC participation is strongly influenced by market sector. Clearly, then, the ICC indicates that the effects of sector must be controlled in our model of TAC participation using the HNLM methodology outlined above.

As our first dependent variable (TAC participation) is an ordered count we use a Poisson sampling model with the canonical log link function (Long

TABLE 5.4 *1998/2003 Estimated Effects of Organizational and Network Variables on the Number of TACs (Unstandardized Regression Coefficients with SEs in Parentheses)*

Fixed Effect	Eq. 1	Eq. 2	Eq. 3
Constant	-1.8765^{**}	-2.5693^{**}	-2.6677^{**}
	(.1780)	(.4651)	(.4725)
Year = 2003	–	$-.5656^{**}$	$-.5753^{**}$
		(.1188)	(.1168)
Organizational Variables			
Capital Intensity	–	.05801	.0393
		(.0729)	(.074)
Foreign Subsidiaries	–	$.1271^{**}$	$-.0285$
		(.057)	(.052)
Firm Size	–	$.4037^{**}$	$.1696^{*}$
		(.059)	(.067)
PAC Expenditures	–	$.0029^{**}$	$.0022^{**}$
		(.0008)	(.0008)
Network Variables			
Board Interlocks	–	–	.0117
			(.012)
Policy Network Affiliations	–	–	$.2125^{**}$
			(.046)
Bus. Roundtable	–	–	$.5245^{**}$
			(.150)
Random Effect	*Variance (df)*	*Variance (df)*	*Variance (df)*
Sector Mean μ_{Oj}	$.9942^{**}$	1.147^{**}	1.0107^{**}
	(57)	(57)	(57)
Level-1 Effect, r_{ij}	$.6491^{**}$	$.5677^{**}$	$.5470^{**}$
Compound Symmetry Parameter	$.2690^{**}$	$.1080^{**}$	.0626

* p < 05 ** p < 01

1997).[11] Additionally, because approximately two-thirds of the sample firms appear during both sample years, it is possible that the error structure is temporally dependent (i.e., displays serial autocorrelation). Because there

---

[11] Poisson regression, which assumes that the conditional mean is equal to the conditional variance, was too restrictive to be employed in our models (Long 1997). Thus, we estimated our models using SAS's GLIMMIX macro, which corrects for overdispersion in multilevel count models.

are only two panels of data and the populations differ in each panel, standard corrections for serial correlation, such as the first-order autocorrelation coefficient, are not indicated (Ostrom 1978). Thus, we correct for temporal dependency in the error vector in two ways. First, we add a dummy variable for one of the observational years to shift any *unique* residual time dependency into the X vector. This is an important statistical precaution because systematic variation unique to a single time period may yield biased standard error *and* slope estimates if left unmodeled (Green, Kim, and Yoon 2001). Second, we utilize SAS's compound symmetry residual transformation procedure to correct for error dependency among firms with two observations in the combined dataset (i.e., firms listed in the FF500 directories in *both* study years).

Equation 2 (Table 5.4) presents a hierarchical non-linear model (HNLM) of combined 1998/2003 TAC participation (N = 966). Size, foreign subsidiaries, and PAC expenditures yield statistically significant, positive coefficients in the organizational baseline model (Eq. 2, Table 5.4). Four key findings emerge from these results. First, foreign subsidiaries are significant in the predicted direction. Multinational firms, which stand to benefit the most economically from reduced international transaction costs, are more likely to advise government officials on foreign trade policy. The significance of this relationship is not entirely surprising given the historic role of globalizing MNCs in promoting free trade. Second, firm size is strongly associated with participation in trade policy formation. As both class cohesion and interest group theories would predict, large corporations are more likely to engage the state due to their greater capacity to mobilize resources for political purposes. Third, the PAC expenditures variable yields a significant, positive coefficient. Consistent with expectations, this finding suggests that political expenditures increase the odds of firm political activism even when controlling for the effects of firm size. Fourth, and finally, the dummy variable for firm year is significant and negative, indicating that the mean rate of TAC affiliation decreased in 2003. This finding is unsurprising considering that the unconditional rate of FF500 TAC affiliation decreased from 23 percent to 13 percent between 1998 and 2003.[12]

---

[12] We also estimated the models separately for each panel. Because coefficient confidence intervals for the significant predictors of TAC participation overlap in the uncombined models, the observed drop in total participation may simply indicate an absolute decline in mean participation more than a significant change in the predicted direction of key explanatory variables.

In Table 5.4 (Equation 3), the four network variables are included in the model.[13] Their inclusion nullifies the statistical significance of the foreign subsidiaries variable, although size, PAC spending, and the variance component estimate of two-digit sector grouping remain statistically significant.[14] Consistent with a class cohesion perspective, Business Roundtable membership, policy network affiliation, board interlocks, and membership in temporary trade policy alliances significantly increase the odds of TAC participation. Business Roundtable membership increases the expected count of TAC participation by 36%, indicating that members of this organization are significantly more likely to serve as state policy advisors.[15] Similarly, (non–Business Roundtable) policy network affiliation significantly correlates with TAC participation: membership in a policy organization, such as the Emergency Committee on American Trade, increases the expected count of TAC affiliation by 23%. Corporations that engage in lobbying and public campaigns through a temporary trade policy alliance (TPA) are significantly more likely to also be appointed to a TAC: the odds that a firm participates in a TAC are 48.7% greater when they are also a member of a TPA. Board interlocks are associated with a moderate increase in the odds of participation in a Trade Advisory Committee: for a hypothetical firm with ten board interlocks, the odds of appointment to a TAC are 19.8% greater than for a firm with zero board interlocks.

Among the organizational variables, a $100,000 increase in PAC expenditures increases the expected count of TAC participation by 2.3%. Additionally, a one-standard deviation increase in the principle

---

[13] We also estimated Equation 3 using several measures of capital dependence and profitability (again, using *Compustat* data). Because we found no significant relationship between capital dependence or profitability and TAC participation (nor a significant improvement in model fit), we omit them from the results presented here. In addition, although we have no theoretical reason to suspect that firms in certain regions would be more likely to participate in a TAC, we also estimated Equation 3 with regional dummy controls, using census region codes for firm headquarters (Northeast, South, Midwest, and West, with West as the reference category). Since we found no significant regional effect, and because their inclusion did not significantly improve model fit, we omit them here for parsimony.

[14] Comparing the separate 1998 and 2003 models of TAC participation reveals both similarities and differences. Policy network affiliation and PAC expenditures are the most consistent predictors, yielding significant, positive coefficients in both saturated models (See Appendix 3). Additionally, Business Roundtable membership is significant in both observation years if a one-tailed test is accepted. Among the main differences, firm size reaches statistical significance in the 2003 saturated model but is null in 1998.

[15] The coefficient transformation to estimate the percent change in the expected count of a Poisson model is given by Long (1997): [(exp b) – 1]100.

component factor of firm sales, assets, and employees (size) increases the expected count of TAC participation by 18%. These findings largely confirm our main hypothesis that embedded firms are more likely to participate in trade policy, even when the influence of sector and size is controlled.

Thus, three factors seem critical to TAC participation. First, the largest firms in certain sectors, especially those influenced by, or dependent upon, trade (e.g., SICs 28 and 36, chemical and electronic manufacturers, respectively), are more likely to serve as state advisors. Second, *political action* through PAC expenditures is positively correlated with the odds of TAC participation. This suggests, perhaps unsurprisingly, that firms that contribute larger sums to federal elections are more likely to secure influential government advisory positions. Finally, network position within board interlock, policy group, and temporary alliance networks – associative mechanisms that link together a larger, business class-segment – significantly influence the odds of participation. In other words, participation as an advisor on trade policy is predictably patterned by firm sector and size, while political and network influences predominate within any given sector.

PARTICIPATION IN TEMPORARY POLITICAL ALLIANCES

Table 5.5 presents the results of a logistic regression of 1998/2003 trade policy alliance (TPA) participation.[16] As with the models of TAC participation, the one-way ANOVA with random effects (Table 5.5, Eq. 1) of 1998/2003 TPA participation yields a large intra-class correlation coefficient. Fully 61% of the variability in TPA participation is *across* sectors, confirming the importance of nesting firms within sector to allow for different rates of mean affiliation (i.e., different intercepts), and to mitigate potentially contaminating effects of heteroskedasticity in the error structure.

In Equation 2 (Table 5.5), the results of the baseline organizational model are presented. Size, PAC expenditures, and foreign subsidiaries yield significant coefficients in the predicted direction. Consistent with an organizational interests model (c.f., Milner 1988), the proxy for firm

---

[16] Again, for the 1998 models TPA participation is measured in the America Leads on Trade and/or USA ENGAGE coalitions and the 2003 models TPA participation is measured in the US Trade and the Business Coalition for US-Central America Trade (See Chapter 5 for a discussion of these coalitions and their campaigns).

TABLE 5.5 *1998/2003 Estimated Effects of Organizational and Network Variables on the Odds of TPA Participation (Unstandardized Reg. Coefficients with SEs in Parentheses)*

Fixed Effect	Eq. 1	Eq. 2	Eq. 3
Constant	−1.3934**	−2.7264**	−2.8522**
	(.165)	(.643)	(.623)
Year = 2003	−	−.8882**	−.9804**
		(.193)	(.196)
Organizational Variables			
Capital Intensity	−	−.0012	−.05317
		(.101)	(.098)
Foreign Subsidiaries	−	.7060**	.5190**
		(.093)	(.091)
Firm Size	−	.5823**	.0907
		(.135)	(.132)
PAC Expenditures	−	.00591**	.004*
		(.001)	(.001)
Network Variables			
Board Interlocks	−	−	.04288*
			(.019)
Policy Network Affiliations	−	−	.5628**
			(.109)
Bus. Roundtable	−	−	.6877**
			(.232)
Random Effect	*Variance (df)*	*Variance (df)*	*Variance (df)*
Sector Mean μ_{Oj}	.7972**	.7853*	.6485*
	(57)	(57)	(57)
Level-1 Effect, r_{ij}	.5075**	.8226**	.7141**
Autocorrelation Cov. Parameter	.3658**	.1810**	1509*

+ p < .10 * p < 05 ** p < 01

multinationality significantly correlates with TPA participation, even after various controls are introduced. Firms with greater foreign economic interests are more likely to engage in temporary alliances promoting trade expanding policy initiatives (e.g., PNTR with China). Additionally, firms with greater PAC contributions are also more likely to participate: a $100,000 in PAC expenditures increases the odds of participation by 4.6%.

In Equation 3 (Table 5.5), board interlocks, policy network, and Business Roundtable affiliations significantly correlate with TPA participation, while size falls below statistical significance. Similar to the TAC models, Business Roundtable membership and policy network affiliation have a strong, positive effect. Business Roundtable membership increases the odds of participation by approximately 100%, while policy network affiliation increases the odds by 76%. Consistent with prior research (Dreiling 2000), Roundtable members are significantly more likely to bring leadership to trade policy advocacy, promoting policies of interest to the broader corporate community through business lobbying coalitions and public campaigns.

Similarly, board interlocks are associated with a moderate increase in the odds of participation in Equation 3 (Table 5.5): for a hypothetical firm with ten board interlocks, the odds of TPA participation are 53% greater than for a firm with zero board interlocks. Finally, the dummy for firm year is again significant and negative, indicated that the mean rate of alliance participation declined in 2003. This finding is unsurprising because the two policy groups analyzed in the 2003 wave (USTrade and the Business Coalition for DR-CAFTA) experienced lower rates of FF500 participation than the 1998 alliances (USA Engage and ALOT). While this finding may suggest a downward trend in firm affiliation with trade alliances in later years – something claimed by several trade policy scholars (Cohen et al. 2003; Destler 2005) – this result also reflects a relative decrease in overall trade policy conflicts following September 11, 2001. While the initiative to expand NAFTA to numerous Central American countries between 2003 and 2006 was met by broad labor, human rights, and environmental opposition, the challenges did not amount to the scale of mobilization against the NAFTA, the WTO, or China PNTR in the 1990s. Corporate political mobilization to protect and pass the initiatives in the 1990s was thus more vigorous. The widespread opposition to neoliberal trade in the 1990s was comparably diminished after 2001. In short, the negative effect of year 2003 is suggestive of a decrease in overall trade policy conflicts, not just corporate activism, although a fully satisfactory interpretation is beyond the scope of this research.

PARTICIPATION IN CONGRESSIONAL TESTIMONY

Equation 1 of Table 5.6 presents the results of a one-way ANOVA with random effects of congressional testimony by firm sector. The "congressional testimony" variable measures the number of instances of firm testimony in support of trade *expanding* policy initiatives, such as the NAFTA. As with the models for TAC and TPA participation, mean rates of activism (i.e., instances of testimony) significantly vary across industry. Specifically, slightly more than 22.6% of the variability in congressional testimony is *across* sectors, again suggesting the importance of nesting firms within sector to control for differences in the mean rate of activism. In the baseline organizational model of 1998/2003 congressional testimony (Eq. 2, Table 5.6), firm size, foreign subsidiaries, and PAC expenditures are statistically significant in the predicted direction. In Equation 3, board interlocks, policy network, and Business Roundtable membership yield positive and significant coefficients, while only the proxy for size remains statistically significant in the predicted direction.[17] As with the single wave models, Business Roundtable membership and policy network affiliation positively correlate with testimony. Roundtable membership increases the expected count of testimony by 83%, while membership in a policy organization increases the expected count by 52%.[18] Additionally, while board interlocks fall just below significance in the single wave models, they are significant in the combined model. Increasing board interlocks by ten increases the expected count of testimony by 44%, a finding consistent with Useem's (1984) "inner circle" hypothesis that executives (and, consequently, the firms they represent) are more likely to assume a leading role in business advocacy within government (as with congressional testimony).

Overall, the results of the combined testimony model suggest that network position has a larger effect on the likelihood that a firm will testify at

---

[17] In the single year models (See Appendix 2), the 1998 model and the 2003 model produced divergent outcomes with the capital intensity variable. The observed negative relationship between testimony and capital intensity is not entirely surprising for the 1998 firm sample. This is because previous studies of this period (Dreiling 2000) found that the inverse of capital intensity (i.e., labor intensity) was significantly correlated with leadership in support of the NAFTA. Thus, the significant negative effect of capital intensity is likely explained, in part, by the fact that the 1998 sample includes multiple instances of corporate testimony in favor the NAFTA. Specifically, the NAFTA hearings included several large (and relatively labor-intensive) service and light manufacturing firms, such as Wal-Mart, JC Penny, and Gillette, while at the main trade hearing for the 2003 wave (China PNTR) a preponderance of relatively capital-intensive financial and high technology firms, such as Bank of America, Chase, HP, and Motorola, testified. Specifically, the mean capital intensity of firms that testified at the PNTR hearing was 30 percent larger than the 1998 average, while in the aggregate, the capital intensity of firms that testified in support of free trade initiatives was 20% larger in 2003.

[18] The inclusion of the network parameters in the 2003 single year model (See Appendix 3) nullifies the statistical significance of size and foreign subsidiaries, while policy network affiliation and Business Roundtable membership significantly correlate with congressional testimony. Roundtable membership in particular has a large impact, increasing the expected count by 173%.

TABLE 5.6 *1998/2003 Estimated Effects of Organizational and Network Variables on the* Count *of Congressional Testimony (Unstandardized Reg. Coefficients with SEs in Parentheses)*

Fixed Effect	Eq. 1	Eq. 2	Eq. 3
Constant	-2.1883**	-4.3826**	-3.7312**
	(.175)	(.672)	(.654)
Year = 2003	–	.03145	-1282
		(.187)	(.194)
Organizational Variables			
Capital Intensity	–	.1228	-.04676
		(.101)	(.105)
Foreign Subsidiaries	–	.410**	.1173
		(.093)	(.088)
Firm Size	–	.5017**	.1739+
		(.089)	(.103)
PAC Expenditures	–	.0024*	.00096
		(.001)	(.001)
Network Variables			
Board Interlocks	–	–	.03680*
			(.016)
Policy Network Affiliations	–	–	.4217**
			(.072)
Bus. Roundtable	–	–	.6038*
			(.280)
Random Effect	*Variance (df)*	*Variance (df)*	*Variance (df)*
Sector mean μ_{0j}	.3917+	.8727*	.6375*
	(57)	(57)	(57)
Level-1 Effect r_{ij}	1.339**	.7976**	.7736**
Autocorrelation Cov. Parameter	.4524**	.1948**	.1352*

+ p<.10 * p<.05 ** p<.01

a congressional trade hearing than organizational factors. Additionally, the null effect of the organizational variables in the combined model (with the exception of sector), together with the significant coefficients for the Business Roundtable, board interlock, and policy network variables, suggest that the odds of corporate testimony at a trade hearing are more strongly influenced by network position and product market than organizational attributes such as size or foreign subsidiaries.

For quite some time, social scientists have discussed the importance of "situational constraints," that is, structural embeddedness (Granovetter

1985). However, as Emirbayer (1997) has argued, the application of a structural approach within a rigorously specified empirical model has often proved elusive. In this chapter, corporate trade policy activism was measured as a contingent function of *both* organizational attributes and network position in class embedded networks. Confirming the hypotheses laid out in Chapter 3, organizational attributes significantly predicted corporate political action for neoliberal trade policy. The reasons for this are not difficult to ascertain. Large, multinational firms in trade-dependent product markets typically benefit from lower transaction costs on intrafirm exchange: they have an organizational interest in free trade. Interpreting the effects of the network parameters, however, is somewhat less direct and warrants additional consideration. Following the work of Burris (2005), Domhoff (2006), Mizruchi (1992), and Useem (1984), the proxies for network embeddedness, such as policy group affiliation, capture processes of class-coalescence that produce a variable capacity to articulate the broader interests of business. With respect to trade policy in particular, class-networks spanning between state and non-state institutions channel the resources of well-connected corporations toward strategically defined policy initiatives.

One could argue that the proxies for network participation presented in this chapter do not measure relational phenomena *per se*, but the general effect of firm size on policy activism. In this regard, a number of studies indicate that firm size is strongly correlated with common indicators of inner circle status (e.g., the Business Roundtable), because the heads of the largest firms have historically been most active in these organizations (Mizruchi and Koenig 1991: 308; Useem 1984). To the extent that the network parameters actually capture the effects of size, a model of business political fragmentation becomes more plausible: large firms are more politically active not because of the structural constraints imposed by network position, but because their organizational capacity to produce political change is so great that independent political action produces an adequate economic return. From this perspective, interfirm networks do not exert an independent influence on political activism, but follow as an ancillary consequence of the individual pursuit of favorable policy outcomes by the largest companies. While our data cannot disconfirm this hypothesis conclusively, we would not have expected the network variables to achieve statistical significance after controlling for the effects of size and political spending (eq. 3) were participation primarily driven by firm size. This is especially evident given that other studies of firm political behavior, albeit using different dependent variables, have found that policy

network affiliation via the Business Roundtable is not statistically significant at conventional levels when size and other organizational measures
are controlled (Mizruchi and Koenig 1991: 307). With respect to the
current study, while TAC participation is not evenly distributed across
all levels of firm size, there are TAC participants present in each quartile of
the distribution. While almost 50 percent of FF500 TAC participants have
a size ranking in the seventy-sixth percentile or higher, an additional
40 percent are distributed in the twenty-sixth through seventy-fifth per-
centiles. Thus, while larger firms are considerably more likely to participate in a TAC, there are a significant number of "smaller" participants
(relative to the population mean size). This suggests, together with the
significant partial correlations of the network and political spending variables, that raw organizational capacity and sales rank are not the only
determinants of TAC participation. In the next chapter, an explicitly
relational model of corporate networks is evaluated. Below, additional
network heuristics are offered to clarify the results presented thus far.

CONTRASTING CORPORATE POLITICAL NETWORKS

Thus far, analyses of the "policy" and "board interlock" networks and
their influence on trade policy formation has focused on aggregate patterns of correlation between prominent policy groups and the three forms
of trade policy activism. In might be useful, therefore, to re-examine the
structure of a subset of these relationships visually, analyzing how firms
are related to one another by, for example, board interlocks and policy
discussion groups. Parallel to the three network graphs presented in
Chapter 4, the network heuristics provide a (nonstochastic) methodology
for visually analyzing the characteristics of the political and economic
networks that connect large corporations.

Using network heuristics again, Figures 5.1 and 5.2 map the connections
of two "actor-subgroups" through board of director interlocks and the
policy groups introduced in Chapter 4.[19] The first subgroup consists of
the population (N=11) of 2003 FF500 firms that participated in *each* of the
three forms of trade policy activism analyzed in this study: testimony at
congressional trade hearings, trade policy alliances, and appointment to

---

[19] These organizations are the Business Roundtable, Business Council, Conference Board,
Emergency Committee on American Trade, National Association of Manufacturers,
Council of the Americas, Trilateral Commission, and the United States Council for
International Business.

a TAC. These corporations are unique in their span of activism and can perhaps be conceptualized as a "core" group of FF500 actors lobbying for liberalization of US trade relations in this period. The second actor subgroup consists of eleven firms matched to the "core" group by sector and size.[20] These firms provide a "reference" group against which to compare the board interlock and policy network affiliations of the eleven politically active firms. The purpose of this section is to visually examine the divergence (if any) in network embeddedness between the "core" group of politically active firms and the comparably sized reference firms that did not participate in the three domains of trade policy activism.[21]

Using data on policy network affiliation and board interlocks, the corporations are plotted analogous to the board interlock and policy network graphs in previous chapters. The plotting method within both subgroups is a function of (1) the presence of a tie (indicated by an arc) and (2) the similarity of firm ties, which is measured using nonmetric multidimensional scaling (MDS) coordinates. As discussed previously, MDS coordinates plot the distance between two firms in terms of the similarity of their relations to *other firms in this subnetwork*. If two firms have nearly identical ties to other firms in the subgroup, their graphed locations will be similar.[22] This technique, similar to that applied by Burris (1992a), Burt (1983), and Dreiling (2001), approximates a measure of structural equivalence between two actors in the network. Structural equivalence is a measure of the extent to which a pair or group of actors in a network share similar ties with the other actors in the network.

Figure 5.1 depicts the board interlock ties within each actor subgroup, with the "core" group appearing at the top of the figure (section A) and the eleven nonactive reference firms appearing at the bottom (section B). The most significant difference between the two actor subgroups is the greater number of network isolates in the reference group. Network isolates, in this graph, indicate the absence of a board tie with the other

---

[20] Specifically, each firm in the "core" group was matched to a firm in the same two-digit SIC code with the closest size ranking. Prior to matching, firms that participated in some aspect of trade policy advocacy (e.g., TACs, TPA, or testimony) were removed from the sample.

[21] It may be noted that while network analysis may reveal different patterns of affiliation across different subgroups, the network plots (Figures 5.1 and 5.2) should not be thought of as a formal test of a falsifiable hypothesis. Rather, these plots are mainly shown for heuristic purposes, to illustrate the differing levels of policy network affiliation and board interlocking – suggested by the participation models presented above – across two subpopulations within the FF500.

[22] MDS values, which are a rank preserving transformation yielding two coordinates (i.e., x, y), were computed using Pearson product moment correlations (see Mizruchi 1992).

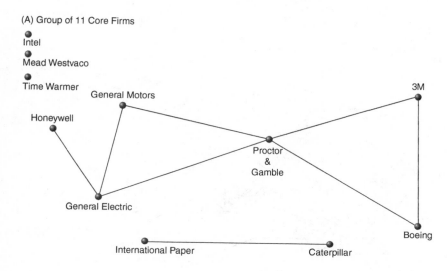

(A) Group of 11 Core Firms

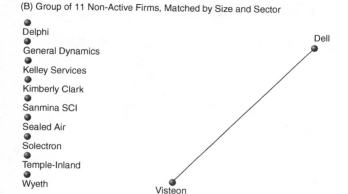

(B) Group of 11 Non-Active Firms, Matched by Size and Sector

FIGURE 5.1 Board of Director Interlocks among Two Actor Subgroups Plotted with Non-Metric Multidimensional Scaling (minor adjustments made to improve visibility of nodes).

ten firms in the subgroup. Among the active subgroup (section A), three firms are isolated from the board network, while in the reference subgroup (section B) nine firms are isolates. Likewise, in the active subgroup (section A) six of the eleven firms can "reach" one another through a direct or indirect board tie, only two actors share a board tie. At the center of the active subgroup's board network, Procter & Gamble shares four directors with other companies, while four other firms (GE, GM, 3M, and Boeing)

(A) Group of 11 Core Firms

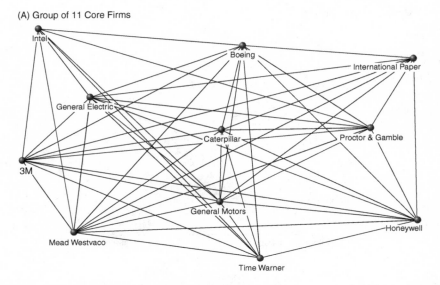

(B) Group of 11 Non-Active Firms, Matched by Size and Sector

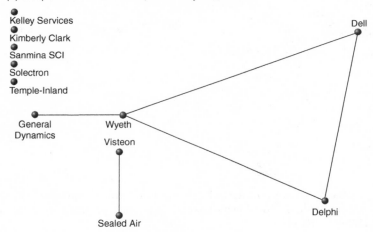

FIGURE 5.2 Policy Network Affiliations for Two Actor Subgroups
Plotted with Non-Metric Multidimensional Scaling (minor adjustments made to
improve visibility of nodes).

share two directors. In the reference subgroup's board network, conversely, no firms share more than one director.

Figure 5.2 presents a similar analysis, this time plotting the interconnections within the two actor subgroups to eight prominent policy discussion groups. Two main findings are suggested by this comparison. First, the frequency of interfirm ties within the policy network is greater than that within the board interlock network. This finding is perhaps to be expected because firms can connect through one or more of several organizations in Figure 5.2. Second, the active subgroup (section A) possesses significantly more ties to the policy network than firms in the reference subgroup (section B). As with the board interlock network, the core firms possess significantly more ties to one another than the reference group. For example, while each firm in the active subgroup (section A) is connected to at least two other firms through a policy organization, five firms are network isolates in the reference group (section B).

Overall, the four subgroup networks presented in Figures 5.1 and 5.2 suggest that firms more active in the three domains of trade policy activism are more embedded within the board interlock and policy networks. Consistent with the regression models presented above, politically active firms (e.g., TAC and TPA participants) are moderately more connected to one another through board interlocks and possess significantly more ties to the policy network.[23]

ANOTHER GLANCE AT THE BUSINESS ROUNDTABLE

Given the significance of common membership in the Business Roundtable across our models and the broader understanding within the literature of the historic role of the Roundtable in advancing neoliberal reforms in tax, regulatory, education, and trade policy, further elaboration of our findings is in order.[24] To illustrate why the networks among firms matter and why, in particular, the Business Roundtable appears so salient, two samples of thirty-five firms each from the 2003 FF500 were selected. Using coordinates from a multidimensional scaling of each co-membership matrix, Figure 5.3

---

[23] Although it should again be noted that in the firm participation regression models board interlocks are measured vis-à-vis the entire FF500, whereas in the Figures 5.1 and 5.2 they are specific to the given subgroup.

[24] Recalling our discussion from Chapter 4, the Business Roundtable was formed in 1972 by a group of CEOs previously involved in the Labor Law Research Group (Gross 1995). Originally the group consisted of fewer than 100 CEOs of some of the largest corporations in the United States. It is the resource commitment of these CEOs, their stature as heads of very large corporations, their frequent meetings with each other and government officials, and the direct involvement of these CEOs in lobbying that makes the Business Roundtable such a potent political force (Domhoff 2006). As the work of Burris (1992a, 2008) reveals, the Business Roundtable emerged at the center of the corporate policy-planning network and played a decisively more aggressive political role than its predecessors with whom it shares a high level of membership overlap, e.g., the Business Council.

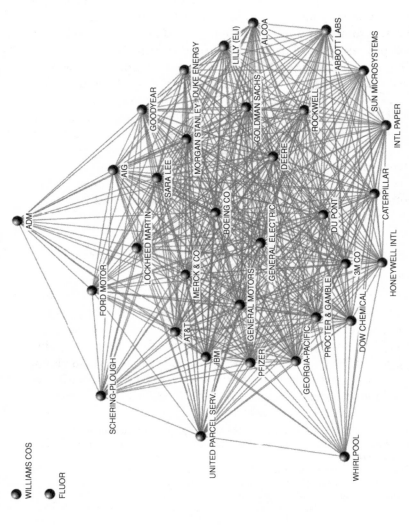

FIGURE 5.3 Sample of 2003 FF500 Business Roundtable Members' Co-membership in Policy-Planning and Ad Hoc Trade Alliance Organizations

Plotted with Non-Metric Multidimensional Scaling (minor adjustments made to improve visibility of nodes) *Connectedness, 0.887; Compactness, 0.849; Density 0.810.*

plots the affiliations among 2003 FF500 Business Roundtable (BR) members that result from their membership in our policy planning and trade advocacy organizations. This intercorporate network is contrasted with a similar plot in Figure 5.4 of a sample of thirty-five non-BR firms from the 2003 FF500. In these figures, each node depicts a corporation, and an arc between two nodes indicates shared membership in at least one other policy planning and advocacy organization.

As is clearly apparent in Figures 5.3 and 5.4, Business Roundtable members diverge significantly from their non-BR counterparts in the mean frequency of ties to the larger policy planning and advocacy network. The sheer intensity of membership overlap among Business Roundtable corporations across the policy-planning organizations indicates a distinct level of organizational embeddedness among these firms. In contrast, the non-BR firms are markedly more isolated from that interorganizational milieu. Table 5.7 presents a two-sample t-test of the mean affiliations of both samples, indicating significantly different mean affiliations.

These network plots support the inference that Business Roundtable co-membership is significant in our model not simply because of the characteristics of the organization per se, but because of the associational dynamics among corporate CEOs that place the Roundtable and those CEOs at the *center* of a much broader intercorporate policy network involving many of the largest corporations in the United States. Irreducible to interests derived from corporate attributes, this relational context facilitates political cohesion and shared political objectives among the CEOs and top executives of large corporations. These corporate elite may be attracted to prominent policy groups for a variety of organizational or ideological purposes. The important point is not so much *why* firms choose to participate in a group but, rather, how the networks created by this association function to channel corporate resources toward strategically defined policy initiatives. The intercorporate network thus connotes not only a complex of interfirm ties but also a social formation with political consequences: a cooperative, business *class segment* that transcends the economic concerns of specific industries (Domhoff 1990; Mills 1956; Mizruchi 1989, 1992; Useem 1984). Our research extends this sociological insight of corporate embeddedness and, as with other empirical accounts that have identified the centrality of the Business Roundtable in corporate policy-planning networks, confirms that these network sources of business unity impact political behavior across the institutional contours of the state (Akard 1992; Burris 1992a, 2008). The significance of Roundtable membership in all three

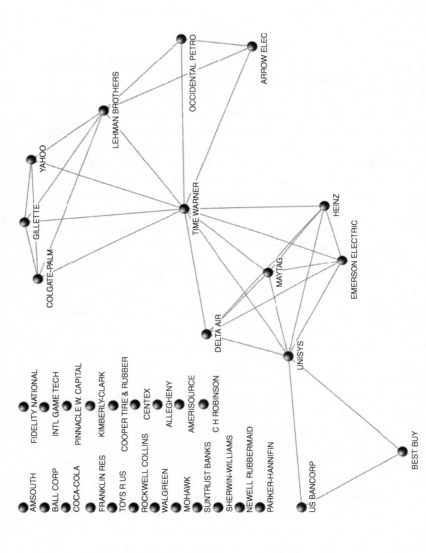

FIGURE 5.4 Sample of 2003 FF500 (Non-Business Roundtable) Corporations' Co-membership in Policy-Planning and Ad Hoc Trade Alliance Organizations.

Plotted with Coordinates from Non-Metric Multidimensional Scaling (minor adjustments made to improve visibility of nodes) *Connectedness, 0.153; Compactness, 0.101; Density 0.055.*

TABLE 5.7 *Two-Tailed T-Test (n = 70), 2003 FF500 Business Roundtable (1) and Non-BR (0) Corporations' Mean Affiliations to Policy and ad Hoc Trade Alliance Organizations*

Group	Observed	Mean	Std. Err.
0	35	.8286	.22635
1	35	4.600	.47844
Mean Diff.		3.7714	

df: 68 H$_0$: mean(1) − mean(0) = diff. = 0; H$_1$: diff. ≠ 0
t = 7.125***
*** $p < .000$

facets of trade policy echoes Useem's (1984: 74) point that inner-circle corporate actors receive the political advantages offered by "the stature and resources of the premier business associations" which facilitate not only cohesion, but heightened visibility and access to "government circles ... and special hearings."

Substantively, there is no doubt that the Roundtable is a major advocate of neoliberal trade. Jerry Junkins, speaking on behalf of Texas Instruments and the Business Roundtable before the Committee on Ways and Means, spoke plainly to this point: "Liberalized trade and investment simply means getting governments, both at home and abroad, out of people's economic affairs and letting free markets work efficiently ... the Roundtable believes that fast-track should be reauthorized for use in both multilateral and bilateral negotiations" (US House of Representatives 1995: 67). Less obvious is the "class relevant selectivity" of state structures (Jessop 1990) that adjoin organized segments of large firms, such as Roundtable members, to the political process. This dynamic is reflected in the multiple network ties and testimony of James D. Robinson III, former CEO of American Express. As one of the founders of the USA*NAFTA ad hoc trade advocacy group, James D. Robinson III was also a co-chair of the Business Roundtable (1988–1994) and the chair of the ACTPN (Advisory Committee on Trade Policy Negotiations to the President). Testifying before Congress, he declared that the US Trade Representative "met with the private sector representatives ... nearly 1000 times ... over the course of the negotiations. We had regular, detailed, substantive input into the process" of developing and negotiating NAFTA (US Senate, 1992: 102).

DISCUSSION

While many analysts examine organizational sources of corporate trade policy advocacy, few consider the impact of what Gulati and Gargiulo (1999) term "positional embeddedness," that is, the effect of interfirm ties through board interlocks or policy organizations on trade policy activism. This is not to say that organizational factors are unrelated to corporate political behavior – indeed, firm activism in all three domains is strongly patterned by sector and, less consistently, by multinationality and size. However, while most research focuses on these *organizational* sources of participation, the effect of positional embeddedness is rarely considered.

The models presented here suggest that "strictly" organizational accounts of firm trade policy activism rest on shaky empirical foundations through their omission of key explanatory variables (e.g., measures of network position within board and policy networks). More theoretically, the strictly organizational approach of the trade policy literature is based on the (empirically tenuous) assumption that firms are "inward looking," and pursue their political objective independent of other economic actors. In other words, organizational behavior is conceptualized vis-à-vis the attributes of the corporate unit. Most important, we find that net significant differences in participation by industrial sector, corporate membership in class cohesive policy groups and board interlocks overcome industry differences to suggest concerted interindustry cooperation on trade. This is one of the criteria for class cohesion that we discussed in Chapter 2 – corporate elite, through their policy memberships and board interlocks, pursue interests that are not clearly reducible to their own firm or industry. Yet the results presented here suggest that corporate behavior is also strongly influenced by relational factors, not simply self-referential interests.

Thus, to understand corporate political behavior, we must consider not only organizational characteristics, such as size and product market, but also network position within board interlock and policy networks. Across each of the three political settings, Business Roundtable membership and policy network affiliation strongly influence the odds of firm activism (Eqs. 3, Tables 5.4, 5.5, and 5.6). The consistently positive effect of these variables in different settings provides strong support for the hypothesis that policy organizations function as a crucial "anchoring point" in the corporate community, facilitating the transfer of corporate resources toward strategically defined policy objectives. The "resource" transfer these organizations facilitate assumes a variety of forms, from sizable monetary contributions to fund the expenses of temporary policy alliances to the ongoing costs associated with directing a certain percentage of executive time to policy activism, as with TAC participation and congressional testimony.

Because positional factors, such as Business Roundtable membership, appear to systematically influence corporate political behavior, this raises the theoretical question, noted earlier, whether such ties also influence the *unity* of corporate political behavior in the trade policy arena. Analyzing actual outcomes of unity in the next chapter moves us in a direction to think about how, net of industry and other firm-specific interests, shared relationships work to produce class cohesion among large corporations. As described in previous chapters, one way to assess this question is to restructure the firm-level data such that the unit of analysis becomes *all possible* relations within the network,[25] and the outcome is not participation by single firms per se but the political unity of corporate-pairs within the group. This stochastic network approach has the advantage of allowing for a more granular specification of shared corporate ties, for example, through direct *and* indirect board interlocks or involvement in specific policy organizations. Whereas in the participation models presented above, these measures are more general and measure the frequency of *firm*-level ties to the entire group (e.g., through board interlocks), in the "relational" model we are able to measure the presence of a *specific* tie between two actors. In the chapter to follow, results are presented from several relational models of corporate political unity across the three domains of trade policy advocacy. An extended discussion of those results serves for a revisit of theories concerning the role of class agency in shaping the institutional framework of neoliberal globalization.

---

[25] Specifically, the upper or lower triangle of a firm-by-firm matrix with N^2 elements measuring the presence of a shared tie in each of the dependent measures.

6

Fusing Class Agency to a State Trade
Policy Apparatus

> The corporations are the organized centers of the private property system:
> the chief executives are the organizers of that system.
>
> – C. Wright Mills, *The Power Elite* (1956: 119)

In this chapter, the eight central hypotheses of corporate unity presented at the end of Chapter 3 are examined through dyadic models to assess the relative significance of class associative determinants of corporate political action for neoliberal trade policy. As with the firm-level models in the previous chapter, corporate political behavior is analyzed across the three institutional domains of trade policy advocacy: congressional testimony, appointments to trade advisory committees, and temporary trade alliances geared to influence the media and public debate over trade policy. Each domain of political action is further examined with an extended discussion of the political fight to "normalize" trade with China in 1999–2000, which prepared China for accession to the World Trade Organization in 2001. The case for normalizing trade with China is particularly compelling because of the broad nature of the business coalition that was mobilized to support it and the consequence of trade liberalization with China, which has been nothing short of a world-historical shift in the geography of global manufacturing.

Figure 6.1 plots employment in US manufacturing from 1980 to 2012. Economists from a variety of theoretical persuasions identify trade liberalization with China as the key factor in the dramatic drop in manufacturing employment in the United States. As a share of world manufacturing output (measured in value), the trend put China on track to surpass the United States in 2011 and become the world's largest manufacturing

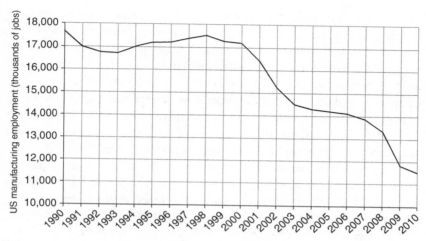

FIGURE 6.1 US Manufacturing Employment, 1990–2010
Source: US Bureau of Labor Statistics, 2011.

economy. Economists estimate that China PNTR and China's entry into the WTO, net other factors, reduced the manufacturing sector in the United States by about 3 million jobs over seven years, more than the 900,000 manufacturing jobs lost in the first year of the Great Recession (Autor et al. 2012). Liberalized trade and China's entry into the WTO contributed to a watershed drop in US manufacturing employment (Pierce and Schott 2012).

The transformation in global manufacturing associated with China's accession reveals the significance of neoliberal political action in shaping the contours of the world *economic* order. We are reminded that economic activity and mobility of capital alone do not lead to the kind of market transformations observed here. Capital mobility hinges on institutional protections. For this reason, class political agency works in concert with state actors to construct the institutional frameworks that secure capital mobility through trade and investment. In the pages that follow, the dyadic models and the case study discussion of China PNTR reveal the crux of why class agency is an appropriate conceptualization of the kind of corporate political unity observed around neoliberal trade policy. Recall from the discussion in Chapter 4 how the creation of the WTO with the conclusion of the Uruguay Round of the GATT changed the character of international trade, especially in terms of finance and trade in services. That overview of major policy and global economic developments explained how trade policy goals shifted in the 1980s from selective tariff reduction toward the elimination of *nontariff* barriers (NTBs), liberalized trade in services, agriculture, financial services, and the transnational governance of property rights. These economic goals required the assertion of new institutional authorities for market governance in bodies like the WTO or NAFTA's "tribunal" (Chorev 2007). Chapter 4 explained how these goals were formulated within corporate policy and lobbying organizations that maintained close overlapping memberships with the United States' trade advisory system. Class and state actors collaborated to facilitate this transfer of authority globally. With China's entry to the WTO hinging on the US decision to permanently normalize trade in 2000, more was at stake than a bilateral trade relation. Every major business association signed on to support it, and a concerted, high-stakes campaign was initiated to secure the congressional votes to forever change trade with China. Conceptually, the sociological picture of class actors working in concert with state actors remains theoretically salient and consistent with the larger historical narrative on trade policy in the 1990s. As a best match to that narrative, the methodological approach in this chapter raises the bar in terms of what is actually measured – and tested – in the statistical models. In the concluding chapter, we consider parallels with the corporate organizations and state officials within the Obama Administration who led the campaign for a Trans-Pacific Partnership (TPP), a multilateral market governance apparatus that extends throughout the Pacific Rim a series of transnational investor protections equivalent to NAFTA's bitterly disputed chapter 11 provisions.[1]

MEASURING CORPORATE UNITY: DYADS

Because corporate political unity is often conceptualized as a characteristic of large groups of firms at the local or national level, this study's

---

[1] The investor-state dispute settlement provisions in NAFTA (chapter 11) were widely criticized by opponents to the deal. Over twenty years later, most of the challenges from investors through these provisions took issue with Canada's strong environmental and public sector procurement laws. A recent study by the Canadian Centre for Policy Alternatives (Sinclair 2015) notes that the United States has never lost a case under the rules, while both Mexico and Canada have been compelled to settle with investors $207 million and $170 million, respectively. One of the most notable cases involved a suit from the Ethyl Corporation where Canada, which banned a fuel additive (also banned in California for its carcinogenic effects), was compelled to allow use of the compound and pay the company $15 million in damages. Since NAFTA, these investor protections were included in numerous other trade agreements and represent a key reason for the controversy over the Trans-Pacific Partnership in 2015.

analytic focus on corporate dyads requires some elaboration. The discussion of the "business unity" literature in Chapter 2 might suggest, for example, that in order to study corporate political unity business as a whole, or some large grouping of firms, would be an appropriate unit of analysis (e.g., all FF500 firms). While this approach has the advantage of allowing us to focus on business as a collectivity of actors, it has one significant disadvantage: it prevents us from analyzing direct connections between variables (Mizruchi 1992: 86). For example, suppose we seek to analyze TAC participation in two groupings of firms, Business Roundtable members and the 200 largest non–Business Roundtable FF500 firms. If, say, we found that the Business Roundtable grouping had higher levels of interlocking and higher levels of committee participation, we could not establish whether the interlocked firms in the group are also the firms involved with the advisory committees (ibid.). Instead, we only know that the Business Roundtable grouping has higher levels of interlocking and participation (expressed, for example, as a raw frequency of the number of interlocks and advisory committee memberships within the group).

Measuring political unity at the firm level of analysis creates similar problems. First, a firm-level approach does not allow us to model unity, or *similarity* of political behavior because our data, by definition, can only describe the activity of a *single* firm. Second, and more technically, a firm-level approach does not permit analysis of the association between *specific* ties and some outcome. To illustrate this point, consider the case of board of director interlocks. One way to measure interlocks is to compute a raw or composite score of the total number of board interlocks between a firm and some sample or population (e.g., the FF500). If, for example, we were interested in predicting whether a firm is invited to testify before Congress, we could model the correlation between the odds of testimony and total board of director interlocks. However, even if we were to determine that board interlocks significantly correlate with the odds of testimony, the problem with this methodological approach is that we are unable to determine whether firms that testify are actually connected *to each other* via board interlocks (Mizruchi 1992: 87). We only know that firms with more ties in general are more likely to testify.

Given the results from the firm-level models presented in Chapter 5 and the historical-network analyses in Chapter 4, it is important to step back and recall a few of the substantive differences between models of corporate networks at the firm-level versus dyadic approaches (see Appendix 2 for additional discussion on the data for these analyses). Common to both approaches are efforts to bring statistical tests to network variables. But dyadic models allow stochastic modeling on *actual* ties between groups of actors, assessing the probabilities of specific associations occurring given the presence or absence of other ties that are measured in the model. In this way, dyadic analysis provides a more robust empirical framework for assessing interstitial sources of political unity. This is an important methodological advantage because the influence of two actors' shared ties is closely linked to the "steps" between them. As elaborated in the literature on intercorporate networks (Chapter 2), it is expected that firms with direct (step 1) or indirect (step 2) ties will display greater political unity than those connected at further distances (Burris 2005; Granovetter 1974; Mizruchi, Stearns, and Marquis 2006). Similarly, it is expected that a direct board tie or PAC dollars allocated to the same political candidates between a pair of firms is more consequential to their political unity than a count of the raw frequency of their combined ties to the entire network of FF500 boards or a sum of their total campaign contributions (e.g., to every firm in the FF500). Because a firm-level approach is unable to distinguish between these two forms of connection or PAC donations (i.e., within the pairing and to the entire network), dyadic analysis is a preferred method for testing network effects on political unity. This is more than a technical consideration, since it is possible that dyadic analysis will support different substantive conclusions from a firm-level methodological approach.

Now, consider a dyadic approach to the problem. Within this framework, our research question is not whether any *given* firm testifies, but whether *two firms testify in common*. Dyadic political unity thus refers to whether a pair of companies (a corporate dyad) share a common political trait (e.g., both dyadic subunits participate in the same temporary political alliance). Operationally, a dyad, such as Dow Chemical and Pfizer, is a single case with unique measures on each variable. Using this methodology, our predictors become measures of *shared* attributes, for instance, whether two firms share a director, or whether they are both members of the Business Roundtable. At the dyadic level, we are able to assess whether one set of ties (e.g., via board interlocks) directly relate to another (e.g., common testimony before Congress) (Mizruchi 1992: 87).

To more fully examine how class cohesion networks facilitate intercorporate unity and class agency, the empirical question analyzed in this chapter is not whether a given *corporation* gets involved in trade policy activism, but whether *pairs* (or dyads) of corporations exhibit political unity in any of the three domains of policy activism. To assess this question, a different data structure is utilized to model corporate behavior where the unit of analysis is the corporate dyad and variables measure the presence of *shared* behaviors or attributes.[2] As a network concept, unity in a dyad implies a symmetric edge between nodes (in this case, corporations). Shared ties, or positive edges, in a dyad capture a fundamental feature of the interorganizational network in which all firms are embedded. Modeling *all possible* dyadic pairs (N = 232,807) across the multiple corporate networks in this study provides a powerful empirical framework to examine the role of these networks among the largest corporations in the United States across the three domains of trade policy influence.

In our discussion, the concept of "cohesion" – figures prominently. The social network dimensions of this concept are widely discussed. Because actors who share ties with one another are frequently tied to other similar actors, the concepts of cohesion and structural equivalence are often indistinguishable empirically (Burt 1987). As Mizruchi (1990) explains, actors with similar ties to another set of actors share a structural equivalence and are also likely to maintain cohesion. Similar behavior is a likely outcome. Dyadic unity in our models thus predicts political unity. This is not just an abstract formula; it also makes theoretical sense. Corporations with multiple independent paths to other actors are able to better coordinate their political behavior. Figure 6.2 maps a sequence of a dyadic relationship to reiterate our argument (Chapter 2) about the conditions that facilitate corporate class agency. When dyadic unity emerges from class-cohesive, interindustry associations, we consider the political action of the pair to represent class unity. As represented in Figure 6.2, two actors who share a common path with a third actor (or set of actors), such as the Business Roundtable, have a positive tie, or unity, on that relationship. We expect the unity in that relationship, net of organizational interests, to increase the likelihood of unity in one of our outcome measures, such as joint testimony in Congress or common appointments to advisory posts on trade policy.

Network graphs (Figure 6.3) provide powerful methods for visualization, logical tests, and analytically meaningful contrasts. Chapter 4 presented a sample of this approach with the intercorporate networks among leaders of the NAFTA campaign. The two-mode affiliation network plotted in Figure 6.3 builds on these analyses to highlight the basic structural properties of complex networks examined in this

---

[2] Refer to Appendix 2 for a more detailed discussion of the methods and variable construction utilized in the dyadic regression models.

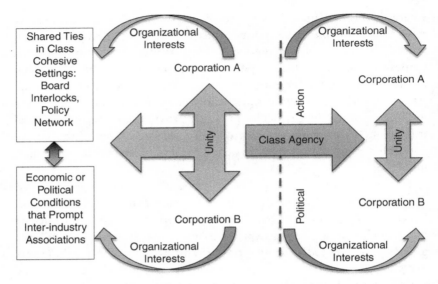

FIGURE 6.2 Conceptual Model of Corporate Dyadic Unity in Class-Cohesive Networks and Class Agency in Political Action

chapter.[3] For example, structural properties among corporations, policy organizations, and the trade advisory committees prominently include a *core-periphery* feature. At the center of the plot, we observe the policy-planning and lobbying organizations like the Roundtable and trade advisory committees (plotted as square nodes). The fifty corporations are plotted around the periphery, defining the hub-spoke structure to this network.[4] As central hubs to the corporate network, groups like the Roundtable and Emergency Committee on American Trade (ECAT) bring the specific interests and concerns of corporate executives to a common forum where more general interests are identified, discussed, and acted upon. Likewise, the government trade advisory committees operate functionally to bring diverse economic interests together in a forum where specific policy interests are identified and developed. More integrative in their operations, organizations such as the BRT and Business Council

[3] Each node is plotted in this figure using correspondence analysis that calculates coordinates for similarly connected nodes and locates them in proximate two-dimensional space.
[4] These structural characteristics are observed in other complex organization networks as well. Galaskiewicz (1979) illustrates how the roles of more integrative organizations occupy positions in the center of graphs while specialized organizations form the periphery (see also Dreiling 2001).

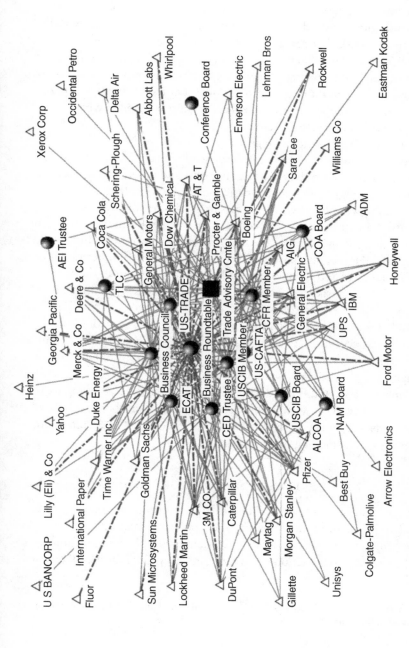

FIGURE 6.3 Two-Mode Network of Fifty Most Central FF500 Corporations with Policy-Planning Organizations and Trade Advisory Appointments, 2003

Plotted using Fruchterman-Reingold layout algorithm. *Connectedness, 0.314; Compactness, 0.236; Density 0.191.*

operate as sites where particular policy projects acquire, through dialogue with the governmental advisory bodies, the generalized vision and aims of large corporations. Indeed, it is in the interorganizational exchange at the core of the network that particular interests are discussed, organized, and communicated as general aims to be pursued in the policy-making arenas of the government. With the most central organizations possessing the most frequent links to the more integrative policy bodies, their influence and broad vision offer to the larger business community a lesson in what Useem (1984) calls the "classwide principle."

Based on the visualization in Figure 6.3, substantive differences between the dyadic and firm-level models can be gauged. For the firm-level models, all network effects are measured as a count of ties to other organizations in the network. A single company is a case, such as Hewlett-Packard, and the policy-planning variable is equal to the sum of ties to any policy-planning organizations in the network. The count of total policy-planning ties is then evaluated along with all other cases in the regression model. But in the dyadic model, Hewlett-Packard is not treated as a single firm but rather as a subunit of a dyad and is paired with all other corporations in the sample. The statistical analysis then assesses all possible pairs of companies to determine if the presence (or absence) of a dyadic attribute changes the likelihood of them also participating together, as a dyad, in any of the trade-policy political actions (dependent variables): the trade advisory committees, testifying before Congress, or joining together in a public relations campaign. The model thus evaluates how actual measures of corporate unity impact the likelihood of corporate collective action, allowing us to ascertain the extent to which shared memberships in class associative organizations and policy networks match the theoretical expectations of class agency on the making of neoliberal trade policy.

STATISTICAL METHODS: DYADIC MODELS

We utilize dyadic regression to model the determinants of corporate political *unity* in three domains of trade policy formation: (1) shared involvement in trade policy alliances, (2) shared congressional testimony, and (3) common participation in a Trade Advisory Committee.[5] The first

---

[5] The data set of corporate dyads was created with an algorithm in *STATA* that converts the ~484 firms in each study year into a larger data set of ~118,000 corporate dyads. Specifically, this creates a data set of all possible *pairs* created by the sample of 484 companies, for example, the elements of the upper triangle of a firm-by-firm matrix less the diagonal.

measure of unity is a dichotomous indicator of whether both dyadic subunits participated in the same temporary trade policy alliance.[6] The second dependent measure is a dummy indicator of whether each dyadic subunit testified in agreement ("shared testimony") at a congressional trade policy hearing.[7] The third and final dependent measure is a *count* of the number of shared trade policy advisory committee memberships. For the testimony and TPA measures, which are dichotomous, we utilize binary logistic regression. For the TAC model, which is a count, we utilize a variant of Poisson regression that corrects for overdispersion.[8] The general form of the equation predicting political unity of firms i and j is given by:

$$\text{Political Unity}_{ij} = \beta_{0j} + \beta_{1j}(\text{Subsidiaries}) + \beta_{2j}(\text{Cap. Inten.}) + \beta_{3j}(\text{Size})$$
$$+ \beta_{4j}(\text{PAC}) + \beta_{5j}(\text{Sector}) + \beta_{6j}(\text{Pol. Network})$$
$$+ \beta_{7j}(\text{Bus. Roundtable}) + \beta_{8j}(\text{Direct Interlocks})$$
$$+ \beta_{9j}(\text{Indirect Interlocks}) + \beta_{10j}(\text{State}) + \beta_{11j}(\text{Year}) + r_{ij}$$

Our use of corporate dyads in a multiple regression model poses several statistical issues that must be considered. Most important, repeated observations of the same dyadic subunits (i.e., individual firms) produce contemporaneous autocorrelation of the error structure.[9] This violates the least squares assumption of independent error terms and results in overly optimistic coefficient variance estimates. Even though autocorrelation does not affect slope estimates (Beck and Katz 1995), the standard computation of coefficient variance will generally yield biased estimates, confounding statistical inference about the effect size of different parameters. One solution to this problem is the incorporation of a dummy variable for each firm, that is, to use a "fixed effect" or "least squares dummy variable" (LSDV)

---

[6] Again, these alliances refer, for the 1998 wave, to America Leads on Trade and/or USA Engage, and for the 2003 wave, to the Business Coalition for US-Central America Trade and/or USTrade.

[7] Because there were only twenty-six dyads with two instances of shared testimony (the maximum observed value), the testimony variable is dichotomized to facilitate interpretation. It should be noted, however, that the results do not alter significantly if a rare event, ordered count model is utilized, such as Negative Binomial regression.

[8] Specifically, the dyadic TAC model is estimated using the *STATA*'s negative binomial regression procedure (nbreg) nested within a quadratic assignment procedure bootstrap routine.

[9] Specifically, this is because the error terms associated with dyads that contain a common firm are likely to covary.

approach.[10] While this is an effective (but statistically inefficient) method for modeling the dependency of the error vector (Sayrs 1989), the main problem with LSDV is that it treats variation unique to a specific firm as a spurious effect. For example, if an interlocked firm shares high levels of political unity in a number of dyadic pairings, the statistical covariance between interlocks and political unity in dyads involving this firm is absorbed by the dummy parameter. Thus, LSDV may be overly conservative, resulting in a greater risk of type-two statistical errors (Mizruchi 1992: 114).

Given the limitations of the LSDV model, many analysts employ quadratic assignment procedure (QAP) regression to analyze dyadic data (Burris 2005; Gulati and Gargiulo 1999; Mizruchi 1992). QAP is a nonparametric method yielding a percentile ranking for each of the observed coefficients that is substantively analogous to standard-error-based tests of statistical significance. The basic idea of QAP is that the independent variables are held constant while the row and column values of the dependent variable matrix are randomly permuted. Similar to the bootstrap procedure (Efron 1979), the model is estimated after each successive permutation of the dependent variable matrix. This procedure is repeated many times (1,000 times in our models) yielding a distribution of coefficient estimates. The QAP distribution is then compared with the empirical coefficient estimates. Typically, a threshold is set such that empirical coefficient estimates below or above a certain percentile (e.g., the 2.5th and 97.5th) are deemed statistically significant.[11]

DEPENDENT VARIABLES

In this section, a brief revisit to the variables used to test the hypotheses raised in Chapter 3 is warranted because the methodology for dyadic analysis involves some important data transformations. The first dependent

---

[10] All but one firm was assigned a dummy variable such that, within each dyad, the dummy variable associated with each subunit was set to one (the sole exception being the reference firm's dummy, which is always null).

[11] Because there are only two waves of data and the population differs in each wave, standard corrections for serial correlation, such as the first-order autocorrelation coefficient, are not indicated (Ostrom 1978). For these dyadic models, temporal dependency in the error vector is of less concern because QAP regression uses a non-standard-error-based test of coefficient significance (as described above). However, a dummy indicator was also included in the dyadic models to correct for any unique dependency in the error vector associated with a specific observational year (e.g., where the mean rate of a given outcome differs across study years).

variable, which measures dyadic involvement in a Trade Advisory Committee, is a proxy for corporate trade policy activism in the executive branch. The second dependent variable, which measures the unity of corporate testimony at congressional trade policy hearings, is a proxy for direct corporate lobbying of the legislature. The third dependent variable, trade policy alliance participation measures dyadic involvement in nonstate advocacy groups lobbying Congress and conducting public campaigns for specific trade policy outcomes.

Because US trade policy development is distributed across numerous federal agencies and congressional committees, corporations seeking to influence trade policy must channel their resources into multiple "leverage points" in the policy-formation process. Thus, focus on any single leverage point may not reveal a comprehensive picture of the factors that encourage firms to engage in trade politics. In the sections to follow, each of these three measures of trade policy activism (testimony, TAC, and TPA) are described in greater detail.

Trade Advisory Committee Appointments (TACs)

Recall that the Trade Act of 1974 created a three-tiered system of federal trade policy advisory committees that allow industry representatives to provide policy input and recommendations to US trade negotiators. In addition to their evaluative function, TACs also provide direct input into active US trade negotiations. It is common, for example, for TAC members to communicate directly with US officials during active trade negotiations to provide input on the language of a treatise or to make other requests.[12]

In Table 6.3, we measure TAC participation as a count of the number of *shared* committee memberships within the corporate dyad. For example, a dyad in which each firm is a member of one TAC is coded one, while a dyad in which both firms in the dyad are involved in two committees is coded two, and so on.

Testimony Before Congress

In this study, the congressional testimony of the FF500 at US trade policy hearings during the period 1993–2004 was examined and

---

[12] Information obtained in a 10/4/2005 interview with Angela Cazada, a Department of Commerce official who oversees the trade policy committees.

coded.[13] Similar to Mizruchi's (1992) study, testimony was measured across several years because in any given year there are insufficient instances of FF500 congressional testimony to permit statistical modeling. The testimony data were collected by compiling a list of major trade policy initiatives (such as NAFTA, FTAA, China PNTR, and CAFTA) during the period under investigation and analyzing the invited testimony of FF500 corporate representatives. For each trade policy initiative, a variable measuring dyadic unity in support or opposition was created by coding the testimony of each FF500 firm that appeared at the congressional hearing as being in support of or in opposition to the pending legislation.[14] Each instance of testimony was coded by two researchers to augment inter-rater reliability. Overwhelmingly, the relatively small number of FF500 firms that testified *together* before Congress professed unambiguous support for pending trade initiatives (nearly all sought to further liberalize US trade relations),[15] which simplified the coding process.

In the dyadic models below, testimony was modeled as a dummy variable indicating whether two firms testified together in support of a trade-expanding policy initiative, such as the NAFTA. A separate model predicting dyadic opposition (i.e., a model of whether the two corporate subunits of the dyad opposed one another at a trade hearing) was deemed unnecessary because opposition is almost perfectly predicted by whether or not one of the dyad's subunit is a steel producer.[16]

---

[13] Specifically, testimony for the period 1999–2004 was measured for the 2003 wave of companies, while testimony for the period 1993–1998 was measured for the 1998 wave.

[14] Mizruchi's (1992) research on corporate congressional testimony (on any policy, not simply trade related) employed an "unrelated" category to describe some instances of shared testimony. However, this was deemed unnecessary in the present study because nearly all recorded instances of FF500 testimony were either clearly supportive or clearly opposed to the pending trade legislation, making a third category unnecessary.

[15] Steel firms were the only major exception to this, as they tended to oppose certain tariff and NTB reductions.

[16] While Mizruchi (1992) models opposition and agreement in one equation using OLS regression on a three-item ordinal scale ranging from –1 to 1, this practice is somewhat questionable statistically because it treats a unit change in the dependent variable as comparable across all variable values. This is problematic because a unit change from, for example, opposition (–1) to no shared testimony (0) may not be the same as a unit increase from no shared testimony to agreement (1). Despite these limitations, the dyadic models were estimated using a measure comparable to Mizruchi's analysis with little substantive difference in the coefficient estimates. Thus for parsimony's sake and to simplify interpretation analyses are limited to instances of shared FF500 testimony in *favor* of trade-expanding policy initiatives such as the NAFTA.

Temporary Alliance Participation

The third dependent variable, trade policy alliance (TPA) participation, measures corporate involvement in four prominent political alliances that lobbied Congress in support of Fast Track Renewal, PNTR with China, the Free Trade Area of the Americas, and the Central American Free Trade Agreement. The first coalition, America Leads on Trade (ALOT), was formed in 1997 by the Business Roundtable and several other protrade business coalitions to lobby Congress to renew President Clinton's Fast Track negotiating authority (Neil 1997). By the end of its campaign, ALOT had spent over $2 million on ad-buys and lobbyists in support of the legislation and organized a "grass-roots" corporate campaign in multiple states. The second coalition, USA Engage, was formed by several prominent corporate CEOs – including Halliburton's CEO, Dick Cheney – to lobby the legislature and build public support for congressional ratification of permanently normalized trade relations with China, among other trade and sanctions legislation. The third coalition, the Business Coalition for US–Central America Trade, was an intersector coalition of US companies and associations that lobbied Congress to enact a free trade agreement (modeled after NAFTA) with the governments of Costa Rica, the Dominican Republic, El Salvador, Guatemala, Honduras, and Nicaragua. This agreement was later passed by Congress as the "DR-CAFTA" bill and was implemented by the signatories in 2006. The final organization, USTrade, was formed by approximately 250 large corporations to lobby Congress in support of the (NAFTA-like) "Free Trade Area of the Americas" (FTAA).

Shared participation in a TPA was operationalized as a dummy indicator of whether each firm participated in a temporary trade policy alliance in each wave. For the 1998 wave, alliance participation was measured by shared firm involvement in America Leads on Trade and/or USA Engage, while for the 2003 wave alliance participation was measured by shared firm involvement in the Business Coalition for US–Central America Trade and/or USTrade.[17]

---

[17] Because each five-year period included two trade advocacy groups, this variable could assume one of three values (0=null, 1=shared membership in one group, 2=shared membership in both groups). We dichotomized (0, 1) this variable to simplify interpretation. Re-estimation of the model using a technique for ordered counts (e.g., Poisson) did not change the substantive interpretation of the findings.

ORGANIZATIONAL PREDICTORS

The first organizational measure, capital intensity, was computed using financial data on firm assets and employees. For the dyadic model, Mizruchi's (1992) operationalization[18] was utilized, which takes the absolute value of the *difference* in the natural log of the asset-to-employee ratio. That is, for dyadic subunits *i* and *j*:

$$(Capital\ Intensity)_{ij} = \text{abs}(\log(assets/employees)_i - \log(assets/employees)_j)$$

Eq. 1

To facilitate interpretation, Stata's reverse scoring procedure was utilized that creates a variable with perfect negative correlation with the original. After this transformation, larger values indicate greater *unity* in dyadic capital intensity.

The second organizational predictor, size, was estimated using data on firm sales, assets, and employees. Because these three attributes assume variable importance in different sectors, principal factor analysis was used to extract a single factor solution for firm size. For the dyadic models, the geometric mean of the firm factor scores was employed as a control for size:

$$Size_{ij}\sqrt{(Size\ Factor)_i \times (Size\ Factor)_j}$$

Eq. 2

The geometric mean provides a weighted average of each subunit's size, such that two firms with a moderately high value in the size factor will yield a larger dyadic value than two firms with the same *summed* value but unequal contributions to the total (e.g., one large firm and one small firm) (see also Mizruchi 1992). Unlike the capital intensity variable (Eq. 1 above), the control for size in the dyadic regressions was not a measure of the *unity* of the two subunits scores but, rather, a proxy for the combined size of the dyad. In other words, the expectation was not that two comparably sized small firms or two firms of mixed size (e.g., one small and one large), would display greater than average political unity. Rather, it was expected that dyads of the largest firms should exhibit greater than average political unity.

---

[18] Other operationalizations of dyadic capital intensity, such as taking the geometric mean of the subunits' logged capital intensity ratios, were also investigated. Generally, it was determined that Mizruchi's formula provided the best model fit. Thus, to maintain consistency with Mizruchi's (1992) research, we opted to use his operationalization.

The third organizational predictor, multinationality, is a function of firm subsidiary operations in foreign countries. For the dyadic model, multinationality was operationalized as a count of the number of geographic regions in which both dyadic subunits operate a foreign subsidiary operation.[19]

The fourth organizational interest predictor, product market, is measured using primary two-digit firm Standard Industrial Classification coding[20] (SIC). For the dyadic models, sector was modeled using Mizruchi's (1992) operationalization: Firms in the same two-digit sector are coded one and zero otherwise.

The fifth organizational predictor is shared region, operationalized similar to Mizruchi's (1992) as a dummy indicator for whether each subunit's headquarters are in the same state.

The sixth predictor, political donations, measured FF500 PAC expenditures in the 1996, 1998, 2000, and 2002 election cycles to House, Senate, and presidential candidates. The 1996 and 1998 election cycle data were assigned to the 1998 F500 sample firms, while the 2000 and 2002 election cycles data were assigned to the 2003 sample. The geometric mean of firm-level PAC expenditures was employed as a control for the effect of political donations:

$$Expenditures_{ij} = \sqrt{(PAC\ Expenditures)_i \times (PAC\ Expenditures)_j} \qquad Eq.\ 3$$

NETWORK VARIABLES

The seventh predictor, firm-level board interlocks, was created in two steps. First, FF500 directorate rosters were used to create a firm-by-director matrix of affiliations. Next, this matrix was transformed to produce a square firm-by-firm matrix of board interlocks. In the dyadic model, interlocks were measured using two *dichotomous* measures of "direct" and

---

[19] Subsidiary operations were coded into the following regions: North America, Central America, South America, Western Europe, Central Europe, Eastern Europe, Northern African, Sub-Saharan Africa, the Middle East, Asia, and Oceana.

[20] The Standard Industrial Classification is a four-digit coding scheme that describes the product market(s) in which a firm operates. Each digit, from the first to the fourth, describes in ascending detail the firm's product market attributes. For example, SIC code 5 refers to restaurants, wholesale firms, and retail outlets, while SIC code 57 refers to the subgrouping of home furniture, furnishings, and equipment stores.

"indirect" board ties between the dyadic subunits.[21] Direct ties measure whether a dyad was linked by one or more shared directors, while indirect ties measure whether a dyad's boards were tied through a third company. For example, dyadic subunits "A" and "B" are indirectly tied to one another if each has a director who participates in some third company, "C." Indirect ties were computed by taking the (matrix) square of the firm-by-firm interlock matrix (Wasserman and Faust 1994).

The eighth predictor, Business Roundtable membership, is a measure of firm affiliation with the Business Roundtable. This variable was simply set to one only if both firms in the dyad were members of the Business Roundtable.

The ninth predictor, policy network affiliation, measures firm ties to the following business advocacy organizations: the Business Council, Conference Board, Emergency Committee on American Trade, National Association of Manufacturers, the Council of the Americas, Trilateral Commission, and the United States Council for International Business. The policy network variable is a count of *shared* firm ties to each of these organizations.[22]

CORPORATE TRADE ACTIVISM IN THE EXECUTIVE BRANCH: MODELING CORPORATE UNITY IN TRADE ADVISORY COMMITTEES (TACS)

Correlations between each of the dependent and independent dyadic variables are presented in Table 6.1. None of the zero-order correlations exceed 0.5, and the variance inflation factor estimates for each of the predictors are well within accepted limits. Table 6.2 presents the results of two multiple regression equations where common (dyadic) participation in a Trade

---

[21] We also modeled the effects of interlocking in the dyadic models using the geometric mean of board interlocks (see also Gulati and Gargiulo 1999). As expected, this variable was positively correlated with direct and indirect interlocks (most likely because firms with more board ties to the entire network will, *ceteris paribus*, have a higher probability of being tied to each other). Entering the variables in separate models (i.e., direct/indirect ties in one model and the geometric mean of Freeman centrality in another) tended to produce similar estimates of model fit and did not change the substantive interpretation of the other predictors. Thus, because of the correlation between the measures, as well as the fact that the coefficients for direct and indirect interlocks are easier to interpret than the geometric mean of Freeman centrality scores, the former were used in the dyadic regression models below.

[22] For example, if each unit of a dyad is a member of the Trilateral Coalition and the Business Council, the variable is set to two.

TABLE 6.1 *Means, Standard Deviations, and Intercorrelations (N = 232,807)*

	Mean	St. Dev	1	2	3	4	5	6	7	8	9	10	11	12
1: TACs	0.082476	0.461478												
2: Testimony	0.0014089	0.0375088	0.3184											
3: TPA	0.0449901	0.2072827	0.0616	0.0935										
4: Size	9.975951	0.691613	0.1599	0.1921	0.0593									
5: Common State	0.0548609	0.227709	0.0072	0.0191	0.008	0.0109								
6: Foreign Subs.	1.36931	2.041381	0.1914	0.3073	0.0651	0.2222	0.0356							
7: Capital Intensity	1.628652	1.274772	0.0744	0.0797	0.0024	-0.1113	0.0109	0.1231						
8: Common Sector	0.039973	0.1958963	0.0262	0.0203	0.0052	0.0007	0.0125	0.0273	0.1384					
9: PAC Expenditures	15.75412	30.43744	0.1698	0.1837	0.0584	0.469	-0.002	0.139	0.0075	0.0416				
10: Direct Interlocks	0.0137668	0.1165217	0.0491	0.064	0.0191	0.0809	0.0811	0.0613	0.0075	-0.0064	0.0628			
11: Indirect Interlocks	0.0978407	0.2970998	0.1066	0.1491	0.0285	0.2285	0.0374	0.1589	0.0339	0.0102	0.16	-0.0389		
12: Policy Network	0.0829013	0.3714649	0.2592	0.3278	0.1174	0.3114	0.0504	0.3269	0.0381	0.0182	0.299	0.09	0.1849	
13: Bus. Roundtable	0.0529752	0.2239845	0.2235	0.2974	0.0852	0.2273	0.0072	0.2557	0.0667	0.0171	0.2708	0.0695	0.1622	0.3504

TABLE 6.2 *1998/2003 Estimated Effects of Organizational and Network Variables on the Count of Shared TAC Committee Memberships (Unstandardized Reg. Coefficients with QAP Probabilities in Parentheses)*

	Eq. 1	Eq. 2
Constant	-10.4592^{**}	-7.9180^{**}
	(.000)	(.000)
Year = 2003	-1.8437^{**}	-1.9117^{**}
	(.000)	(.000)
Organizational Variables		
Capital Intensity	.46467**	.40126**
	(.000)	(.000)
Common Subsidiary Operations	.255488**	.18732**
	(.000)	(.000)
Firm Size	.80343**	.536772**
	(.000)	(.000)
PAC Expenditures	.00001**	.00008**
	(.000)	(.002)
Geographic Proximity	.05545	$-.12176$
	(.20)	(.164)
Common Sector	.08551	$-.09675$
	(.48)	(.19)
Network Variables		
Direct Interlocks	–	.44256**
		(.001)
Indirect Interlocks	–	.26638*
		(.012)
Policy Network Affiliations	–	.69034**
		(.000)
Bus. Roundtable	–	.92647**
		(.000)

+ $p < .10$ * $p < .05$ ** $p < .01$

Advisory Committee for the combined years of 1998/2003 is the dependent variable.[23]

In Table 6.2, the results of the 2003 baseline models/2003 shared TAC affiliation analysis contrast a model including only the organizational variables with a saturated model including the network measures.

---

[23] Though we only report the results of the combined 1998/2003 data, each year was analyzed separately using the same models. The analyses of each individual year were roughly consistent with what is reported for the combined years.

Model 1 gives the parameter estimates for the baseline organizational model. Each of the organizational predictors yields significant coefficient estimates in the predicted direction, with the exception of geographic proximity and shared sector. The null finding on geographic proximity is perhaps unsurprising given that TACs consider *international* trade issues that are (generally) not specific to geographic areas.[24] With respect to the other organizational variables, the control for size positively correlates with shared participation. A one-unit increase in size increases the expected count of shared firm committee memberships by 118 percent. Likewise, operating a foreign subsidiary in the same regions increases the expected dyadic count by 29 percent, while the proxy for shared dyadic industry produces a comparable effect, increasing the expected count by 24 percent. The capital intensity variable[25] is statistically significant[26] and positive. Consistent with expectations, the positive coefficient indicates that as dyadic capital intensity becomes more similar, the odds of political unity *increase*. Lastly, the remaining organizational variable, PAC expenditures, significantly correlates with shared TAC affiliation in Equation 2: an increase of $10,000 in the PAC expenditure variable is associated with an 11 percent increase in the expected count of TAC affiliation.

In model 2 of Table 6.2, the network variables are introduced. Their introduction diminishes the coefficient estimates of the organizational variables, although size, foreign subsidiaries, capital intensity, and PAC expenditures remain statistically significant. Policy network affiliation produces a significant increase in the odds of TAC membership: The presence of a shared policy group membership increases the expected count of common TAC affiliations by 99 percent, while the presence of two shared ties increases the expected count by nearly 300 percent. This is an extraordinary finding that supports the independent effects of shared corporate associations in the policy-planning network. Similarly, common Business Roundtable membership is associated with a positive change in shared TAC affiliation, alone increasing the expected count by

[24] Geographic proximity was included because previous research has argued for the importance of corporate headquarters as a factor shaping corporate political interests (Burris 1987; Mizruchi 1992).

[25] Capital intensity measures the absolute difference of the dyadic subunits' capital-intensity ratios. To simplify interpretation, the variable was reverse scored so that larger values indicate greater similarity in dyadic capital intensity.

[26] The use of the term "statistical significance" when describing the dyadic models refers, specifically, to the QAP probabilities for each coefficient estimate, not conventional significance tests based on the standard error parameter.

152 percent. This finding is consistent with prior studies (Akard 1992; Burris 1992a, 2008; Mizruchi 1992; Useem 1984) that emphasize the uniquely influential role of the Business Roundtable in coordinating firm lobbying activities and increasing corporate political cohesion over the last three decades. Finally, direct and indirect board ties significantly increase the odds of shared TAC affiliation. Compared to having no ties, one or more direct ties increases the expected count by 55 percent, while having one or more indirect ties is associated with a 31 percent increase.

To summarize, the organizational variables PAC expenditure and size significantly increase the expected count in both sets of models. Likewise, and for the network variables, policy network affiliation and Business Roundtable membership produce a large, positive increase in the expected count. These findings support conclusions by others that industry consultation programs, such as the TACs, provide direct avenues for business organizations to influence policy in both process and substance (Moore et al. 2002).

CORPORATE TRADE ACTIVISM IN THE PUBLIC SPHERE:
CORPORATE UNITY IN THE TRADE POLICY ALLIANCES

Table 6.3 presents the results of two multiple regression equations where common membership in a temporary trade policy alliance was the dependent variable.[27] In the baseline model (model 1, Table 6.3), the QAP probabilities for size, foreign subsidiaries, capital intensity, and PAC expenditures are all statistically significant in the predicted directions. Foreign subsidiaries produce a significant and positive change in political unity: Operating in the same foreign region increases the odds of shared TPA involvement by 41 percent, while operating in two common regions approximately doubles them. In addition, PAC expenditures positively correlate with political unity: A $10,000 increase in the PAC expenditure variable is associated with a 52 percent increase in the odds of corporate unity in the TPA.

In Equation 2, each of these organizational parameters remains statistically significant, although the inclusion of the network variables diminishes their estimated effect on the odds of shared participation. Each of the hypotheses on the effect of network position also finds support

---

[27] America Leads on Trade and USA Engage were the trade policy alliances analyzed in the 1998 wave, while the Business Coalition for Central America Trade and USTrade were the alliances analyzed in the 2003 wave.

TABLE 6.3 *1998/2003 Estimated Effects of Organizational and Network
Variables on the Odds of Shared TPA Affiliation (Unstandardized Reg.
Coefficients with QAP Probabilities in Parentheses)*

	Eq. 1	Eq. 2
Constant	−10.308**	−8.2056**
	(.000)	(.000)
Year = 2003	−1.3726**	−1.4964**
	(.000)	(.000)
Organizational Variables		
Capital Intensity	.38555**	.3426**
	(.000)	(.001)
Common Subsidiary Operations	.42076**	.34709**
	(.000)	(.000)
Firm Size	.68356**	.46830**
	(.000)	(.000)
PAC Expenditures	.00008**	.00004*
	(.000)	(.037)
Geographic Proximity	.16320+	.00932
	(.06)	(.449)
Common Sector	−.01702	−.03931
	(.48)	(.377)
Network Variables		
Direct Interlocks	−	.43320**
		(.000)
Indirect Interlocks	−	.35498**
		(.003)
Policy Network Affiliations	−	.60920**
		(.000)
Bus. Roundtable	−	1.20679**
		(.000)

+ $p < .10$ * $p < .05$ ** $p < .01$

in Equation 2. The coefficients for direct and indirect interlocks, policy
network affiliation, and Business Roundtable membership are all in the
predicted direction and yield QAP probabilities below .05. Having one or
more direct board interlocks was associated with a 54 percent increase in
the odds of shared participation, while indirect ties produced a 43 percent
increase. Both Business Roundtable membership and policy network
affiliation were again positively associated with political unity. Common
affiliation in a policy discussion group increased the odds of shared TPA
participation by 84 percent. As an example of the policy group

commitments, the National Foreign Trade Council [NFTC] is quite vocal about its attempts to direct members toward a neoliberal vision of international trade policy. The NFTC, which "consists of approximately 500 U.S. ... firms having substantial international operations or interests ... [and] collectively account for over 60% of U.S. non-agricultural exports ..., strongly opposes calls to condition trade liberalization on meeting certain social objectives" (US Congress, House 1995: 88). Similarly, Business Roundtable membership is associated with an even more dramatic change, increasing the odds of shared involvement by approximately 234 percent: a stunning result supporting network and power structure conceptions of corporate political action. Taken together, the results suggest that political unity in temporary trade policy alliances is strongly influenced by shared organizational attributes, such as size and foreign subsidiaries, as well as interorganizational ties within board interlock and policy networks.

CORPORATE TRADE ACTIVISM IN THE LEGISLATURE: CORPORATE UNITY IN CONGRESSIONAL TESTIMONY

In Table 6.4, the results of the 1998/2003 shared congressional testimony QAP regressions are presented. In the baseline model (Eq. 1, Table 6.4), only size and foreign subsidiaries reached statistical significance. In Equation 2, the coefficient estimates of size and subsidiaries diminish somewhat but remain statistically significant. For this complete model, the Business Roundtable is associated with a strong, positive increase in the odds of shared testimony (346 percent). Substantively, the role of the Business Roundtable as a prominent actor in Washington, DC, should not be overlooked, and the fact that our model captured its importance corresponds to other accounts of business influence in Congress (Akard 1992; Mizruchi 1992). Representatives of the organization are also quite explicit in their aims with regard to trade policy. Testifying with Kellogg's and Time-Warner CEOs, Harold McGraw III – representing McGraw-Hill Companies and the Business Roundtable – reminded the Senate Finance Committee that "the Business Roundtable has always been in the front lines of U.S. efforts to open markets" (US Senate 2004: 20). The effect of shared Business Roundtable membership is perhaps more readily described in terms of frequencies: Of the 159 dyads with shared trade testimony in the 2003 wave, 109 (70 percent) were (common) members of the Business Roundtable. Likewise, the effect of foreign subsidiaries was significant, increasing the odds of shared testimony by 26 percent. Finally, a one-unit

TABLE 6.4 *1998/2003 Estimated Effects of Organizational and Network Variables on the Odds of Shared Congressional Testimony (Unstandardized Reg. Coefficients with QAP Probabilities in Parentheses)*

	Eq. 1	Eq. 2
Constant	−17.105**	−15.536**
	(.000)	(.000)
Year = 2003	−09181	−1.7015**
	(.11)	(.000)
Organizational Variables		
Capital Intensity	.05519	−.00937
	(.64)	(.57)
Common Subsidiary Operations	.36405+	.23858**
	(.08)	(.000)
Firm Size	.90523**	.75230**
	(.000)	(.004)
PAC Expenditures	.00004	.00001
	(.15)	(.395)
Geographic Proximity	.46307+	.30171
	(.08)	(.149)
Common Sector	.30201	.21788
	(.18)	(.214)
Network Variables		
Direct Interlocks	−	.15991
		(.355)
Indirect Interlocks	−	−.04170
		(.551)
Policy Network Affiliations	−	.31183
		(.102)
Bus. Roundtable	−	1.49467**
		(.000)

+ $p < .10$ * $p < .05$ ** $p < .01$

increase in the control for size increases the odds of shared testimony by 112 percent.

Of the four network variables, only common Business Roundtable membership yielded a significant QAP probability. Likewise for the organizational variables, only size and foreign subsidiaries reached statistical significance. Undoubtedly, the relatively weaker findings of the congressional testimony models (i.e., compared to the dyadic TAC and TPA models) can be explained, in part, by the fact that shared *trade* testimony is somewhat rare: Less than 1 percent (.14%) of the corporate dyads in

1998 or 2003 appeared together (in agreement) at a trade-related congressional hearing.[28] Thus there was very little variance to explain, making it somewhat difficult for the predictors to reach statistical significance.[29] As a point of contrast, 3 percent and 4 percent of sample 1998/2003 dyads shared participation in a temporary trade policy alliance or Industrial Sector Advisory Committee, respectively.

While Mizruchi (1992) found a generally stronger effect of direct and indirect board interlocks on the likelihood of *shared* congressional testimony, the results of his models can only be nominally compared to the present study because they included *all* forms of shared congressional testimony (not only trade related) among large manufacturing firms (whereas the present study analyzes companies from an array of sectors).[30] Thus, with few studies available to directly compare these results against, the only hypothesized influences that the shared testimony model unambiguously supports are size, foreign subsidiaries, and shared Business Roundtable membership.

Exploring the facets of class agency in advancing neoliberal trade policy in the United States, these analyses examined the role of corporate collective action across three institutional settings to further test the organizational and class cohesion hypotheses concerning corporate involvement in trade policy. Overall, most of the class cohesion hypotheses find support in the dyadic regression models for each trade policy domain. In the combined TAC and TPA models (Tables 6.2 and 6.3), each of the network variables successfully predicts corporate political unity as an outcome in trade policy advocacy. In the testimony models, the network variables produce a less consistent change, with only Business Roundtable membership achieving statistical significance. Consistent with prior research, the important influence of Business Roundtable membership across the three domains of trade policy formation supports the hypothesis that this organization "funnels" corporate CEOs (and, more important, their vast resources) into strategic leverage points in the state

[28] It is also likely that testimony before Congress is more likely, in general, to be a solo-act. Less than 1 percent of dyads demonstrated agreement at the same trade hearing but over 7 percent of the FF500 appeared at one or more trade hearings (with or without other firms).

[29] Rerunning the testimony analyses using a restricted sample consisting of dyads where each subunit testified in at least one hearing (but not necessarily the same hearing) produced similar results.

[30] In Mizruchi's analysis (1992), approximately 5 percent of the sample appeared in agreement at one or more congressional hearings.

apparatus. Additionally, the effect of direct and indirect ties in the TAC and TPA models suggests that board interlocks increase corporate political cohesion.

While the proxies for board interlocking do not measure actual communication per se, their significant partial correlations suggest, as is commonly asserted in the business unity literature, that interlocks facilitate information exchange and persuasion, which, in turn, increases corporate political unity (Mintz and Schwartz 1985; Mizruchi 1992; Useem 1984). Also, consistent with Burris's (2005) research on executive political cohesion, these findings suggest that direct ties are relatively more consequential (if rarer) than indirect ties. In most models, the estimated effect (after exponentiation) of direct interlocks is approximately twice that of indirect interlocks.[31]

Among the organizational hypotheses, the proxies for size, multinationality, PAC expenditures, and capital intensity each significantly correlate with political unity in most models.[32] Somewhat surprisingly, however, market sector was not associated with a significant change in any of the saturated equations. Chapter 5 showed that firm-level participation in trade policy activism exhibited a significant difference in mean affiliation (i.e., the intercepts) across two-digit market sector classifications; sector does not appear to exert a comparable effect on the political unity of paired firms. Drawing from the analyses in Chapter 5, this finding suggests that while sector influences the odds that a *given* firm will engage in trade policy advocacy, other factors are more important to the structure of the relational networks created when two or more firms *collectively* engage in trade policy advocacy. In other words, market sector does not strongly predict which firms, in a network consisting of all possible ties in the dependent variables, will share a connection.

With the exception of market sector, each of the organizational variables appears to produce a more consistent change in the odds of unity than they do in the participation models presented in the previous chapter.[33] While

---

[31] While Mizruchi (1992) found that *indirect* board ties through financial institutions produce a stronger effect on political unity than direct ties, this study analyzes different forms of corporate political activism, making it difficult to speculate on the causes of these differences.

[32] The main exception in the testimony model exists where capital intensity and PAC expenditures fall just below statistical significance.

[33] In the firm-level model of TAC participation (Eq. 3, Table 5.4), size and PAC expenditures are the only organizational variables that reach statistical significance, whereas in the combined dyadic model (Eq. 2, Table 6.2), size, PAC expenditures, foreign subsidiaries, and capital intensity are statistically significant in the predicted direction. Likewise,

this finding may simply reflect the fact that the organizational variables measure different attributes in the participation and dyadic models, their generally stronger effect in the latter suggests that organizational structure more strongly influences political unity than *firm-level* participation. It is possible, then, that firm-level factors condition the probability of association among organizationally similar corporate political actors. Taken together, the results strongly suggest that *both* organizational and network variables influence corporate political action.[34] In order to understand business unity over trade policy, then, we must consider how a commonality of material interests (such as subsidiary operations) and network embeddedness can influence political cohesion. Consistent with literature on corporate political action, neither a strictly organizational account, which currently enjoys primacy in the trade policy literature, nor a strictly "network" or class cohesion account provides a comprehensive account of the factors that generate political unity. As with previous research on corporate political action, our results acknowledge the significance of organizational factors, but critically affirms several "mediating mechanisms" that form the network embedded context in which corporate unity is achieved (Mizruchi 1992). Mizruchi stresses that unity is a process, certainly impacted by organization-level factors, but he concludes that "it is not size or concentration *per se*, but rather corporations' economic, organizational, and social *interaction* that unify and empower them" (1992: 254).

in the TPA participation model (Eq. 3, Table 5.5), subsidiaries and PAC expenditures are the only organizational variables to reach statistical significance, while in the combined dyadic TPA model (Eq. 2, Table 6.3) capital intensity and size reach statistical significance in addition to these variables. Lastly, whereas none of the organizational variables is significant in the firm-level congressional testimony model (Table 5.6), size and subsidiaries reach statistical significance in the dyadic shared testimony model (Table 6.4).

[34] Our models also suggest a historical effect indicated in the negative coefficient for year 2003 in all three models. This result suggests an overall decrease in corporate trade policy activism in the second period (though the continued significance of network determinants remains evident). This finding is consistent with the relative decrease in broader political conflicts over trade policy after September 11, 2001. While the initiative to expand NAFTA to numerous Central American countries between 2003 and 2005 was met by broad labor, human rights, and environmental opposition, the challenges did not amount to the scale of mobilization against the NAFTA, the WTO, or China PNTR in the late 1990s. Corporate political mobilization to protect and pass the initiatives in the 1990s was consequently more vigorous. The widespread opposition to neoliberal trade in 1990s was comparably diminished after 2001. In short, the negative effect of year 2003 is suggestive of a decrease in overall trade policy conflicts, not just corporate activism, though a fully satisfactory interpretation is beyond the scope of this study.

CLASS AGENCY AND THE STATE: PRESSING CHINA-PNTR AND THE WTO

In contrast to the prevailing depictions of corporations as atomistic political actors vying for their specific company or industry interests in trade policy, the dyadic analyses presented above help explain how organizations like the BRT facilitate class cohesion and political mobilization toward trade policy in recent decades. Peak corporate leadership organizations like the BRT, NAM, COC, and USCIB bring together top executives and owners to help formulate policy priorities, educate and mobilize members, and collaborate with state agencies to reshape the global market context in which US-based multinational corporations (MNCs) pursue their economic interests. Corporate elite work with state actors to maintain the economic power of American capital in a more competitive global economy. We have argued that this network embeddedness of large corporations captures processes of class-coalescence that generate a unique capacity (relative to other societal actors) to cohere a wide spectrum of business interests and corporate leaders, often transcending more narrow sector and firm-level interests. With respect to trade policy in particular, the class-networks spanning state and nonstate institutions channel the resources of well connected corporations toward strategically defined policy initiatives. These relationships impact political behavior from the relatively rare example of shared testimony before Congress to the more common and arguably less influential shared membership in ad hoc "interest groups."

An alternative reading of our results might view the significance of our network measures as proximate to the social processes they are intended to capture but distant in their importance to actual policy outcomes. This is the "so what" question, most forcefully advanced by Block (1987). From this perspective, China PNTR, for example, was ratified because it was in the state's interest to do so, irrespective of preceding political actions by business elite. This state-centered view of trade policy has an obvious limitation. Both NAFTA and China PNTR, for example, did not initially have sufficient House and Senate votes to pass, and both received widespread opposition in public polls (Woodall et al. 2000). While, as discussed in Chapters 3 and 4, the Department of Commerce and its associated trade advisory committees strongly support global trade expansion, federal law requires that the House and Senate ratify bilateral and multilateral trade agreements. Corporate interests must therefore assert their presence in policy formation at multiple levels (e.g., legislative, public opinion, and the Executive Branch) precisely because the motivation for elected officials to support neoliberal trade initiatives is not static and is subject to reversal when influenced by competing constituencies in the legislature. For this reason, successful corporate political strategies in support of these agreements must involve a multipronged approach aimed at influencing policy development in the executive branch, lobbying and testimony in the legislature, and public mobilization to influence opinion in congressional districts, thereby shaping votes over ratification in Congress. Hence, in our models, corporate policy activism in the legislature (via temporary trade alliances and congressional testimony) coincides empirically with corporate appointments to the trade advisory committees (TACs) in the executive branch. State structure effects the organization of class agency, and conversely, the institutional contours of the state are drawn, as in the case of the 1974 Trade Act, to facilitate alliances and input from powerful and connected segments of the corporate elite. This interactive character of business class and state relations is well theorized in other contexts (Carroll and Fennema 2004; Domhoff 1990; Evans 1995; Prechel 2000).[35]

Consider the class and state dynamics involved in the case of the China PNTR campaign, where a multipronged strategy involving the Clinton White House and leading corporate policy and lobbying organizations was developed in order to swing votes in congressional districts throughout the country. The historical trajectory prior to the heated fight over China PNTR included the conflict over NAFTA (1991–1993), the WTO (1995), and, of course, the explosive conflict in Seattle, Washington, in November 1999 that blocked substantive agreements at the ministerial meetings of the WTO. In the years prior, the antiglobalization movement had developed enduring coalitions bridging labor unions, human rights groups, and environmental causes, and an antisweatshop campaign elevated labor and human rights issues in China.[36] Finally, legislation related to bilateral trade with China was advanced in Congress at the same time

---

[35] In the final chapter, the broader theoretical implications of class-state relations are addressed. Prechel's (2000) "capital-dependence" theory offers important avenues for synthesis with theories of global capitalism.

[36] The revelation of several high-profile child labor cases associated with major US apparel brands also politicized trade and globalization. Students made significant strides across campuses in the United States, peaking by the late 1990s with a series of highly public antisweatshop campaigns. China's labor conditions were also front-and-center in those public outcries, particularly as Wal-Mart's Kathy Lee brand brought considerable attention to the low-cost retail giant's contracting practices (Klein 2002).

that global justice activists trained for mass demonstrations at the 1999 Ministerial Meetings of the WTO in Seattle.[37] As a result, China PNTR emerged in a highly politicized context over global labor and human rights causes. H.R. 4444, which ultimately passed and was signed into law in May 2000, ended the annual review of China's trade status in Congress and granted unconditional and permanent access for Chinese-made goods into the US market. Corporate lobbyists recognized the challenges facing the bill, and they understood that China PNTR, along with China's bid to enter the WTO, would require considerable political effort. This was even clearer after the mass demonstrations against the WTO in Seattle in November and December of 1999. Bill Morley, the chief lobbyist for the US Chamber of Commerce, acknowledged the context: "Seattle happened with plenty of time for us to get that wake-up call" (quoted in Salant 1999:4B).

Despite an energized opposition from the left and the right, the corporate campaign would ultimately outstrip its opponents in what some observers have termed the most expensive lobbying campaign in US history (Woodall et al. 2000). Because PNTR was coupled to China's entry into the World Trade Organization, interests among large US corporations were magnified by hopes of market opportunities that an opening of China's economy would harbor (Cohen et al. 2003). Business leaders structured several new organizations for this fight, many of these leaders relied on extensive connections with current and former government officials. Their campaign was swift and extensive, working all faces of the state.

CLASS-STATE COLLABORATION FOR CHINA-PNTR
IN THE EXECUTIVE BRANCH

The Clinton Administration worked aggressively with corporate leaders to secure support for the passage of China PNTR (Sanger 2000). Indeed, most of President Clinton's cabinet was drawn into the White House "PNTR War Room," that included over 150 staff devoted to passage of the bill (Woodall et al. 2000). Within the White House, China PNTR and trade liberalization more generally were framed as a beacon for democratic change in China, a great "opening." Public relations campaigns using this message involved current and former secretaries of state,

---

[37] The first piece of legislation was comprised mostly of unilateral market opening steps by China to prepare for accession to the WTO. This legislation passed in November 1999, but did not take effect until China officially became a member of the WTO in December 2001.

asserting a new dawn for China and the world. Echoing the administration's promises of reform in China, the Business Roundtable published a report arguing that US business practices operating in China would contribute to "improvements of social, labor and environmental conditions in China" (Business Roundtable 2000: 1). This discourse of "reform" was quite persuasive and became the dominant message heard from the White House.

High-profile press events and fund-raisers featured prominent foreign policy leaders, often in their roles as private consultants. Figures like Henry Kissinger, Colin Powell, Alexander Haig, and Madeline Albright endorsed PNTR publicly in multiple contexts (Powell 2000). And in instances where these individuals had ties to companies that would benefit from China PNTR, public disclosure did not occur. For example, Kissinger had personally helped US corporations, like Disney, American International Group, and Chubb, gain access to the Chinese market (Woodall et al. 2000). In the case of Alexander Haig and Colin Powell, both served as board members to corporations that held membership in pro-PNTR corporate coalitions (MacArthur 2000: 180). Former secretary of defense Dick Cheney spoke for China PNTR with multiple roles: as CEO of Halliburton, as co-founder of USA*ENGAGE, and as former secretary of defense. One of the Chamber of Commerce's (COC) chief lobbyists at Public Strategies Washington was Joe O'Neill, the son of former Democratic house speaker Tip O'Neill. The COC's other key trade policy lobbyist hired for this campaign was Mayer, Brown & Platt, the former law firm of Commerce Secretary William Daley. Mayer, Brown & Platt led the PNTR campaign for the White House (MacArthur 2000: 169, 180).

Ambassador Barshefsky – the US Trade Representative under Clinton in 2000 – cited affirmations from Chinese human rights activists who claimed that China's preparations for joining the WTO were "the most important reforms in two decades" (Barshefky 2000). Among familiar observers of the policy debate, Secretary of State Madeline Albright was incredibly persuasive on the cause of trade normalization with China. Her public speeches and testimonies before Congress delivered seamless arguments rooted in the values of liberal internationalism and American exceptionalism.[38] For example, testifying before the House International

---

[38] In 2001, former secretary of state Albright established a consulting firm and a private equity partnership that would later become members of the US China Business Council. The board of advisors included former executives from Citigroup, President of the

Relations Committee, Secretary Albright explained how approval of PNTR would serve US goals for liberalizing China: "Once in the WTO, China will be required to follow international trading rules, open its regulations to public scrutiny and reduce the role of state-owned enterprises. This will encourage growth in the rule of law, and hasten the development of a more open society" (Albright 2000: 1).

As is evident from these brief examples, state actors collaborated across political parties and branches of government. These state actors worked closely with the broad-based corporate coalition to lobby Congress. The combination of asserting global authority from the stature of executive branch authorities alongside a very specific mobilization aimed at members of Congress proved to be central strategic elements of the corporate campaign to pass China PNTR. The corporate coalition's efforts leveraged multiple points of the political process, assembling over $113.1 million in corporate monies specifically directed to the passage of the bill (Woodall et al. 2000).[39] From within the state, executives acted as non-elected governmental advisors to build political consensus within a divided congressional body (ibid.). Operating outside the state, these actors utilized prominent business associations as a vehicle for resource mobilization, political lobbying, and astroturfing to shape public opinion.

MOVING THE HOUSE: A CLASS POLITICAL MOBILIZATION

With clear support for China PNTR within the Clinton Administration, several influential business organizations undertook an extensive investigation to determine the minimum number of congressional swing votes needed to pass the legislation. By December 1999, the Business Roundtable had targeted seventy-one congressional districts in which members were encouraged to devote resources for lobbying and advertisements (Salant 1999). During the course of a single month, the organization raised over $4.2 million in political contributions for the bill (Woodall et al. 2000). Directed toward specific regions and congressional districts, several business advocacy groups organized radio and television advertising campaigns to promote the legislation. According to one

Chamber of Commerce, and other officials from the Clinton Administration. Bloomberg Business Week, http://investing.businessweek.com/research/stocks/private/snapshot.asp?privcapId=2514851 accessed May 12, 2011.

[39] These organizations included ALOT, the Business Roundtable, the Chamber of Commerce, the National Association of Manufacturers, and several other advocacy organizations (Woodall et al. 2000).

observer, this strategy "was used to great success earlier in the year when Congress voted to renew normal trade relations with China for one year" (Salant 1999:4B).

Corporate lobbying involved the traditional work on Capitol Hill, though with some interesting innovations and twists. The Business Roundtable, for example, organized with ALOT a "CEO fly-in" lobbying blitz. The CEO of FMC Corp., Robert N. Burt, told the *Wall Street Journal* the thrust of their message to Congress: "We aim our donations ... at people who support free enterprise and what we see as the free-enterprise system. Free trade is certainly one element that goes into that" (Woodall et al. 2000: 9). The connection between votes and campaign financing was very direct and in some instances explicit. After Minority Leader Richard Gephardt (D-MO) announced his opposition to PNTR, an unnamed lobbyist told *Roll Call* that anti-PNTR positions by Democrats would have repercussions and that "they better believe it's going to hurt them in terms of money in November" (Crabtree 2000: 8). Days before the vote, US Chamber of Commerce President Thomas Donohue summed it up to the *Wall Street Journal*: "If somebody's on the margin and they screw up this vote, they'd better not look to me for money" (Woodall et al. 2000: 9).

Between January 1999 and May 2000, Business Roundtable members assembled over $58 million in PAC and soft money contributions. These political expenditures were frequently directed toward key representatives whose vote on the China bill was uncertain (Kahn 2000). A spokesman for Rep. Merrill Cook (R-UT), for example, divulged that the congressman was offered $200,000 in corporate PAC money to change his "no" vote to a "yes" (Woodall et al. 2000: 8–23). Dozens more congressional fundraisers for undecided representatives were hosted by the Chamber of Commerce, the Emergency Committee on American Trade (ECAT), and the National Association of Manufacturers (Crabtree 2000; Salant 1999). Undecided Rep. Max Sandlin (D-TX), struggling under a large campaign debt, had a fund raiser hosted by the ECAT a month before the vote. Opponents to PNTR expected Sandlin to vote against the bill given his ties to labor and his working-class district. He voted for it (*National Journal*: 2000a). Another example, involved Rep. Martin Frost (D-TX), who reportedly phoned Motorola before he made his decision to vote for PNTR and asked the company to sponsor a fundraiser for him. They suggested that Frost would be supported (*National Journal*: 2000b).

China PNTR was not just about trade with China. Many large US companies had invested heavily in China in the years prior. For example, the American International Group (AIG), one of the world's oldest insurance companies, maintained significant interests in China at the time. In fact, AIG was the first foreign insurer to enter China's market, in 1992. During the first half of 2000, AIG spent $1.7 million lobbying Congress, including on many trade issues, but eight of its in-house lobbyists worked on PNTR, more than twice as many as on any other issue (Brostoff 2000). Like AIG, Motorola had invested in China for years. By 2000, the company boasted $3.4 billion in manufacturing investments in China (*Los Angeles Times* March 10, 2000, cited in Woodall et al. 2000). Motorola, like so many other electronics firms, was investing heavily in manufacturing in China before PNTR, but the promise of permanent liberalization with China's accession to the WTO inspired considerable activism from the high-tech sector. Hewlett-Packard president and CEO Carly Fiorina declared in a *Los Angeles Times* op-ed: "In reality, a vote against trade with China is a vote against US businesses" (*Congress Daily* February 9, 2000: 10). Individual CEOs flew in and out of Washington lobbying on behalf of the Business Roundtable and for the Electronic Industries Alliance, including CEOs of Lucent, Sony, and Qualcomm.

The week of the vote, the Business Coalition for US China Trade delivered baskets with cell phones, computer chips, Pepsi, and candles to 300 House Members (*Agence France Presse* 2000, cited in Woodall et al. 2000). While certain sectors were more active, the overwhelming effort to pass China PNTR came from the broad, interindustry corporate associations of the COC and the BRT. On the day of the vote, the Chamber of Commerce alone dedicated at least one lobbyist for each undecided House member, fielding at least fifty lobbyists to cover the legislators the *New York Times* reported as still undecided on the morning of the vote (cited in Woodall et al. 2000). A Chamber of Commerce publication described the PNTR vote as "the most important trade vote in decades," and its China lobbyist called the vote the Chamber's "top legislative priority" (Salant 1999: 4B).

Attempts to persuade the public were mostly focused on undecided congressional districts. But national advertising campaigns were integral and spending on advertising far outstripped previous trade campaigns or the campaign against Clinton's health care initiative. Examples abound. In a *New York Times* advertisement on May 12, 2000, ExxonMobil described the PNTR vote as "one of the most important policy decisions faced by the Congress of the United States" (quoted in Woodall et al. 2000). The *Public Citizen* analysis in Woodall et al. (2000) showed that at least $13.75 million was spent on advertising in the three months prior to the vote. Corporate leaders in the Business Roundtable also ran a national television ad campaign on CNN that was supplemented in specific congressional districts with print and radio expenditures, all totaling $4 million (ibid).

The *Christian Science Monitor* reported how the campaign became theater when the Business Roundtable hired hundreds of young temporary workers in Washington, DC, to wear pro-PNTR T-shirts and appear at "spontaneous" rallies in support of pro-PNTR Congressional members (Chaddock 2000). The campaign climaxed with an astroturf effort the week of the China PNTR vote when the BRT hired temporary workers to pass out free ten-minute telephone calling cards to commuters exiting Metro stations all over Washington, DC. The cards represented $40,000 worth of calling minutes (quoted in Woodall et al. 2000: 12). Organized labor vigorously opposed the bill, but their political expenditures were outstripped 11:1 by the Business Roundtable alone (ibid.). Although it is estimated that 79 percent of Americans opposed the legislation, prominent US firms and their associated business interest groups had, by the end of the campaign, secured enough House and Senate votes to pass the bill 237–197 (Woodall et al. 2000: 4–7).

Since the passage of China PNTR and China's accession to the WTO, China has become the largest manufacturing economy in the world, surpassing the United States in 2011. Massive amounts of foreign direct investment (FDI) poured into China while exports surged. In the ten years after passage of China PNTR, several economists made estimates on the US jobs lost as US investors contracted with or moved production to China. The liberal-leaning Economic Policy Institute estimated 2.4 million jobs lost in the United States between 2001 and 2008 as a result of the increased trade encouraged by the agreement. Figure 6.4 outlines this dramatic shift with the passage of China-PNTR and the subsequent explosion of the US-China bilateral trade deficit as imports to the United States from China grew quickly. A world-historic economic transition was underway, and this economic context added new pressure on US corporations operating globally to press the US state for more aggressive investor protections for corporate interests in the growing economies of Asia. In 2011, the former governor of Michigan, John Engler, left his role as executive director at NAM to become president of the Business Roundtable. In that same year, these two organizations, along with the smaller ECAT, initiated a campaign for a Trans-Pacific Partnership (TPP). They wrote a letter to President Obama outlining the desire to move the TPP (begun under President

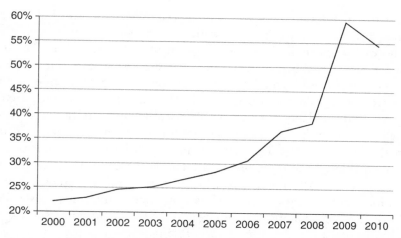

FIGURE 6.4 China's Share of US Global Trade Deficit (Percentage), 2000–2010
Source: US Bureau of the Census, US Trade in Goods and Services, August 15, 2011.

Bush) to the front of the agenda on trade negotiations and to dramatically expand investor protections. Specific concern was expressed about several "agreements between ASEAN and China and ASEAN and India, reflecting the deepening of commercial ties between key emerging-market partners across Asia, which leave the United States at risk of being excluded from these vital growth markets" (ECAT 2011: 1). After the Great Recession (2007–2010), corporate and state elite continued to guide the project of neoliberal globalization.

NEOLIBERAL TRADE POLICY AS A CLASS PROJECT

Recent institutionalist accounts of trade policy are correct to note that the historical form of institutions (i.e., the state) matters (Campbell 2004; Chorev 2007; Duina 2006). Chorev (2007) regards the political and institutional transformations of American trade policy as the key to understanding the rise of neoliberal trade and the larger manifestations of globalization. Like Jessop's (1990, 2002) structural Marxist account of the state, the "form" of the state shapes the strategic orientation of political actors. For Chorev (2007) and Duina (2006), the ascent of trade liberalization in American trade politics is intricately tied to the slow drift of the state's decision-making apparatus on trade matters from the legislature to the executive, something that has occurred over a seventy-five-year period.

Our research does not dispute this important course of historical change and, in fact, acknowledges this critical development. However, and as Chorev (2007) similarly argues, these historical shifts cannot be adequately explained by a strict focus on the choices of state actors alone; "strategic political actors" also play an important part. Action on the part of free trade "interests," particularly large corporations, factor significantly in Chorev's (2007) historical-institutional arguments as well as in Duina's (2006) explanations for the rise of free trade policies in the United States. The research presented here offers statistically grounded insight into the organizational mechanics of those corporate "strategic actors" or interests. However, the results presented better conform to the expectations of class unity models. Indeed, as argued in Chapter 3, a class unity conceptualization of "free trade interests" offers a more robust theorization of corporate political action than the very generic imagery of "interest group" or "strategic actors." In the context of sustained, multidecade political action geared toward restructuring the global economy, treating corporate leadership in the Business Roundtable – whose members' combined annual revenues approach half of the US GDP – as a form of class agency offers much greater theoretical parsimony for the two scales of analysis, from the interorganizational to the macrohistorical, pursued here.

Mirroring the bifurcation of the trade policy apparatus since the Reciprocal Trade Agreement Act, corporate promotion of trade policy has centered on *both* the executive and legislative branches of government. The form of the state matters. In the legislature, corporations promote and defend trade initiatives such as NAFTA and China PNTR through temporary trade policy alliances, which, in turn, are formed by the more enduring policy organizations, usually the Business Roundtable. Within the executive branch, a deeper form of corporate influence is evident. Under the banner of industry consultation programs, state actors work in concert with strategic business allies to form the policy objectives and broader trade programs ultimately advanced by the Department of Commerce, the US Trade Representative, and US President. The distinct political dynamics within the executive and legislative branches result in diverse strategies involved in trade policy development and implementation. On the one hand, the executive branch, essentially captured by industry interests in *this* policy domain, offers predictable support for trade expansion initiatives. On the other, trade policy outcomes in the legislature are more contested, given the greater number of actors competing for influence in Congress.

Clearly, the institutional structure of the trade policy apparatus worked to attract corporate leaders who were already active in other policy-related associations. Thus in addition, two theoretical propositions can be derived from this observation. First, as observed by Martin (1994), the state acts to facilitate corporate unity. Political officials use and build state structures for the purpose of securing allies in the business community. *Facilitative state* structures promote business unity for political purposes. For this reason, it is imperative that we take seriously the role of preceding actions on the part of state actors in constructing political opportunities for corporate leaders to act collectively (Martin 1994). In the case of trade policy, facilitative state structures created the opportunity in 1974 – alongside structural transformations in the international economy – for state actors to forge strategic links to a politicized and dominant corporate class segment. Situated directly under the president, the Office of the US Trade Representative and the numerous trade advisory committees provide an influential and strategic forum for formulating and advancing international institutions, such as NAFTA, that are favorable to the economic opportunities of US-based multinational corporations.

Second, the presence of these facilitative state structures enabled the most organized corporate leaders to reproduce class leadership and authority. In this way, prominent corporate actors exert influence within the state policy apparatus *and* the political organization of the wider business sector. As a result, class agency is enhanced by the dual-function of state facilitation and intraclass associative mechanisms. The economic capacities of corporations and policy organizations are transformed into political capacities. These conditions make for a durable structure of power forged in the context of trade policy that is wedded to the highest sources of solidarity among the economic and political elite. In some ways, these institutional and organizational dimensions converge around Mills's (1956) discussion of the power elite's structural position at the "command posts" of society. Prominent policy-planning organizations, such as the Business Roundtable, secure the attention of state elite and provide ready-made vehicles for collective discussion and mobilization. Extant networks among corporations and across industries then serve as a source for political leverage. Together, class structure and state organizations meet, making it possible for these structures to provide, as Prechel observed, "class segments with the mechanisms to exercise control over the state" (1990: 664), in this case over trade policy.

Class agency in trade policy – conceptualized here as sustained corporate political unity geared toward the transformation of economic and political influence – is detectable as a unified political force stretching across three fields of government decision making. The discernible consequences of class agency are also evident in the advance of neoliberal globalization. This does not deny that organizational interests are unimportant. To the contrary, as Mizruchi's (1992) synthesis of organizational and social class models reveals, even ties created for "organizational purposes could have the consequence of facilitating interfirm political unity" (1996: 280). The research presented here highlights this point even further by linking these network conditions to corporate political behavior. Corporate embeddedness filters corporate collective action through a prism of class and state institutions. Institutional context, in this regard, makes the social class models even more interesting because class agency among corporate elite must respond to state institutional structures.

Ample evidence shows (see Chapters 3 and 5) that economic conditions facing business in America changed between the 1970s and 2000 (Dumenil and Levy 2011). Considerable evidence also demonstrates that those economic changes prompted ideological and political shifts in America's corporate elite (Domhoff 2013; Mizruchi 2013; Prechel 2000). Neoliberalism as an ideology and institutional project took root in this context, fitting the historical argument in Prechel's (2000: 11) "contingent capital-dependence theory," which argues that "capitalists mobilize politically in order to overcome historically specific barriers to profit making." Drawing on this proposition, the model developed here examined the relationship between corporate unity, class agency, and state institutions. The close coupling of the corporate policy milieu to government policy making highlights the need for greater conceptual clarity on state-class relations in the period of neoliberal economic restructuring. By conceptualizing class agency as a contingent outcome of inter-corporate networks that are shaped in a broader economic context of capital accumulation (Prechel 2000), a strictly instrumentalist view of the state becomes problematic. The political influence of corporate groups and executives via class-embedded networks is clearly an important factor to incorporate into political theories of globalization.

Prechel's (2000, 2003) capital-dependence theory fuses these organizational and macro-historical dimensions of change in business and state relations. Prechel argues that state autonomy is contingent on broad, but specifiable historical conditions. As Prechel (1990, 2000, 2003), Akard (1992), and others argue, this contingency nonetheless is bound to a structural imperative for shaping economic institutions favorable to capital accumulation, a condition that in turn advances a state-economy linkage between leading governmental agencies and powerful class segments. These linkages reinforce the "societal content," or "class-relevant selectivity" of state structures and discourses that privilege business (Jessop 1990). As Prechel (2000: 273) argues, "[w]hen severe constraints on capital accumulation or crises emerge the capitalist class unifies and mobilizes politically to advance particular policies to resolve obstacles to their economic agenda." Prechel continues that the policy strategies and political alliances among corporate elite are also conditioned by the impacts of those policies and political strategies on class segments as well as the power of competing social and economic interests. The political pursuit of neoliberal globalization is thus an example of corporate leaders responding politically to diminished profitability in an increasingly competitive global economy. The promise of low-cost export platforms from Mexico to China induced a political project of global market restructuring.

Indeed, corporate political unity around trade policy points to still deeper questions concerning the relationship between class and state actors in the politics of globalization. The old debate between unity and disunity theorists – between pluralist and institutionalist models of democratic states that rest on the assumption of business fragmentation, or class-cohesion models based on the assumption of corporate solidarity – is also advanced. Despite different arguments concerning the character of the modern state, a loosely held assumption among corporate disunity theorists (pluralist, institutionalists, as well as state-centered) holds that business is not capable of sustaining unified, class-oriented political action (Bauer, Pool, and Dexter 1972; Berry 1999; Block 1987; Lindblom 1977; Poulantzas 1973; Salisbury 1992). This unnecessarily strong assumption creates a dilemma for theories of political and economic globalization. When business is seen as a fragmented political actor because business is assumed to be in competition economically, the sources of foreign economic policy (including international trade) will be found in the strategic initiatives of "autonomous" government policy makers, whether they are presumed to act on behalf of capitalists or of the nation. Class actors do not enter the conceptual fray.

The observations presented here offer a link to a more cogent theory of neoliberal globalization, one that accounts for the close coupling of state and class actors in the creation and protection of neoliberal market projects. As Sassen argues (1996: 25), the role of private agents in constructing the new global trade apparatus is both a political and economic affair; it is not enough to argue that the "state is in decline," swallowed and increasingly impotent in the seemingly inevitable advance of liberalized global markets. Rather, "the new geography of global economic processes, the strategic territories for economic globalization, have to be defined in terms of both the practices of corporate actors . . . and the work of the state in producing or legitimizing new legal regimes" (ibid.). If these processes are to be better grasped, it is not only the economic practices of corporations that must be examined, but, as has been the concern of this chapter, the political as well. To more fully understand the dramatic transformation of nation states and markets in the neoliberal era, it is worth considering recent trade policy as a more general phenomenon in which *both* state and class actors, in spite of significant levels of public resistance, set in motion a transfer of market authority from the national to the transnational, continental level. The larger historical argument, that we will turn to in the concluding chapter, details how neoliberal trade policy emerged as a solution to the economic constraints – import competition, labor and environmental regulations, wage growth – on profits for American business in the 1970s and 1980s, a solution that achieved widespread acceptance among every major business association in the United States. Corporate leaders offered this program as a new hegemony geared toward the construction of a global free market utopia where American commercial interests would thrive.

7

Conclusion: Agents of Globalization

Fligstein (2001: 28) has remarked that "it is necessary to think systematically about how government capacity and the relative power of government officials, capitalists, and workers figure into the construction of new market rules to define the forms of economic activity that exist in a given society." Fligstein's theoretical project urges an approach to markets and globalization that considers the varying capacity of social actors to influence government actors and shape market rules and institutions around their interests. As an answer to this call, our approach has renewed a theoretical and empirical sociology of class political action to make sense of the unique structural power and agency of large US corporations amid the historical transition to neoliberal globalization. Our findings suggest that the ascent of neoliberal trade institutions relied on the consistent collective action of large firms working in collaboration with state actors. The nature of this collective action, we posit, is best conceptualized as class agency.

RATIONALE AND RESULTS

The main finding of this study is that position within class-cohesive networks influences corporate policy activism and political unity across several political settings inside and outside the state. We have measured corporate trade policy activism as a contingent function of both organizational attributes and position within class-cohesive networks. Confirming our general hypotheses, organizational attributes significantly influence corporate political behavior. Large, multinational firms in trade-dependent product markets typically benefit from lower transaction costs on intrafirm exchange: they have an organizational interest in free trade. Such firms are therefore more likely to engage – individually and, as a consequence of their shared economic interests, collectively – in trade policy formation and advocacy.

In addition to the organizational factors, however, the results of this study show how network position has significant, independent effects on corporate political activism and unity. The thesis that policy organizations and board interlocks influence corporate political behavior is by no means new to power structure researchers. Nonetheless, these factors rarely enter into the explanatory framework and methodology of trade policy analysts. While many trade policy studies highlight how firm attributes create organizational "interests" that, in turn, lead to political participation and collective action, few analysts consider how corporate political behavior is historically situated within board and policy networks connecting the largest and most politically active corporations over relatively long periods of time.

Empirically, the problem with the trade policy literature's prevailing emphasis on corporate *economic* interests is perhaps most readily seen in the political participation models presented in Chapter 5. In each of the combined 1998/2003 baseline models (Eq. 2, Tables 5.4, 5.5, 5.6), size, foreign subsidiaries, and sector significantly predict corporate trade policy activism, whereas in each of the full models at least one of these factors falls below significance after network variables are controlled. While this does not suggest that organizational attributes are unimportant to corporate trade policy activism, it does indicate that an exclusive focus on *intra*-organizational factors may inflate the importance of certain variables (e.g., foreign subsidiaries) because the influence of network position is not measured.[1]

In the dyadic unity models, the network and organizational variables do not appear to "compete" with one another to the extent observed in the participation models, suggesting that both exert an important and independent influence on political unity. While the network parameters generally diminish the coefficient estimates in the baseline dyadic unity

---

[1] While the strength of these predictors may occur because their effect is more temporally invariant vis-à-vis other predictors, it should be noted that it is not possible to confirm this hypothesis without further waves of data. More generally, because the statistically significant predictors of corporate policy activism vary from year to year, with some variables achieving significance in one wave but not in subsequent observation periods, the results suggest that future research, in particular of trade related political behavior, may be enhanced by the collection of additional observational years.

models (e.g., Eq. 2, Tables 6.2, 6.3, 6.4), their inclusion typically does not, in contrast to the participation models, move the organizational variables below statistical significance. This finding is consistent with Mizruchi's (1989: 418–419) research and suggests that, at least for corporate political unity, the effects of network position and organizational attributes are nominally independent from one another. Stated more technically, most of the network and organizational variables explain a significant amount of residual variance in political unity even after other factors are controlled.

INTERPRETING THE NETWORK VARIABLES

While most of the network variables, such as policy group affiliation, are associated with a positive change in activism and unity, these empirical correlations are, of course, open to several interpretations and warrant additional consideration. In this study, we have argued that proxies for class cohesion, such as policy group affiliation and board interlocking, capture processes of class-coalescence that produce a variable capacity to articulate the broader interests of business. By directing corporate resources toward a common political agenda, policy groups and other sites of business cooperation promote an expansive, "classwide" business interest (Useem 1984). Whether one views this interfirm coordination as a form of "class-consciousness" among business elite (as in Marx's notion of a class "for itself"), or simply an expression of a commonality of material interests (as in a class "in itself"), is somewhat inconsequential to its political consequences (Mizruchi 1992). That is, the effect of corporate political cohesion is essentially the same regardless of whether firms cooperate for ideological *or* material reasons (see also Mizruchi 1989: 404). With respect to trade policy in particular, firms may be attracted to prominent policy groups for a variety of organizational or ideological purposes. The important point is not so much *why* firms choose to participate in these groups but, rather, how the class-embedded networks created by this association function to channel corporate resources toward strategically defined policy initiatives. The intercorporate network thus connotes not only a complex of interfirm ties but also a social formation with political consequences: a cooperative, business *class segment* that transcends the economic concerns of specific industries (Domhoff 1990; Mills 1956; Mizruchi 1989; Prechel 2000; Useem 1984; Zeitlin 1974). We have argued that proxies for position within this intercorporate network (such as Business Roundtable membership) capture communication and coordination processes that, in turn, have a significant impact on corporate political behavior. In short, our main propositions assert that firms more embedded within board and policy networks will be more likely to (1) engage the state through political activism and (2) pursue their political objectives in concert with other firms.

THE CORPORATE POLICY NETWORK AND DOMINANCE
OF AMERICAN TRADE POLICY

Of the numerous social, political, and economic networks that interconnect the corporate community, perhaps none is more important than the board interlock and policy group networks analyzed in this study (see also Domhoff 2006; Useem 1984). Of the two, policy network affiliation, in particular, appears to consistently influence corporate political activism and unity across several domains of trade policy advocacy. Interlocks, while significant, produce a less consistent and marked effect on the corporate political behavior analyzed in this study. In each of the 1998/ 2003 combined participation models, for example, Business Roundtable membership and policy network affiliation significantly increase the odds that a firm will participate in trade policy formation and advocacy, whereas interlocks produce a smaller and less consistent effect. In the dyadic models, a similar pattern emerges, although policy network affiliation falls just below statistical significance when predicting shared congressional testimony. Even though the proxies for interlocking (i.e., direct and indirect interlocks and degree centrality) often correlate significantly with activism and political unity, their estimated effect was generally smaller than the policy network variables, and less consistently achieved statistical significance.[2] Thus, while both forms of interfirm ties appear to influence corporate activism and political unity, policy network affiliation in particular seems to produce a larger and more consistent effect. Corporations embedded more deeply in the policy network are more likely to act in concert with others from that policy network and dominate American trade policy.

Despite the important function of policy organizations, however, few analysts examine their influence on corporate political behavior and state-

---

[2] In the dyadic models, for example, the coefficient estimates for Business Roundtable membership are consistently larger than the estimate for direct interlocks (both variables being dummy coded). The same relationship also holds in the participation models, although direct comparison is more problematic because interlocks are measured as an ascending count of total firm interlocks to the entire FF500.

firm relations (see Jessop 1990: 150). Organizations like the Business Roundtable and ECAT facilitate ad hoc coalitions for broad-based political advocacy, as with temporary trade policy alliances, but also (and more importantly) provide the stable organizational structures necessary for the development and promotion of a policy agenda consonant with the interests of big business. Because this agenda is not temporally static, inferences about the "general" corporate interest are somewhat problematic (ibid. 152). As Jessop (1990: 159) argues, the "general interests" of business are always articulated vis-à-vis a specific accumulation strategy advocated by a contingent community of capitalists. Corporate "interests," in other words, are not predetermined and must be defined in terms of a specific political economic context (see Prechel 2000). Businesses, as with other social sectors, use associations to articulate and, more crucially, *create* the common interests that underlie political cooperation. Thus, there is no natural law that says corporations must collectively lobby for shared economic interests: this process is instead facilitated by an institutionalized and historically constituted apparatus geared toward political influence over specific state processes.

This is not to say that shared material interests are unimportant to corporate political cohesion. Indeed, it may also be argued that recent efforts by the major policy organizations toward further trade liberalization and globalization have been greatly strengthened by the increasingly multinational structure of FF500 firms (Sklair 2001). Nonetheless, policy issues that draw the interests of firms from multiple sectors, as with NAFTA and China PNTR, are particularly important because they create "legacies" of political coordination that extend beyond a single policy outcome. In effect, localized policy struggles create institutional centers with enduring effect.

With respect to the largest US corporations, it is important to maintain specificity about the different forms of association by which they are connected. In the trade policy literature, for example, most analysts focus on the numerous – indeed, hundreds of – industry-specific trade associations. Focus on industry associations follows, in part, from the trade policy literature's emphasis on corporations as a force for protectionism (usually through narrow industry-level associations). Moreover, some analysts, such as Milner (1988; see also Cohen et al. 2003), argue further that sectoral conflicts undermine broader corporate political cohesion. This occurs, she argues, because the largest firms within a given sector tend to favor trade expansion and foreign investment, while smaller producers (typically) seek import protection because they lack the organizational capacity to exploit foreign market opportunities. From this perspective, trade policy conflicts *diminish* the political power of business because they expose intraindustry divergences in trade policy preferences.

However, Milner's argument implicitly assumes that sector is the principal "grouping unit" around which large firms coordinate their political activity. This assumption perhaps misses the most important point, though: the power of business is not simply derived from its political organization *within* industries, but from the "horizontal" structures that integrate broad sectors of the corporate community. In fact, while Milner's argument may nominally describe the *sectoral* conflict patterns of recent decades, political division over trade policy is not frequently observed among the largest US corporations. Indeed, a remarkable feature of recent corporate trade policy activism is not the conflict it has revealed but, rather, the extensive *agreement* across every major cross-industry business association, from small and medium to large business interests. This is evidenced, for example, by the paucity of FF500 firms testifying before Congress against the hemispheric and global trade regimes developed and ratified in the last twenty years.

Because most models of corporate political behavior in trade policy have been inattentive to the structure of intercorporate organization, we have advanced a theory of class agency that is attentive to firm position within the array of overlapping networks created by policy groups that span industries, board interlocks, and temporary trade policy alliances. At the center of these various networks, prominent business associations such as the Business Roundtable create a stable institutional framework for the expression of broader class interests. Class segments seek to influence the political system because the state will not, in all circumstances, produce business-favorable legislation. In this way, corporate policy activism is best conceptualized as a relational phenomenon: while less connected corporate actors perceive their interests more narrowly, more connected leaders perceive the corporate "interest" in broader, classwide terms, channeling resources toward strategic alliances to promote institutional changes consonant with a neoliberal restructuring of the global economy.

NEOLIBERAL GLOBALIZATION AND CLASS AGENCY

The consequences of over twenty years of neoliberal trade regimes like the World Trade Organization and the contentious Trans-Pacific Partnership (TPP), negotiated over eight years by the Obama administration to the disappointment of liberal Democrats, are significant. As the 2015 debate over the TPP unfolded in the United States, the OECD released a follow-up to their critical 2011 report, *Divided We Stand*, documenting the growing problem of economic inequality and attributing much of its spread to decades of financialization, weakened social protections, and globalization. This latest report states that the OECD countries have reached a "tipping point" on income inequality (OECD 2015). Corporate initiatives from the 1970s were clear in their intent to shift the wage and tax burden from capital to labor. It is not disputable that such a shift has now occurred and that corporate dominance of trade policy has contributed to those outcomes.

Recalling the arguments of Domhoff (2006) and Useem (1984), it is through the organization of the "policy-planning network" that particular company interests are translated into more general interests and policies regarded as beneficial to leading class segments. We observed that business mobilization for neoliberal trade occurred through a complex network of corporate policy organizations. These organizations have longstanding roles as hubs within a larger intercorporate network. The distinctive role of organizations like the Roundtable and ECAT arises from the manner in which they sustain *cross*-industry connections – "business scan" – while also facilitating a classwide orientation among ideologically distinct corporate leaders (Useem 1984). Our results, both statistical and historical, support the general propositions that the policy-planning network offers a resilient, though contingent, basis for sustained class cohesion.

Yet, as several scholars have determined, this network is quite large, consisting of hundreds of associations, think tanks, lobbying groups, and smaller member groups. Our approach has been to focus on the policy organizations where corporate membership leads to an active and visible role in the advance of neoliberal trade programs. As interlocked organizations, these circles of corporate elite are exposed to an evolving spectrum of international trade concerns as well as the political-strategic dilemmas that particular policy agendas face. But each of the organizations included in our data and historical account persists as a force in trade politics and routinely interfaces with the Office of the US Trade Representative, key congressional committees, and the broader public. A significant and recurring overlap between corporate leaders in these policy groups and state agencies responsible for trade policy has gone unabated since the 1974 Trade Act. It is worth recalling that each of the policy groups brings historically distinct forms and functions.

Ample research affirms that the Business Roundtable remains the most important organization within the corporate policy network. Like the

Business Roundtable, the Emergency Committee for American Trade (ECAT) remains "an action-oriented organization of the CEOs of about 60 large US multinational corporations ... to influence public policy in the direction of an open ... international trading, investment, and monetary system" (ECAT 1993: 1). The ECAT's small, but effective staff "keeps track of relevant developments in Congress, the Administration, other organizations, and the media " in order to "communicate those developments to the Chairman and to ECAT members" (ibid.). Working closely with the Roundtable, ECAT "either chairs or plays a leading role in several important coalitions in Washington" all while maintaining "direct contact with the White House ... members of the House Ways and Means, Foreign Affairs, and Senate Finance and Banking Committees" (ibid. 2–3). The neoliberal trade policy network also integrates from the periphery of the network business associations that represent a much broader range of medium to large corporations. The National Association of Manufacturers (NAM) and the Chamber of Commerce (COC) represent a more conservative, broader, and generally smaller cross-section of US business. The leadership of the NAM, with over 12,000 members, has been an advocate of free trade since its inception in 1894. On the other hand, the smaller businesses represented by the Chamber of Commerce have not been as consistent in their approaches to trade policy, although its leadership remains committed to neoliberal trade agendas alongside the larger corporate organizations. Other policy organizations, such as the "hemispheric" Council of the Americas – founded in 1965 by David Rockefeller – keep "members abreast of the ever-shifting business and financial conditions in the region ... [and] plays a critical role in helping them develop a business strategy"(Council of the Americas 1994: 4). In 1994, the NAFTA victory was declared a "realization ... of David Rockefeller's original vision when founding the Council" (ibid.: 5).

Additionally, the neoliberal trade policy network links US corporate leaders to the international corporate world. The US Council for International Business (formed in 1919 as the US affiliate to the International Chamber of Commerce) played a decisive role in the development of the neoliberal trade network. Its leaders, as we argued in Chapter 4, were key founders of the ECAT in 1967 and the group remains poised to mobilize "a cross-sectoral group of companies" (USCIB 1993: i). Its leaders possess a capacity to "broaden the expertise available when the Council develops policy; the wider representation also amplifies the influence of the group" (USCIB 1993: i). With a rather unique role in the international affairs of business, the USCIB "is dedicated to developing and promoting the views of American business before the U.S. Government and in the leading multilateral economic organizations" (ibid.: ii). This role stems "from the Council's status as the formal U.S. affiliate of the ... ICC, the Business and Industry Advisory Committee to the OECD, and the International Organization of Employers" (ibid.: ii). Following the implementation of the NAFTA, for example, the USCIB worked closely with the BRT and ECAT, taking a very active role on the steering committee of the "GATT NOW" coalition, and subsequently nominated numerous advisory posts (with success) to the institutions created under the NAFTA and the side agreements. The USCIB was also the leading advocate to the OECD's plan for a Multilateral Agreement on Investment (MAI) and more recently the Trans-Pacific Partnership (TPP). In 1994, the USCIB honored Allied Signal CEO Lawrence A. Bossidy (also the former vice chair of General Electric) with an international leadership award "for his leadership in the business community's successful effort to pass NAFTA" (USCIB 1994: 7). Bossidy was also a member of the Business Roundtable, the Business Council, and numerous other policy organizations, as well as holding an appointment to the President's Advisory Committee on Trade Policy Negotiations – the leading advisory committee among the labyrinth of trade policy committees under the US Trade Representative.

The membership and leadership of these and other policy groups overlap considerably, linking the organizational apparatus of most large corporations in the United States around a concerted agenda to advance trade and shape the global economic rules, scripted as they are in neoliberalism. Further, as the results presented in this book illustrate, US trade policy is formed in consultation with numerous private-sector advisory committees. The corporate members to this advisory system are tightly networked to the neoliberal policy network. These committees provide the opportunity for corporate leaders to voice their concerns at the policy-making and negotiating tables. While the 1972 Federal Advisory Committee Act (FACA) mandates that bodies such as these TACs remain open to the public and be "fairly balanced in terms of point of view represented and functions to be performed," the actual composition of the TACs is overwhelmingly corporate (Hilliard 1990: i). The second and third tiers consist of seven policy advisory committees and thirty industry sector committees, respectively. As with similar federal panels, however, a broad interpretation of FACA entitles secrecy in trade negotiations, for disclosure could "seriously compromise the development by the United States Government of trade policy, priorities, negotiating objectives or bargaining positions" (ibid.: 114).

Our concept of class agency specifies an important contingency with respect to class-cohesive associations among corporations and their top executives. In particular, the robust findings of the Business Roundtable point to a unique structural dimension of our concept: firms with structurally equivalent relations have cohesive properties. We assume that in the case of the BRT, where the CEO is the member and active body of the BRT, their actions are more or less consistent with the direction of the member corporations. Action by the Business Roundtable, we assert, is derived from class-cohesive networks where the dualism of person and organization are most acutely in line. CEOs, who typically own substantial shares of the company, and the corporation, mutually embedded and circumscribed in broad intercorporate networks thus at times express, in concert with similarly embedded CEOs/corporations, class agency.

The concept of class agency – as collective political action among corporations that is sustained across major economic sectors in the economy and drawn together through cohesive networks – offers a salient framework for explaining three decades of neoliberal trade policy advocacy by corporate elite in the United States. As we have noted, not all intercorporate connections lead to class cohesion, and not all corporate political unity is class agency. Nor does class agency need to be reduced to corporate political action, as we have seen. The policy network possesses structural features that persevere independent of the membership of particular corporations or leaders. For example, in 2011 the leaders of ECAT, the BRT, the USCIB, NAM, and the Chamber of Commerce joined together (once again) in a Trade and American Competitiveness Coalition. Led by the BRT (Business Roundtable 2013), the group includes many of the same corporate members from earlier campaigns for NAFTA, the WTO, and China PNTR, but new members are present as well. What is remarkable is the persistent and unified tone of the coalition. Tactically and strategically, the group – which morphed again in 2013 to the US Business Coalition for the TPP – took a multipronged strategy of influencing the passage of trade promotion authority for the TPP in spring 2015, mimicking the approaches crafted in the early years of ECAT.

Forty-eight years after its founding, the ECAT persists as a powerful lobby for a neoliberal trading system. Some wondered if the presidency of Barack Obama, who urged a renegotiation of NAFTA and other trade deals during his 2008 candidacy, would bring a turn in US trade policy from a neoliberal to a more selective trade agenda. This did not happen. Instead, ECAT, the Business Roundtable, and USCIB have consulted directly with President Obama to press neoliberal trade globalization agendas domestically and internationally. With regard to the TPP, the US-China Business Council, along with the USCIB, ECAT, and BRT conducted early meetings among business leaders through the International Chamber of Commerce to develop the TPP. These interests have developed in close cooperation with the secretaries of commerce and treasury. On this, the Business Roundtable reported: "The Office of the United States Trade Representative is leading the negotiations for the United States and has been consulting with Congress and private sector stakeholders on issues at all stages of the negotiations" (Business Roundtable 2013). Reflecting their multipronged strategy, and anticipating a congressional fight over the TPP, the ECAT and the US Business Council for TPP announced the formation of a bipartisan "Friends of TPP Congressional Caucus" on October 29, 2013. "It's an exciting time for U.S. trade policy," remarked Ambassador Michael Froman, President Barack Obama's newly minted US Trade Representative when he announced that the Trans-Pacific Partnership (TPP) was entering the endgame following nineteen rounds of intense negotiations (TPP Embassies: 2013).

On November 13, 2013, *Wikileaks* posted numerous documents leaked from the highly secretive negotiations for the TPP. Anyone reading the text of these leaked chapters would be lost without a bit of understanding of the history of international trade policy, international property rights, and patent law. What a reader is likely to wonder is how the documents qualify as "trade agreements," which, as a matter of course, is how the TPP was presented to the US Congress for "trade promotion authority" – or fast track approval. The text of the TPP builds directly on the recent investment treaties, including chapter 11 of NAFTA and the TRIPS agreement. It is perhaps more properly understood as an agreement between corporations and multiple governments. But even more basically the TPP sets out to establish transnational rules for investment, property rights, and production standards beyond those found in the WTO. It is an incipient legal doctrine for private interests to assert transnational juridical claims on participating governments, much like the legal force of chapter 11 in NAFTA. Where the TPP departs from these previous agreements is in its more onerous restrictions on governments to align their patent, property, and investment rules to the TPP. It is for this reason, more than trade, that the leak of the documents proved so evocative to critics of neoliberal globalization: the TPP, which is believed to be a forerunner to a second pact for a TransAtlantic Trade and Investment Partnership (TPIP), is a guidebook for global market rules that lock-in power relations among governments and global corporate actors, leaving citizens and labor at the back door.[3]

The evidence presented here warrants a serious consideration of class political agency in the structuring of these world economic institutions and the gross inequalities set in their wake. Clearly the global trade interests of member firms drive their political action, but, as our network models demonstrate, it is their embeddedness in class-cohesive networks that makes their political unity possible, net organizational interests. This class embeddedness of corporate political action is a sorely overlooked empirical fulcrum for explaining the global restructuring of capitalism under neoliberal auspices.

CONCLUSION

The findings in this study support our main hypothesis that corporate policy activism and political unity are driven, in part, through positions within class-cohesive networks, independent of narrow organizational interests. We have argued that corporate involvement in trade policy, both individually and collectively, embodies a class and organizational logic that is structural, not atomistic, in character. The political vision of inner circle actors *qua* leaders of MNCs is a function of their ability to consider and act upon interests of broader concern to the corporate community, as with the promotion of hemispheric and global trade regimes. Their political efficacy is best understood as a product of the "dual-logics" of classwide rationality. While attentive to short-run organizational interests, these actors are relatively unified around a broader vision for a social order that embeds neoliberal assumptions in the institutions and practices of the global economy.

The observations presented here thus suggest the need for a more cogent theory of neoliberal trade and globalization, one that accounts for the close coupling of state and class actors. Prechel's (2000) organizational perspective provides the kind of theoretical synthesis needed for grasping the contingent alignment of organized class segments and the state's trade policy apparatus. The project of neoliberal trade expansion in

---

[3] The release of the TPP documents fell in tandem with various news reports casting doubts about the value of the NAFTA in its first 20 years. As growing evidence implicates neoliberal trade for depressed wages, growing inequality, and increasing shares of national income to the financial sector (itself a contributor to deepening inequality according to the OECD), public conflicts over trade policies are sure to escalate.

the western hemisphere, and across regional economies, cannot be reduced to autonomous actions on the part of state actors, as much of the trade policy literature suggests. Instead, firms populate the state structures responsible for making US trade policy. These state structures are important, of course; but not because they maintain state autonomy. Mediated by important policy-planning organizations, such as the Business Roundtable, the Emergency Committee on American Trade, and the US Council for International Business, large corporations in the US create links to these extant state structures, thereby forging a stable basis for coupling class and state actors. In this way, state advisory committees and the enduring policy groups create an interorganizational system capable of advancing the interests of multinational corporations and the larger political-economic project behind neoliberal globalization.

Neoliberal trade policy initiatives emerged from the active and deliberate participation of class and state actors, also fueling a heightened politicization of global markets. Persistent political drives to cut corporate taxes, liberalize trade, expand transnational investment protections, and drive down wages have come with escalating political tensions. These politics, imbued with strands of class, environmentalism, and nationalism, did not simply arise as reactions to some "anonymous" force of globalization. Rather, politics drove neoliberal globalization to new heights. In this context, it is not enough to argue that the "state is in decline," swallowed and increasingly impotent in the seemingly inevitable advance of liberalized global markets. Neoliberal globalization is not simply an additive phenomenon, that is, a spillover effect of international transactions made on the margin. Far from inevitable, it takes shape by differentiating market factors such as technology, wages, land, and capital, but also by political factors that are conditioned by the coordinated political activities of broad segments of business and supportive state agencies. In this way, the role of class agents in constructing the new global trade apparatus is both a political and an economic affair and brings about political consequences. If these processes are to be better understood, it is not only the economic practices of corporations that must be examined, but, as has been the concern of this study, the political as well. Global markets, then, are both economic and political constructions – and, as such, could be made otherwise.

APPENDIX I

Data and Network Methods for 1991–1993 NAFTA Sample

The use of network analysis for the study of corporate events and behavior dates back some time. Three networks are used in Chapter 4 to capture and represent the structural features of pro-NAFTA, corporate leaders, circa 1991–93. First, as with all forms of network analysis a problem of sampling arises. Sampling a population for its possible ties to other units of observation in that population is problematic because the "observed structure" of ties is likely to diverge from the "true structure" (Holland and Leinhardt 1973). A sampling of actors is not the same as a sampling of relations. Despite the limits arising from measurement error, and the methodological limits to estimating measurement error in network samples, some resolution can be achieved. Frank (1979) offers basic solutions to the problems that arise when "true structure" cannot be obtained. In this study, every effort is made to incorporate appropriate solutions.

Under the circumstances presented by research for Chapter 4, a "quasi-enumeration" of the population of corporate proponents for NAFTA was sought by a snowball sampling of the largest corporations in the coalition (Scott 1991). The population, the USA*NAFTA coalition (1991–1994), is a relatively bounded set of actors comprised of pro-NAFTA business organizations. In this manner, our population consists of only those politically active, pro-NAFTA corporations, not the entire universe of business. Due to the size of the population (2308) and the difficulty of obtaining reliable network data for each actor, a stratified probability sample was obtained initially. For private

companies where data was unavailable for the board interlocks *and* if no
ties were identified in the two policy networks, then the company was
excluded.

This type of purposive snowball sampling incorporates two common
sampling solutions found in use among network analysts. The common
method employed by corporate interlock research is to assign a "cut-off"
at say the "top 200" or "top 50," a strategy analogous to our initial
subsampling procedure. Unfortunately these arbitrary cut-offs leave out
ties to companies ranked below them. Any significance of firms below
the cut-off remain unexamined. This may be particularly problematic for
the study of collective action, where many firms are not Fortune 500.
Another problem common for corporate interlock researchers is
that many smaller to medium firms (as in the USA*NAFTA coalition)
are privately held and are thus exempt from many of the disclosure
rules that large, publicly traded firms face. Board interlock data is
consequently difficult to obtain in a reliable manner. Even so, where
data was accessible, privately held, large and medium-sized firms were
incorporated into the USA*NAFTA analysis in with the snowball
technique. The snowball approach, advocated by Frank and others
thus enables us to draw-in theoretically and empirically important
corporate players, somewhat independent of arbitrary size thresholds
(Frank 1979; Scott 1991). Given our interest in the study of "global"
network properties, this type of network sampling offers the most solid
analytical ground.

The sample of 228 USA*NAFTA members was used to construct three
separate sociomatrices of the thirty-five State Captains in that sample.
The State Captain data forms the basis for our brief analysis in Chapter 4.
The first of the three measured relations consists of a matrix of board of
director interlocks among the sampled companies. This matrix measures
ties between pairs of corporations resulting from shared board members.
Board of director membership for each firm was obtained from raw textual
data output from Compact Disclosure online database of corporate tax
filings.

Thirty-Five State Captains, 1992

3M CO
ABBOTT LABS
ADM
AIG
ALCOA

AT&T
BOEING CO
CATERPILLAR
DEERE
DOW CHEMICAL
DU PONT
DUKE ENERGY
FLUOR
FORD MOTOR
GENERAL ELECTRIC
GENERAL MOTORS
GEORGIA-PACIFIC
GOLDMAN SACHS
GOODYEAR
HONEYWELL INTL
IBM
INTL PAPER
LILLY (ELI)
LOCKHEED MARTIN
MERCK & CO
MORGAN STANLEY
PFIZER
PROCTER & GAMBLE
ROCKWELL
SARA LEE
SCHERING-PLOUGH
SUN MICROSYSTEMS
UNITED PARCEL SERV.
WHIRLPOOL
WILLIAMS COS

A snowball sample of "events" or policy-planning organizations was selected to construct the second of the three relations. Initial inclusion of a corporate policy-planning organization was determined by evaluating the frequency of congressional testimony in support of the NAFTA. Nearly every corporate policy-planning body that sent a representative before Congressional committees was included in this network.[1] The third

---

[1] The National Foreign Trade Council (NFTC) will not disclose its membership and was thus not included in the network. While the Council on Foreign Relations did not testify

network relation measures common membership in a Trade Advisory Committee (TAC) for the US Trade Representative, which is a fixed network of committees in the executive branch of the US government. Appointment to one of these committees is indicated in an actor-by-event co-membership matrix. These two co-membership matrices represent USA*NAFTA–member affiliations with relevant Trade Advisory Committees (TACs) and corporate policy-planning bodies. The policy planning organizations are: memberships in the Business Roundtable, the National Association of Manufacturers executive and three policy teams, the Emergency Committee for American Trade, the Multilateral Trade Negotiation (MTN) coalition, the US Council of the Mexico-US Business Committee (a Chamber of Commerce Bilateral Committee), the Council for the Americas, the US Council for International Business, and the Council on Foreign Relations. These data were derived from multiple sources. For membership in the Trade Advisory Committees, official membership rosters were obtained from the Office of the USTR. Membership for the MTN coalition was obtained from the *Inside US Trade*, May 18, 1990. Policy organization membership was obtained from the annual reports, or equivalent documents from National Association of Manufacturers, 1991–1993; US Chamber of Commerce and the US Council of the Mexico-US Business Committee, 1991–1992; US Council for International Business, 1991–1992; Council of the Americas, 1991–1993; Council on Foreign Relations, 1991–1994; and the Emergency Committee for American Trade, 1991–1993.

In network terminology, two hypergraphs, or affiliation networks measure the number of private sector policy organizations and TACs to which each corporation was affiliated in 1991–1993. Rather than simply representing ties between pairs of actors, as with the board of director network, these affiliation networks possess a duality that allows us to examine patterns of overlapping membership (Breiger 1974). Breiger (1974) emphasizes these properties while demonstrating the use of affiliation networks to study ties between actors, between events, or

---

before congressional committees, it was included in the network for the broad significance given to the CFR in related literature. Moreover, the Council showed indirect support through numerous venues, including its *Foreign Affairs* journal. The US Chamber of Commerce as a whole was not included due to the extreme breadth of participation in the organization. More appropriately, we used the US Council of the US-Mexico Business Committee, a bilateral entity managed by the US Chamber of Commerce. Numerous trade associations specific to market sector concerns were also excluded from this network. Think tanks were excluded from this network as well.

both. Rather straightforward matrix manipulations transform an actor-by-event, or affiliation matrix into an actor-by-actor, or event-by-event matrix.[2] By measuring these ties among corporations it is possible to represent the network structure.

[2] A g × h affiliation matrix, A, records the number of policy affiliations for each corporate actor. The precise relation between the affiliation matrix and a matrix, B, that records the number of "events" (or memberships) that each pair of corporations share in common can be expressed as the product of A and its transpose:

$$B = A \times A'$$

where A′ is the transpose of A.

Similarly, the matrix C, which indicates the number of actors each pair of events share in common, is derived as the product of A′ and A:

$$C = A' \times A.$$

For this study, the original affiliation matrices are not used directly. Rather, matrices representing joint membership between pairs of corporations within each policy network are used as one-mode, symmetric measures of intercorporate relations. In other words, the B matrix above. In addition, a submatrix of event-by-event overlaps, that is, matrix C, measures the extent to which pairs of policy bodies share State Captain members. All matrix manipulations were accomplished using UCINET 6.0, (Borgatti, Everett, and Freeman 1999).

Data and Methods for Measuring and Analyzing Corporate Unity in American Trade Policy

In this Appendix, we describe the data sources, variable measurements, and statistical methods used to test the hypotheses presented at the end of Chapter 3 and the analyses presented in Chapters 5 and 6. In the first section of this appendix the sampling universe and data sources of the study are described. The second section presents descriptions of the three dependent measures of corporate trade policy activism: participation in Trade Advisory Committees (TACs), congressional testimony at US trade policy hearings, and involvement in temporary trade policy alliances. Detailed descriptions of the variable construction for each of the independent measures are presented.

SAMPLING UNIVERSE

A number of important sociological studies have analyzed the policy activism and political similarity of large US corporations. However, much of this research uses cross-sectional firm- and executive-level data from the 1970s and 1980s, and is limited to an analysis of specific business sectors, such as banking (Mintz and Swartz 1985) or manufacturing (Mizruchi 1992). One of the unique contributions of this book is that it integrates a variety of data sources to study firms from an array of sectors during two time periods (1998 and 2003). The main advantage of studying the political behavior of multiple sectors is that it is possible to generalize the findings beyond a single category of corporations, such as manufacturing or banking. Likewise, although two waves of data do not, of course, constitute a time series, the data used in this analysis is nonetheless an advance over previous research. This is because the data allow us to investigate whether observed relationships between, say, board interlocks and trade policy activism, can be observed at more than one observation point – strengthening causal inferences about the stability of various influences over time.

The sampling universe[1] consists of publicly traded (i.e., non–privately owned) firms listed in the 1998 and 2003 *Fortune* and *Forbes* 500 directories (FF500). Because the *Fortune* and *Forbes* lists overlap considerably, the combined firm directories typically contain ~560 public and private companies in a given year. After dropping privately held firms, the sample size for each wave of data is approximately 484. Privately held companies are dropped from the sample because they (typically) do not produce financial statements analogous to the SEC 10k filings incumbent on publicly traded firms, which confounds cross-sectional comparison.

While many trade policy studies model corporate political activism at the sectoral level, the firm-centered approach of this study is preferable because companies within the same industry often possess differing trade preferences (Milner 1988: 20). In addition, international subsidiary operations and board interlocks, for example, often distribute unevenly within sectors, suggesting that an industry-level unit of analysis may obfuscate examination of their effect on corporate trade policy activism (ibid.; see also Useem 1984).

DATA SOURCES FOR 1998 AND 2003

The data sets used in Chapter 5 and 6 were created using multiple corporate and governmental data repositories. Measures of firm sales, assets, employees, primary product market (SIC code), and headquarters location are drawn from Standard and Poor's *Compustat Industrial Annual* database (distributed by Wharton Research Data Services). Data on firm foreign subsidiaries were obtained from Uniworld Business Publications' fifteenth and eighteenth editions of the *Directory of American Firms Operating in Foreign Countries*. For each FF500 firm listed in the Uniworld directory, data on the country and region of its subsidiary operations were recorded. Data on FF500 business advocacy group memberships were obtained from multiple sources. Generally, membership rosters were available from the organization's website or

---

[1] See Chapter 5, footnote 4 for a discussion of sampling universe in this study.

printed annual report.[2] In some cases, organizations were contacted directly for a membership list when these sources were not available. Annual reports, membership rosters, or equivalent documents were obtained for the following organizations: America Leads on Trade, Business Council, Business Roundtable, Conference Board, Emergency Committee on American Trade, National Association of Manufacturers, Business Coalition for US-Central America Trade, Council of the Americas, Trilateral Commission, USA-Engage, US Trade Coalition, and the United States Council for International Business. Similarly, data on corporate participation in federal trade policy advisory committees (TACs) were obtained from the Department of Commerce's Industry Consultation Program.

Board of director interlock data were generated using directorate information produced by the Investor Responsibility Research Council (IRRC), while data on FF500 congressional testimony were obtained through the *Lexis-Nexis Congressional* database. Additionally, some congressional transcripts were obtained directly from the printed version of the Congressional Record or the Government Printing Office's (GPO) online congressional record database. Finally, corporate Political Action Committee (PAC) data were obtained from Federal Election Commission PAC summary files.

The 1998 and 2003 data sets use the following public data sources to model corporate involvement and advocacy in US trade policy formation. Measures of firm sales, assets, employees, primary product market (SIC code), and headquarters location are drawn from Standard and Poor's *Compustat Industrial Annual* database (distributed by Wharton Research Data Services). The *Compustat* database compiles financial data on over 10,000 US and Canadian corporations using a number of public and private data sources and providers, including company shareholder reports, 10K and 10Q Securities and Exchange Commission filings, NASDAQ, *Interactive Data,* and *Fortune.* After compiling the list of corporations in the 1998 and 2003 FF500, relevant firm attribute data were downloaded from the *Compustat* database using firm ticker symbols as the unique identifier.

---

[2] Because the 2003 wave of policy group affiliation data were not collected until 2005, *archive.org* was used to obtain a cached copy of a given organization's membership roster circa 2003. This ensured that corporate membership data were contemporaneous with other attributes, such as sales and subsidiaries.

Data on firm foreign subsidiaries were obtained from Uniworld Business Publications' fifteenth and eighteenth editions of the *Directory of American Firms Operating in Foreign Countries*. For each FF500 firm listed in the Uniworld directory, data on the country and region of its subsidiary operations were recorded.

Data on FF500 business advocacy group memberships were obtained from multiple sources. Generally, membership rosters were available from the organization's website[3] or printed annual report. In some cases, organizations were contacted directly for a membership list when these sources were not available. Annual reports, membership rosters, or equivalent documents were obtained for the following organizations: America Leads on Trade, Business Council, Conference Board, Emergency Committee on American Trade, National Association of Manufacturers, Business Coalition for US-Central America Trade, Council of the Americas, Trilateral Commission, USA-Engage, US Trade Coalition, and the United States Council for International Business. Similarly, data on corporate participation in federal trade policy advisory committees (TACs) were obtained from the Department of Commerce's Industry Consultation Program.

Board of director interlock data were generated using board of director rosters for each FF500 firm. For the 1998 wave, the list of corporate directors for each FF500 company was obtained using *Compact Disclosure*. For the 2003 wave, the *Compact Disclosure* data were no longer available, but a new database of director data created with the same underlying SEC sources was available from the Investor Responsibility Research Council[4] (IRRC). Thus, for the 2003 FF500 wave, director names were obtained from the IRRC database.

Data on FF500 congressional testimony were obtained through the *Lexis-Nexis Congressional* database. Additionally, some congressional transcripts were obtained directly from the printed version of the Congressional Record or the Government Printing Office's (GPO) online congressional record database.[5]

---

[3] Because the 2003 wave of policy group affiliation data were not collected until 2005, *archive.org* was used to obtain a cached copy of a given organization's membership roster circa 2003. This allowed us to ensure that corporate membership data were contemporaneous with other attributes, such as sales and subsidiaries.

[4] While the IRRC database contains additional demographic data on corporate directors, the basic information obtained from *Compact Disclosure* (director and company name) is the same.

[5] This database can be accessed at www.gpoaccess.gov/crecord

Finally, corporate Political Action Committee (PAC) data were obtained from Federal Election Commission PAC summary files. Each summary file was carefully scrutinized to identify PACs operated by FF500 firms. Over 8,000 corporate PACs register in a typical election cycle. PAC expenditures in the 1996 and 1998 election cycles were assigned to the 1998 wave, while the 2000 and 2002 election cycle data were assigned to the 2003 wave of companies.[6]

DEPENDENT VARIABLES

In this section, we outline three dependent measures of individual and dyadic corporate involvement in US trade policy formation and advocacy. The first dependent variable, which measures involvement in a TAC (individual and dyadic), is a proxy for corporate trade policy activism in the executive branch. The second dependent variable, which measures the frequency and similarity of corporate testimony at congressional trade policy hearings, is a proxy for direct corporate lobbying of the legislature. The third dependent variable, trade policy alliance participation, measures individual and dyadic involvement in nonstate advocacy groups lobbying congress and conducting public relation campaigns for specific trade policy outcomes.

Trade Advisory Committees

For the firm-level models (Chapter 5), TAC participation is measured as a *count* of the total number of trade advisory committee memberships. In the class-cohesion dyadic models (Chapter 6), TAC participation is measured as a count of the number of *shared* committee memberships within the corporate dyad.

In the dyadic models, testimony is measured as a dummy variable indicating whether two firms testified together in support of a trade-expanding policy initiative, such as the NAFTA. A separate model predicting dyadic opposition (that is, a model of whether the dyadic subunits opposed one another at a trade hearing) was again deemed unnecessary because opposition is almost perfectly predicted by whether one of the subunits is a steel producer.[7]

---

[6] Expenditure data for the 2003 sample of firms were chosen from the preceding "even" years (2000 and 2002) because they correspond to election years.

[7] While Mizrichi (1992) models opposition and agreement in one equation using OLS regression on a three item ordinal scale ranging from −1 to 1, this practice is somewhat

Testimony Before Congress

FF500 congressional testimony at US trade policy hearings is measured for the period 1993–2004.[8] For the firm-level models, congressional testimony is measured as a *count* of the number of company appearances before Congress in support of trade-expanding policy initiatives (e.g., NAFTA or PNTR with China). In the dyadic models below, testimony was modeled as a dummy variable indicating whether two firms testified together in support of a trade-expanding policy initiative, such as the NAFTA.

Temporary Alliance Participation

In the firm-level models, TPA participation is operationalized as a dummy indicator of whether a firm participated in a temporary trade policy alliance. For the 1998 wave, alliance participation is measured by firm involvement in America Leads on Trade and/or USA Engage, while for the 2003 wave alliance participation is measured by firm involvement in the Business Coalition for US-Central America Trade and/or USTrade.[9]

INDEPENDENT VARIABLES[10]

In this section, we describe variable operationalization for the hypothesized predictors presented at the end of Chapter 3. While the underlying data sources are the same, the firm-level variables predicting participation require a slightly different measurement strategy from the dyadic variables measuring political similarity. For this reason, we describe variable operationalization for both the firm- and dyad-level models.

---

dubious statistically because it treats a unit change in the dependent variable as comparable across all variable values. This is problematic because a unit change from, for example, opposition (−1) to no shared testimony (0) may not be the same as a unit increase from no shared testimony to agreement (1), etc. Despite these limitations, we also estimated the dyadic models using a measure comparable to Mizruchi's analysis and found little substantive difference in the coefficient estimates. Thus, for parsimony's sake and to simplify interpretation, we limit the analysis to instances of shared FF500 testimony in *favor* of trade expanding policy initiatives such as the NAFTA.

[8] Specifically, testimony for the period 1999–2004 were measured for the 2003 wave of companies, while testimony for the period 1993–1998 were measured for the 1998 wave.

[9] As this variable could only assume one of three values (0, 1, 2) it was dichotomized to simplify interpretation. Re-estimation of the model using a technique for ordered counts (e.g., Poisson) did not change the substantive interpretation of the findings.

[10] See Appendix Table A.2 for a summary of variable operationalizations.

Organizational Predictors

The first organizational measure, capital intensity, is computed using financial data on firm assets and employees. For the models of firm participation in trade policy formation and advocacy, we employ the commonly accepted measure of capital intensity: firm assets divided by number of employees[11] (Dreiling 2001; Mizruchi 1992). Because this measure displays a strongly positive distributional skew in the FF500, we take its natural log:

$$(Capital\ Intensity)_i = \log(assets/employees) \qquad \text{Eq. 1.a}$$

For the dyadic model, we utilize Mizruchi's (1992) operationalization,[12] which takes the absolute value of the *difference* in the natural log of the asset-to-employee ratio. That is, for dyadic sub-units i and j:

$$(Capital\ Intensity)_{ij} = \text{abs}\left(\log(assets/employees)_i - \log(assets/employees)_j\right)$$

$$\text{Eq. 1.b}$$

To facilitate interpretation, we utilized Stata's reverse scoring procedure, which creates a variable with perfect negative correlation with the original. After this transformation, larger values indicate greater *similarity* in dyadic capital intensity.

The second organizational predictor, size, is estimated using data on firm sales, assets, and employees. Because these three attributes assume variable importance in different sectors, we used principal factor analysis to extract a single factor solution for firm size. Several other operationalizations for firm size found in the literature, such as summing sales and assets or entering each measure as a separate variable, were also analyzed. In most models, the factor analytic solution produced the best model fit and, therefore, was used for the firm participation models. For the dyadic models, we employ the geometric mean of the firm factor scores as a control for size:

---

[11] Several other operationalizations were investigated, such as standardizing capital intensity by industry or assigning each firm its industry's average value. Because none of these operationalizations significantly improved model fit, we opted to utilize the standard measurement, that is, the quotient of assets divided by employees.

[12] Other operationalizations of dyadic capital intensity, such as taking the geometric mean of the subunits' logged capital intensity ratios, were also investigated. Generally, it was determined that Mizruchi's formula provided the best model fit. Thus, to maintain consistency with Mizrruchi's (1992) research, we opted to use his operationalization.

$$Size_{ij}\sqrt{(Size\ Factor)_i \times (Size\ Factor)_j} \qquad \text{Eq. 2}$$

The geometric mean provides a weighted average of each subunit's size, such that two firms with a moderately high value in the size factor will yield a larger dyadic value than two firms with the same *summed* value but unequal contributions to the total (e.g., one large firm and one small firm) (see also Mizruchi 1992). Unlike the capital intensity variable (Eq. 1), the control for size in the dyadic regressions is not a measure of the *similarity* of the subunits' scores but, rather, a proxy for the combined size of the dyad. In other words, the expectation is not that that two comparably sized small firms, or two firms of mixed size (e.g., one small and one large), will display greater than average political similarity. Rather, it is expected that dyads of the largest firms should exhibit greater than average political similarity.

The third organizational predictor, multinationality, is a function of firm subsidiary operations in foreign countries. For the firm-level participation models, the variable is operationalized as a count of the total number of firm subsidiary operations in foreign countries. Because the variable displayed a strongly positive distributional skew, the natural log was taken. For the dyadic model, multinationality is operationalized as a count of the number of geographic regions in which both dyadic subunits operate a foreign subsidiary operation.[13]

The fourth organizational interest predictor, product market, is measured using primary two-digit firm Standard Industrial Classification coding[14] (SIC). For the firm-level participation models, two-digit SIC code operates as a grouping characteristic in a mixed (hierarchical) regression model.[15] For the dyadic models, sector is modeled using Mizruchi's (1992) operationalization: firms in the same two-digit sector are coded one, and zero otherwise.

---

[13] Subsidiary operations were coded into the following regions: North America, Central America, South America, Western Europe, Central Europe, Eastern Europe, Northern African, Sub-Saharan Africa, the Middle East, Asia, and Oceana.

[14] The Standard Industrial Classification is a four-digit coding scheme that describes the product market(s) in which a firm operates. Each digit, from the first to the fourth, describes, in ascending detail, the firm's product market attributes. For example, SIC code 5 refers to restaurants, wholesale firms, and retail outlets, while SIC code 57 refers to the subgrouping of home furniture, furnishings, and equipment stores. See Appendix A1 for a directory of two-digit SIC codes 01–99.

[15] Statistical methods are described in greater detail below.

The fifth organizational predictor applies only to the dyadic regression models and, similar to Mizruchi's (1992) operationalization, is a dummy indicator for whether each subunit's headquarters are in the same state. Though not theoretically motivated, controls for firm geographic region[16] were also introduced to the firm-level participation models but did not significantly improve model fit. Thus, for parsimony they are omitted from the firm-level models.

The sixth predictor, political donations, measures FF500 PAC expenditures in the 1996, 1998, 2000, and 2002 election cycles to House, Senate, and presidential candidates. The 1996 and 1998 election cycle data are assigned to the 1998 F500 sample firms, while the 2000 and 2002 election cycles data are assigned to the 2003 sample. For the firm-level participation models, the variable is operationalized as the sum of PAC expenditures in the two previous election cycles. For the dyadic models, we employ the geometric mean of firm-level PAC expenditures as a control for the effect of political donations:

$$Expenditures_{ij} = \sqrt{(PAC\ Expenditures)_i \times (PAC\ Expenditures)_j} \qquad \text{Eq. 3}$$

NETWORK VARIABLES

The seventh predictor, firm-level board interlocks, was created in two steps. First, FF500 directorate rosters were used to create a firm-by-director matrix of affiliations. Next, this matrix was transformed to produce a square firm-by-firm matrix of board interlocks. For the participation models, we used the firm-by-firm matrix to calculate the Freeman Degree Centrality score for each firm, which is simply a count of the total number of firm ties to all other actors in the network[17] (i.e., the FF500). The mean number of direct interlocks in the FF500 (to other

[16] Though not theoretically motivated, controls for firm geographic region were also introduced to the firm-level participation models but did not significantly improve model fit. Thus, for parsimony they are omitted from the firm-level models. Region was measured using five categories: West, Midwest, South, Northeast, and Mountain.

[17] Freeman centrality scores were utilized in favor of Bonacich's centrality measure to facilitate interpretation of the regression model coefficients (the Freeman measure is equivalent to a count of actor ties to the network, whereas Bonacich's measure is expressed as a composite value). However, estimating the firm-level model's (see Chapter 4) using Bonacich's centrality measure did not change the substantive findings. For the 1998 data, the Bonacich and Freeman centrality scores were correlated at .9225, while for the 2003 wave, the measures are correlated at .9593.

FF500 firms) is approximately 7, while 118 firms possessed zero board ties across both study years.

In the dyadic model, interlocks are measured using two *dichotomous* measures of "direct" and "indirect" board ties between the dyadic subunits.[18] Direct ties measure whether a dyad is linked by one or more shared directors, while indirect ties measure whether a dyad's boards are tied through a third company. For example, dyadic subunits "A" and "B" are indirectly tied to one another if each has a director that participates in some third company, "C." Indirect ties were computed by taking the (matrix) square of the firm-by-firm interlock matrix (Wasserman and Faust 1994).

The eighth predictor, Business Roundtable membership, is a measure of firm affiliation with the Business Roundtable. For the firm-level model, the variable is simply a dummy indicating membership in the Business Roundtable, while in the dyadic model, the variable measures *shared* affiliation.[19]

The ninth predictor, policy network affiliation, measures firm ties to the following business advocacy organizations: the Business Council, Conference Board, Emergency Committee on American Trade, National Association of Manufacturers, Council of the Americas, Trilateral Commission, and the United States Council for International Business. For the participation model, the policy network variable is a *count* of the number of firm ties to these organizations. For the dyadic model, the policy network variable is a count of *shared* firm ties to each of these organizations.[20]

---

[18] We also modeled the effects of interlocking in the dyadic models using the geometric mean of board interlocks (see also Gulati 1999). As expected, this variable was positively correlated with direct and indirect interlocks (most likely because firms with more board ties to the entire network will, *ceteris paribus*, have a higher probability of being tied to each other). Entering the variables in separate models (i.e., direct/indirect ties in one model, and the geometric mean of Freeman centrality in another) tended to produce similar estimates of model fit and did not change the substantive interpretation of the other predictors. Thus, because of the correlation between the measures, as well as the fact that the coefficients for direct and indirect interlocks are easier to interpret than the geometric mean of Freeman centrality scores, the former were used in the dyadic regression models in Chapter 6.

[19] That is, in the dyadic model the variable is set to one only if *both* firms participate in the Business Roundtable.

[20] For example, if each unit of a dyad is a member of the Trilateral Coalition and the Business Council, the variable is set to two.

TABLE A2.1 *Variable Measures, Participation Models*

Variable	Units and Coding	Source	Predicted Effect
ISAC Participation	Count of total memberships in ACTPN and/or ISACs	US Department of Commerce, 1998, 2003	[DV]
Temporary Trade Policy Alliances	Count of participation in temporary trade policy alliances (for 1998 firms, membership in America Leads on Trade and/or USA Engage, for 2003 firms, membership in the Business Coalition for US-Central America Trade and/or the US Trade Coalition)	Public membership rosters	[DV]
Congressional Testimony	Count of the number of instances of testimony before Congress at trade policy hearings	*Lexis-Nexis Congressional* database. Printed Congressional Record. GPO congressional record database	[DV]
PAC Contributions	Log of combined PAC expenditures in two preceding election cycles (for the 1998 firms, 1996 and 1998 election cycles; for the 2003 firms, the 2000, and 2002 election cycles)	US Federal Elections Commission PAC summary files	+
Foreign Subsidiaries	Count of firm subsidiary operations in foreign countries	Uniworld Business Publications, *Directory of American Firms Operating in Foreign Countries*	+

			Variable
Product Market	Two-digit Standard Industrial Classification (SIC)	1998/2003 *Compustat Industrial Annual*	
Size	Single factor solution for sales, assets, and employees	1998/2003 *Compustat Industrial Annual*	+
Capital Intensity	Log of the quotient of assets divided by number of employees	1998/2003 *Compustat Industrial Annual*	+
Board Interlocks	Count of direct board interlocks	Proxy statement, *Disclosure* (for 1998 firms), *IRRC* director database (for 2003 firms)	+
Policy Network Affiliation	Count of total memberships ties to the Business Council, Conference Board, National Association of Manufacturers, Council of the Americas, Trilateral Commission, and the United States Council for International Business	Public and requested membership rosters	+
Business Roundtable Participation	Dummy indicator of Business Roundtable membership	Publicly available membership roster	+
Year Control	Dummy variable for observation year (1998 = 0, 2003 = 1)	—	−

a: Product market is modeled as a level-2 grouping variable such that firms within each two-digit SIC code are assigned a unique mean rate of ISAC participation (intercept).

TABLE A2.2 *Variable Measures, Dyadic Models*

Variable	Units and Coding	Source	Predicted Effect
ISAC Participation	Count of total shared memberships in ACTPN and/or ISACs	US Department of Commerce, 1998, 2003	[DV]
Temporary Trade Policy Alliances	Count of shared ties to temporary trade policy alliances (for 1998 firms, membership in America Leads on Trade and/or USA Engage, for 2003 firms, membership in the Business Coalition for US-Central America Trade and/or the US Trade Coalition)	Public membership rosters	[DV]
Congressional Testimony	Count of the number of common instances of testimony before Congress at trade policy hearings	*Lexis-Nexis Congressional* database. Printed Congressional Record. GPO congressional record database	[DV]
PAC Contributions	Geometric mean of firm-level PAC expenditures	US Federal Elections Commission PAC summary files	+
Foreign Subsidiaries	Count of the number of common regions in which both dyadic subunits operate a foreign subsidiary operation	Uniworld Business Publications, *Directory of American Firms Operating in Foreign Countries*	+
Product Market	Dummy set to one if both subunits operate in the same two-digit Standard Industrial Classification (SIC)	1998/2003 *Compustat Industrial Annual*	+

Variable	Description	Source	Predicted
Size	Geometric mean of firm level size	1998/2003 *Compustat Industrial Annual*	+
Capital Intensity	Absolute value of the difference in firm level capital intensity (Mizruchi 1992). Variable is reverse coded so that larger values indicate greater similarity	1998/2003 *Compustat Industrial Annual*	+
Board Interlocks	Dummy variables (two) for whether dyad is connected by a direct or indirect board interlock	Proxy statement, *Disclosure* (for 1998 firms), *IRRC* director database (for 2003 firms)	+
Policy Network Affiliation	Count of total *common* memberships ties to the Business Council, Conference Board, National Association of Manufacturers, Council of the America's, Trilateral Commission, and the United States Council for International Business	Public and requested membership rosters	+
Business Roundtable Participation	Dummy indicator of Business Roundtable membership	Publicly available membership roster	+
State	Dummy for whether dyad's headquarters are in the same state	1998/2003 *Compustat Industrial Annual*	+
Year Control	Dummy variable for observation year (1998 = 0, 2003 = 1)	–	+

Standard Industrial Classification (SIC) Codes

01 Agricultural Production Crops
02 Agricultural Production Livestock and Animal Specialties
07 Agricultural Services
08 Forestry
10 Metal Mining
12 Coal Mining
13 Oil and Gas Extraction
14 Mining and Quarrying of Nonmetallic Minerals, Except Fuels
15 Building Construction General Contractors and Operative
16 Heavy Construction Other Than Building Construction
17 Construction Special Trade Contractors
20 Food and Kindred Products
21 Tobacco Products
22 Textile Mill Products
23 Apparel and Other Finished Products Made From Fabrics
24 Lumber and Wood Products, Except Furniture
25 Furniture and Fixtures
26 Paper and Allied Products
27 Printing, Publishing, and Allied Industries
28 Chemicals and Allied Products
29 Petroleum Refining and Related Industries
30 Rubber and Miscellaneous Plastics Products
31 Leather and Leather Products
32 Stone, Clay, Glass, and Concrete Products
33 Primary Metal Industries
34 Fabricated Metal Products, Except Machinery and Transportation
35 Industrial and Commercial Machinery and Computer Equipment
36 Electronic and Other Electrical Equipment and Components,
37 Transportation Equipment
38 Measuring, Analyzing, and Controlling Instruments
39 Miscellaneous Manufacturing Industries
40 Railroad Transportation
41 Local and Suburban Transit and Interurban Highway Passenger
42 Motor Freight Transportation and Warehousing
43 United States Postal Service
44 Water Transportation
45 Transportation by Air
46 Pipelines, Except Natural Gas

47 Transportation Services
48 Communications
49 Electric, Gas, and Sanitary Services
50 Wholesale Trade-Durable Goods
51 Wholesale Trade-Non-Durable Goods
52 Building Materials, Hardware, Garden Supply, and Mobile Homes
53 General Merchandise Stores
54 Food Stores
55 Automotive Dealers and Gasoline Service Stations
56 Apparel and Accessory Stores
57 Home Furniture, Furnishings, and Equipment Stores
58 Eating and Drinking Places
59 Miscellaneous Retail
60 Depository Institutions
61 Non-Depository Credit Institutions
62 Security and Commodity Brokers, Dealers, Exchanges
63 Insurance Carriers
64 Insurance Agents, Brokers, and Service
65 Real Estate
67 Holding and Other Investment Offices
70 Hotels, Rooming Houses, Camps, and Other Lodging Places
72 Personal Services
73 Business Services
75 Automotive Repair, Services, and Parking
76 Miscellaneous Repair Services
78 Motion Pictures
79 Amusement and Recreation Services
80 Health Services
81 Legal Services
82 Educational Services
83 Social Services
84 Museums, Art Galleries, and Botanical and Zoological Gardens
86 Membership Organizations
87 Engineering, Accounting, Research, Management
88 Private Households
89 Services, Not Elsewhere Classified
91 Executive, Legislative, and General Government, Except Finance
92 Justice, Public Order, and Safety
93 Public Finance, Taxation, and Monetary Policy

94 Administration of Human Resource Programs
95 Administration of Environmental Quality and Housing Programs
96 Administration of Economic Programs
97 National Security and International Affairs
99 Nonclassifiable Establishments

References

Agence France Presse. 2000. "U.S. companies mount ferocious campaign to win backing for PNTR," May 23.

Akard, Patrick J. 1992. "Corporate mobilization and political power: The transformation of U.S. economic policy in the 1970s." *American Sociological Review* 57: 597–615.

Albright, Madeline K. 2000. "America and the world in the twenty-first century." *Secretary of State Madeline K. Albright, Statement before House International Relations Committee.* February 16, 2000. Washington, DC. Accessed on May 12, 2015, http://1997-2001.state.gov/www/statements/2000/000216.html.

Appelbaum, Richard P., and William I. Robinson, eds. 2005. *Critical globalization studies.* New York: Routledge.

Arrighi, Giovanni. 1994. *The long twentieth-century: Money, power, and the origins of our times.* London; New York: Verso.

Arthur Andersen & Co. 1979. *Cost of government regulation study for the Business Roundtable.* Chicago: A. Andersen.

Autor, David H., David Dorn, and Gordon H. Hanson. 2012. *The China syndrome: Local labor market effects of import competition in the United States.* NBER Working Paper No. 18054. Cambridge, MA: National Bureau of Economic Research.

Baldwin, Robert E. 1989. *Trade policy in a changing world.* Chicago: University of Chicago Press.

Baran, Paul A., and Paul M. Sweezy. 1966. *Monopoly capital: An essay on the American economic and social order.* New York: Monthly Review Press.

Barnet, Richard J., and Ronald Müller. 1974a. *Global reach: The power of the multinational corporations.* New York: Simon and Schuster.

—1974b. "Companies go abroad, and jobs go along." *New York Times,* December 22, E3.

Barshefsky, Charlene. "China's WTO accession and PNTR: America's choice." Speech to the Women in International Trade, Washington, DC, May 16, 2000. http://www.ustr.gov/speech-test/barshefsky/barshefsky_85.html.

Bauer, Raymond A., Ithiel de Sola Pool, and Lewis A. Dexter. 1972. *American business and public policy: The politics of foreign trade.* Chicago: Aldine-Atherton.

Beck, Nathaniel, and Jonathan N. Katz. 1995. "What to do (and not to do) with time-series cross-section data." *American Political Science Review* 89: 634–647.

Berkowitz, S. D., and Fitzgerald, W. 1995. "Corporate control and enterprise structure in the Canadian economy: 1972–1987." *Social Networks* 17(2): 111–127.

Berle, Adolf A. 1952. *The 20th century capitalist revolution.* New York: Harcourt, Brace & Co.

Berle, Adolf A., and Gardner C. Means. 1932. *The modern corporation and private property.* New York: Harcourt, Brace, & World.

Berry, Jeffrey M. 1999. *The new liberalism: The rising power of citizen groups.* Washington, DC: Brookings Institution Press.

Block, Fred. 1977. *The origins of international economic disorder: A study of United States international monetary policy from World War II to the present.* Berkeley: University of California Press.

—1987. *Revising state theory: Essays in politics and postindustrialism.* Philadelphia: Temple University Press.

Blythe, Mark. 2002. *Great transformations: Economic ideas and institutional change in the twentieth century.* Cambridge: Cambridge University Press.

Boies, John L. 1989. "Money, business, and the state: Material interests, Fortune 500 corporations, and the size of political action committees." *American Sociological Review* 54: 821–833.

Borgatti, Stephen P., Martin G. Everett, and Linton C. Freeman. 1999. *UCINET 6.0.* Natick, MA: Analytic Technologies.

Bourdieu, Pierre. 1994. "Rethinking the state: Genesis and structure of the bureaucratic field." *Sociological Theory* 12: 1–18.

—1999. *Acts of resistance: Against the tyranny of the market.* Translated by Richard Nice. New York: New Press.

—2005. *The social structures of the economy.* Malden, MA: Polity Press.

Bourdieu, Pierre, and Loïc J. D. Wacquant. 1992. *An invitation to reflexive sociology.* Chicago: University of Chicago Press.

Boyer, Robert, and Daniel Drache, eds. 1996. *States against markets: The limits of globalization.* New York: Routledge.

Brecher, Jeremy, and Tim Costello. 1994. *Global village or global pillage: Economic reconstruction from the bottom up.* Cambridge: South End Press.

Breiger, Ronald L. 1974. "The duality of persons and groups." *Social Forces* 53: 181–190.

Brostoff, Steven. 2000. "Life insurer CEOs pushing China trade status." National Underwriter Life & Health Magazine, May 8. www.lifehealthpro.com/2000/05/08/life-insurer-ceos-pushing-china-trade-status.

Bunting, David. 1983. "The origins of the corporate network." *Social Science History* 7: 129–142.

Burch, Jr., Phillip H. 1981. "The Business Roundtable: Its make-up and external ties." *Research in Political Economy* 4: 101–127.

Burris, Val. 1987. "The political partisanship of big business." *American Sociological Review* 52: 732–744.

—1992a. "Elite policy-planning networks in the United States." *Research in Politics and Society* 4: 111–134.

—1992b. "PACs, interlocks, and regional differences in corporate conservatism." *American Journal of Sociology* 97: 1451–1456.

—2001. "The two faces of capital: Corporations and individual capitalists as political actors." *American Sociological Review* 66(3): 361–381.

—2005. "Interlocking directorates and political cohesion among corporate elites." *American Journal of Sociology* 111: 249–283.

—2008. "The interlock structure of the policy-planning network and the right turn in U.S. state policy." *Research in Political Sociology* 17: 3–42.

Burt, Ronald S. 1983a. *Corporate profits and cooptation: Networks of market constraints and directorate ties in the American economy.* New York: Academic Press.

—1983b. *Toward a structural theory of action: Network models of social structure, perception, and action.* New York: Academic Press.

Business Roundtable. 1974. *Coming to grips with some major problems in the construction industry: A Business Roundtable report.* New York: The Business Roundtable.

—1980. The role and composition of the board of directors of the large publicly owned corporation. Washington, DC: Business Roundtable.

—2000. *Corporate social responsibility in China: U.S. Business Practices in China.* Washington DC: The Business Roundtable.

—2013. *Overview of the TransPacific Partnership.* November. http://business roundtable.org/studies-and-reports/trans-pacific-partnership-overview/.

Büthe, Tim, and Helen V. Milner. 2008. "The politics of foreign direct investment into developing countries: Increasing FDI through international trade agreements?" *American Journal of Political Science* 52(4): 741–762.

Cameron, Maxwell A., and Brian W. Tomlin. 2000. *The making of NAFTA: How the deal was done.* Ithaca, NY: Cornell University Press.

Campbell, John L. 2004. *Institutional change and globalization.* Princeton: Princeton University Press.

Campbell, John L., and Ove K. Pedersen, eds. 2001. *The rise of neoliberalism and institutional analysis.* Princeton: Princeton University Press.

Canto, Victor A. 1983. "U.S. trade policy: History and evidence." *CATO Journal* 3: 679–703.

Carroll, William K. 2004. *Corporate power in a globalizing world: A study in elite social organization.* Don Mills, Ontario: Oxford University Press.

—2010. *The making of a transnational capitalist class: Corporate power in the twenty-first century.* London; New York: Zed.

—2012. "Capital relations and directorate interlocking: The global network in 2007." In *Financial elites and transnational business: Who rules the world?* Edited by Georgina Murray and John Scott, 54–75. Cheltenham, UK: Edward Elgar Publishing.

Carroll, William K., and Meindert Fennema. 2004. "Problems in the study of the transnational business community." *International Sociology* 19: 369–378.

Carroll, William, and Jean P. Sapinski. 2010. "The global corporate elite and the transnational policy-planning network, 1996–2006." *International Sociology.* 25: 501–538.

Carroll, William K., and J. P. Sapinski. 2011. "Corporate elites and intercorporate networks." In *Sage Handbook of Social Network Analysis.* Edited by John Scott and Peter J. Carrington, 180–195. London: Sage.

—"Corporate Elites and Intercorporate Networks." In *The SAGE Handbook of Social Network Analysis.* Edited by John Scott and Peter J. Carrington, 180–195. Thousand Oaks, CA: Sage Publications.

Chaddock, Gail R. 2000. "Big vote of 2000 turns Capitol into political theater." *Christian Science Monitor,* May 25. www.csmonitor.com/2000/0525/p2s2 .html. Accessed June 12, 2002.

Chandler, Jr., Alfred D. 1977. *The visible hand: The managerial revolution in America.* Cambridge: Cambridge University Press.

Chase-Dunn, Christopher, Yukio Kawano, and Benjamin D. Brewer. 2000. "Trade globalization since 1795: Waves of integration in the world-system." *American Sociological Review* 65: 77–95.

Chorev, Nitsan. 2005. "The institutional project of neoliberal globalism: The case of the WTO." *Theory and Society* 34: 317–355.

Chorev, Nitsan. 2007. *Remaking U.S. trade policy: From protectionism to globalization.* Ithaca, NY: Cornell University Press.

Clawson, Dan, and Alan Neustadtl. 1989. "Interlocks, PACs, and corporate conservatism." *American Journal of Sociology* 94: 749–773.

Clawson, Dan, Alan Neustadtl, and Mark Weller. 1998. *Dollars and votes: How business campaign contributions subvert democracy.* Philadelphia: Temple University Press.

Cohen, Stephen D., Robert A. Blecker, and Peter D. Whitney. 2003. *Fundamentals of U.S. foreign trade policy: Economics, politics, laws, and issues.* Boulder, CO: Westview Press.

Coleman, James S. 1982. *The asymmetric society.* New York: Syracuse University Press.

Congress Daily. 2000. "High tech industry cites China PNTR as top priority," February 9.

Council of the Americas. 1994. *Annual Report on the Hemisphere.* Washington, DC: COA.

Court, Jamie. 2003. *Corporateering: How corporate power steals your personal freedom – and what you can do about it.* New York: Jeremy P. Tarcher/Putnam.

Crabtree, Susan. 2000. "Matsui blasts PNTR threats. Key backer might vote against deal." *Roll Call News,* April 24.

Dahan, Nicholas, Jonathan Doh, and Terrence Guay. 2006. "The role of multinational corporations in transnational institution building: A policy network perspective." *Human Relations* 59: 1571–1600.

Dahl, Robert A. 1961. *Who governs? Democracy and power in an American city.* New Haven: Yale University Press.

—1970. *After the revolution? Authority in a good society.* New Haven: Yale University Press.

—1985. *A preface to economic democracy.* Berkeley: University of California Press.

Dahrendorf, Ralf. 1959. *Class and class conflict in industrial society*. Stanford: Stanford University Press.

Daley, William M. 2000. "Remarks by Secretary of Commerce William M. Daley to industrial sector advisory committees opening plenary session." Washington, DC: Department of Commerce Press Release.

Darves, Derek, and Michael Dreiling. 2002. "Corporate political networks and trade policy formation." *Humanity and Society* 26: 5–27.

Davis, Gerald, and Mark Mizruchi. 1999. "The Money Center cannot hold: Commercial banks in the U.S. system of corporate governance." *Administrative Science Quarterly* 44: 215–239.

DeBièvre, Dirk, and Andreas Dür. 2005. "Constituent interests and delegation in European and American trade policy." *Comparative Political Studies* 38: 1271–1296.

Department of Commerce. 2000. "Industry consultation program mission and history." http://www.ita.doc.gov/td/icp/home.html. Accessed January 14, 2005. Link no longer available.

Destler, I. Mac. 1995. *American trade politics*. 3rd ed. Washington, DC: Institute for International Economics.

—2005. *American trade politics*. 4th ed. Washington, DC: Institute for International Economics.

Dicken, Peter. 2007. *Global shift: Mapping the changing contours of the world economy*. New York: The Guilford Press.

Diebold Jr., William. 1971. "Timely advice from the Williams Commission." *Columbia Journal of World Business* 6: 9–17.

Domhoff, G. William. 1967. *Who rules America?* Englewood Cliffs, NJ: Prentice-Hall Inc.

—1971. *The higher circles*. New York: Vintage Books.

—1978. *The powers that be: Processes of ruling class domination in America*. New York: Vintage Books.

—1990. *The power elite and the state: How policy is made in America*. New York: A. de Gruyter.

—2000. *Who rules America? Power and politics in the year 2000*. Mountain View, CA: Mayfield Publishing Co.

—2006. *Who rules America? Power and politics and social change*. New York: McGraw-Hill.

—2013. *The myth of liberal ascendancy: Corporate dominance from the great depression to the great recession*. Boulder, CO: Paradigm Publishers.

—2014. "Is the corporate elite fractured, or is there continuing corporate dominance? Two contrasting views." *Class, Race and Corporate Power*. 3 (1). http://digitalcommons.fiu.edu/classracecorporatepower/vol3/iss1/1.

Dreiling, Michael. 2000. "The class embeddedness of corporate political action: Leadership in defense of the NAFTA." *Social Problems* 47: 21–48.

—2001. *Solidarity and contention: The politics of security and sustainability in the NAFTA conflict*. New York: Garland Publishing.

Dreiling, Michael, and Derek Y. Darves 2011. "Corporations in American trade policy: A network analysis of corporate-dyad political action." *American Journal of Sociology* 116(5): 1514–1563.

Duina, Francesco. 2006. *The social construction of free trade: The European Union, NAFTA, and MERCOSUR*. Princeton: Princeton University Press.

Dumenil, Gérard, and Dominique Lévy. 2004. *Capital resurgent: Roots of the neoliberal revolution*. Cambridge: Harvard University Press.

—2011. *The Crisis of neoliberalism*. Cambridge: Harvard University Press.

Dye, Thomas R. 1990. *Who's running America now: The Bush restoration*. Englewood Cliffs, NJ: Prentice Hall.

ECAT 2011. Testimony of Calman Cohen, president of the Emergency Committee for American Trade (ECAT) before the Subcommittee on Asia and the Pacific of the House Committee on Foreign Affairs, March 31.

Edsall, Thomas B. 1985. *The new politics of inequality*. New York: W. W. Norton & Company, Inc.

Efron, B. 1979. "Bootstrap methods: Another look at the jack-knife." *Annals of Statistics* 7: 1–26.

Ehrlich, Sean D. 2008. "The tariff and the lobbyist: Political institutions, interest group politics, and U.S. trade policy." *International Studies Quarterly* 52: 427–445.

Emirbayer, Mustafa. 1997. "Manifesto for a relational sociology." *American Journal of Sociology* 103: 281–317.

Epstein, Gerald A. 2005. *Financialization and the world economy*. Cheltenham, UK: Edward Elgar Publishing.

Evans, Peter B. 1995. *Embedded autonomy: States and industrial transformation*. Princeton: Princeton University Press.

Fairbrother, Malcolm. 2007. "Making neoliberalism possible: The state's organization of business support for NAFTA in Mexico." *Politics Society* 35(2): 265–300.

—2014. "Economists, capitalists, and the making of globalization: North American free trade in comparative-historical perspective." *American Journal of Sociology*, 119(5): 1324–1379.

Feenstra, Robert C. 1998. "Integration of trade and disintegration of production in the global economy." *Journal of Economic Perspectives* 12: 31–50.

Fennema, M. 1982. *International networks of banks and industry*." The Hague: Martinus Nijhoff Publishers.

Ferguson, Thomas, and Joel Rogers. 1986. *Right turn: The decline of the Democrats and the future of American politics*. New York: Hill & Wang.

Fligstein, Neil. 1990. *The transformation in corporate control*. Cambridge: Harvard University Press.

—2001. *The architecture of markets: An economic sociology of twenty-first-century capitalist societies*. Princeton, NJ: Princeton University Press.

Fones-Wolf, Elizabeth A. 1994. *Selling free enterprise: The business assault on labor and liberalism, 1945–60*. Champaign: University of Illinois Press.

Foster, John B. 2007. "The Financialization of Capitalism," *The Monthly Review* 58: 1.

Foster, John Bellamy, and Fred Magdoff. 2009. *The great financial crisis: Causes and consequences*. New York: Monthly Review Press.

Foster, John Bellamy, and Robert W. McChesney. 2012. *The endless crisis: How monopoly-finance capital produces stagnation and upheaval from the U.S.A. to China.* New York: Monthly Review Press.

Fourcade, Marion. 2006 "The construction of a global profession: The transnationalization of economics." *American Journal of Sociology* 112(1): 145–195.

Fourcade-Gourinchas, Marion, and Sarah l. Babb. 2002. "The rebirth of the liberal creed: Paths to neoliberalism in four countries." *American Journal of Sociology* 108(3): 533–579.

Frank, Oliver. 1979. "Estimation of population totals by use of snowball samples." In *Perspectives in social network research.* Edited by P. W. Holland and S. Leinhardt, 78–92. New York: Academic Press.

Frieden, Jeff. 1988. "Sectoral conflict and foreign economic policy, 1914–1940." *International Organization* 42: 59–90.

Galaskiewicz, Joseph. 1979. *Exchange networks and community politics.* Sage Publications.

Galbraith, John K. 1971. *The new industrial state.* Boston: Houghton Mifflin.

Garrett, Geoffrey. 2000. "The causes of globalization." *Comparative Political Studies* 33: 941–991.

Gates, Leslie C. 2009. "Theorizing business power in the semiperiphery: Mexico 1970–2000." *Theory and Society* 38:57–95.

Gereffi, Gary. 1995. "Global production systems and third world development." In *Global change, regional response: The new international context of development.* Edited by Barbara Stallings, 100–142. Cambridge: Cambridge University Press.

Gill, Stephen. 1990. *American hegemony and the Trilateral Commission.* New York: Cambridge University Press.

Glasberg, D. 1987. "The ties that bind? Case studies in the significance of corporate board interlocks with financial institutions." *Sociological Perspectives* 30: 19–48.

Gold, David. 2006 [1970]. "Statistical tests and substantive significance." In *The significance test controversy: A reader.* Edited by Denton E. Morrison and Ramon E. Henkel. Piscataway, NJ: Transaction Publishers.

Goldstein, Judith. 1988. "Ideas, institutions, and American trade policy." *International Organization* 42: 179–217.

Goldstein, Judith L., Douglas Rivers, and Michael Tomz. 2007. "Institutions in international relations: Understanding the effects of the GATT and the WTO on world trade." *International Organization* 61: 37–67.

Granovetter, Mark S. 1974. *Getting a job: A study of contacts and careers.* Cambridge: Harvard University Press.

—1985. "Economic action and social structure: The problem of embeddedness." *American Journal of Sociology* 91: 481–510.

Green, Donald P., Soo Yeon Kim, and David Yoon. 2001. "Dirty pool." *International Organization* 55: 441–468.

Griffin, Larry J. 1993. "Narrative, event-structure analysis, and causal interpretation in historical sociology" *American Journal of Sociology* 98: 1094–1133.

Gross, James. 1995. *Broken promises: The subversion of U.S. labor relations policy, 1947–1994.* Philadelphia: Temple University Press.

Gulati, Ranjay, and Martin Gargiulo. 1999. "Where do interorganizational networks come from?" *American Journal of Sociology* 104: 1439–1493.

Haggard, Stephan. 1988. "The institutional foundations of hegemony: Explaining the reciprocal trade agreements act of 1934." *International Organization* 42: 91–119.

Harvey, David. 2005. *A brief history of neoliberalism.* Oxford: Oxford University Press.

Hayek, Friedrich A. von. 1944. *The road to serfdom.* London: G. Routledge & Sons.

Helleiner, Eric. 1994. *States and the reemergence of global finance: From Bretton Woods to the 1990s.* Ithaca, NY: Cornell University Press.

Hilferding, R. 1981 [1910]. *Finance capital: A study of the latest phase of capitalist development.* Trans. M. Watnick and S. Gordon. London: Routledge & K. Paul.

Hilliard, Tom. 1991. Trade advisory committees: Privileged access for polluters. Washington, DC: Public Citizen.

Hillman, Amy J., Gerald D. Keim, and Douglas Schuler. 2004. "Corporate political activity: A review and research agenda." *Journal of Management* 30: 837–857.

Hirst, Paul Q., and Thompson, Grahame. 1999. *Globalization in question: The international economy and the possibilities of governance.* 2nd ed. Cambridge, UK; Malden, MA: Polity.

Holland, P. W. and S. Leinhardt. 1973. "The structural implications of measurement error in sociometry." *Journal of Mathematical Sociology* 3: 85–111.

Howard, Michael C., and John E. King. 2008. *The rise of neoliberalism in advanced capitalist economies: A materialist analysis.* New York: Palgrave Macmillan.

Hunter, Floyd. 1953. *Community power structure: A study of decision makers.* Chapel Hill: University of North Carolina Press.

Ikenberry, G. John, David A. Lake, and Michael Mastanduno. 1988. "Approaches to explaining American foreign economic policy." *International Organization* 42: 1–14.

Inoue, Hiroko. 2011. "The rise of neoliberalism in advanced capitalist economies: A materialist analysis." *International Sociology* 26: 237–240.

Jackson, John H. 1997. *The world trading system: Law and policy of international economic relations.* 2nd ed. Cambridge: MIT Press.

Jacobs, David. 1999. *Business lobbies and the power structure in America: Evidence and arguments.* Westport, CT: Quorum.

Jessop, Bob. 1990. *State theory: Putting capitalist states in their place.* Cambridge: Polity Press.

—2002. *The future of the capitalist state.* Cambridge: Polity.

—2007. *State power: A strategic-relational approach.* Cambridge: Polity.

Jones, Brendan. 1967. "MONETARY shifts urged by WATSON: Credit expansion called for at world business." *New York Times*, May 20, p. F43.

—1968. "Business group seeks free trade." *New York Times*, March 17, p. F10.

—1970. "Free traders fear a 'war' with Tokyo on textiles." *New York Times*, March 29, p. 128.

—1973. "Business lauds, assails trade plan: Addressed Harvard club importers concerned meany scores bill." *New York Times*, April 12, p. 75.

Kahn, Peter. 2000. "Executives make trade with China a moral crusade." *New York Times*, February 13.

Kennedy, Peter. 2003. *A guide to econometrics*. Cambridge: The MIT Press.

Kentor, Jeffery, and Yong Suk Jang. 2004. "Yes, there is a (growing) transnational business community." *International Sociology* 19: 355–368.

Kiel, Paul. 2008. "Greenspan says 'I still don't fully understand' what happened." ProPublica, October 23.

Klein, Naomi. 2002. *Fences and windows: Dispatches from the front lines of the globalization debate*. New York: Picador.

Krueger, Anne O. 1995. *American trade policy: A tragedy in the making*. Washington, DC: American Enterprise Institute Press.

Krugman, Paul. 2007. "Trade and Inequality, Revisited." http://voxeu.org/index .php?q=node/261.

Ladewig, Jeffery W. 2006. "Domestic influences on international trade policy: Factor mobility in the United States, 1963 to 1992." *International Organization* 60: 69–103.

Lamoreaux, Naomi. 1985. *The great merger wave in American business, 1895–1904*. New York: Cambridge Press.

Lenin, Vladimir I. 1916. *Imperialism: The Highest stage of capitalism*. New York: Penguin Publishing.

Lewis, Charles, and Margaret Ebrahim. 1993. "Can Mexico and big business USA buy NAFTA?" *The Nation*, June 14, 826–839.

Lindblom, Charles. 1977. *Politics and markets: The world's political economic systems*. New York: Basic Books.

Lipson, Charles. 1982. "The transformation of trade: The sources of regime trade." *International Organization* 36: 417–455.

Long, J. Scott. 1997. *Regression models for categorical and limited dependent variables*. Thousand Oaks: Sage Publications.

Lovett, William A., Alfred E. Eckes, Jr., and Richard L. Brinkman. 1999. *U.S. trade policy: History, theory, and the WTO*. Armonk, NY: M.E. Sharpe.

Lundburg, Ferdinand. 1937. *America's 60 families*. New York: Vanguard Press.

MacArthur, John R. 2000. *The selling of "free trade": NAFTA, Washington, and the subversion of American democracy*. New York: Hill & Wang.

Mahoney, James. 2000. "Path dependence in historical sociology." *Theory and Society* 29: 507–548.

Martin, Cathie J. 1994. "Business and the new economic activism: The growth of corporate lobbies in the sixties." *Polity* 27: 49–76.

Martin, Cathie J., and Duane Swank. 2004. "Does the organization of capital matter? Employers and active labor market policy at the national and firm levels." *American Political Science Review* 98: 593–611.

Marx, Karl. 1972. "The civil war in France." In *The Marx-Engels reader*, 2nd ed. Edited by Robert C. Tucker, 618–652. New York: W. W. Norton and Company.

McKeown, Tim J. 1984. "Firms and tariff regime change: Explaining the demand for protection." *World Politics* 36: 215–333.

McMichael, Philip. 1990. "Incorporating comparison within a world-historical perspective: An alternative comparative method." *American Sociological Review* 55: 385–397.

—2001. "Revisiting the question of the transnational state: A comment on Williams Robinson's 'social theory and globalization.'" *Theory and Society* 30: 201–210.

—2005. "Globalization." In *The Handbook of Political Sociology: States, Civil Societies, and Globalization*. Edited by Thomas Janoski, 587–606. New York: Cambridge.

—2012. *Development and social change: A global perspective.* 5th ed. Los Angeles: SAGE.

Miliband, Ralph. 1969. *The state in capitalist society.* London: Weidenfeld & Nicolson.

Mills, C. Wright. 1956. *The power elite.* New York: Oxford University Press.

—1988. *Resisting protectionism: Global industries and the politics of international trade.* Princeton: Princeton University Press.

—1997. *Interests, institutions, and information: Domestic politics and international relations.* Princeton: Princeton University Press.

Milner, Helen V., and Peter Rosendorff. 1996. "Trade negotiations, information, and domestic politics: The role of domestic groups." *Economics and Politics* 8: 145–189.

Milner, Helen V., and David B. Yoffie. 1989. "Between free trade and protectionism: Strategic trade policy and a theory of corporate trade demands." *International Organization* 43: 239–272.

Mintz, Beth, and Donald Palmer. 2000. "Business and health care policy reform in the 1980s: The 50 states." *Social Problems* 47(3): 327–359.

Mintz, Beth, and Michael Schwartz. 1985. *The power structure of American business.* Chicago: University of Chicago Press.

Mirowski, Phillip, and Dieter Plehwe, eds. 2009. *The road from Mont Pèlerin: The making of the neoliberal thought collective.* Cambridge: Harvard University Press.

Mizruchi, Mark S. 1982. *The American corporate network, 1904–1974.* Beverly Hills: Sage.

—1989. "Similarity of political behavior among large American corporations." *American Journal of Sociology* 95: 401–424.

—1992. *The structure of corporate political action: Interfirm relations and their consequences.* Cambridge: Harvard University Press.

—1996. "What do interlocks do? An analysis, critique, and assessment of research on interlocking directorates." *Annual Review of Sociology* 22: 271–298.

—2004. "Berle and Means revisited: The governance and power of large U.S. corporations." *Theory and Society* 33: 579–617.

—2013. *The fracturing of the American corporate elite.* Cambridge: Harvard University Press.

—2004. "Berle and Means revisited: The governance and power of large U.S. corporations." *Theory and Society* 33: 579–617.

Mizruchi, Mark S., and Thomas Koenig. 1991. "Size, concentration, and corporate networks: Determinants of business collective action." *Social Science Quarterly* 72: 299–313.

Mizruchi, Mark S., and Michael Schwartz. 1987. "The structural analysis of business: An emerging field." In *Intercorporate relations: The structural analysis of business.* Edited by Mark S. Mizruchi and Michael Schwartz, 3–22. New York: Cambridge University Press.

Mizruchi, Mark S., Linda B. Stearns, and Christopher Marquis. 2006. "The conditional nature of embeddedness: A study of borrowing by large U.S. firms, 1973–1994." *American Sociological Review* 71: 310–333.

Moore, Gwen, Sarah Sobieraj, J. Allen Whitt, Olga Mayorova, and Daniel Beaulieu. 2002. "Elite interlocks in three U.S. sectors: Nonprofit, corporate, and government." *Social Science Quarterly* 83: 726–744.

Morck, Randall, Jungsywan Sepanski, and Bernard Yeung. 2001. "Habitual and occasional lobbying in the U.S. steel industry: An EM algorithm pooling approach." *Economic Inquiry* 39: 365–378.

Mudge, Stephanie Lee. 2008. "What is neo-liberalism?" *Socio-Economic Review* 6: 703–731.

Mundo, Philip A. 1999. *National politics in a global economy: The domestic sources of U.S. trade policy.* Washington, DC: Georgetown University Press.

Murphy, Kevin M., Andrei Shleifer, and Robert W. Vishny. 1993. "Why is rent seeking so costly to growth?" *American Economic Review* 83: 409–414.

Murray, Georgina. 2006. *Capitalist networks and social power in Australia and New Zealand.* Aldershot, UK: Ashgate.

Murray, Georgina, and John Scott, eds. 2012. *Financial elites and transnational business: Who rules the world?* Cheltenham, UK: Edward Elgar Publishing.

National Journal. 2000. "Art of the deal," May 19.

National Journal. 2000. "Inside Washington," May 27, p. 1657.

Neil, Terry M. 1997. "Business leaders gear up lobbying and ad campaign for 'fast track' bill." *Washington Post*, September 17, p. A4.

Newport, Frank. 1993. "NAFTA slightly more likely to be opposed than supported." *Gallup Poll Monthly.* September (336): 13–14.

Nollert, Michael. 2005. "Transnational corporate ties: A synopsis of theories and empirical findings." *Journal of World Systems Research* 11: 289–314.

O'Halloran, Sharyn. 1994. *Politics, process, and American trade policy.* Ann Arbor: University of Michigan Press.

OECD. 2011. *Divided we stand: Why inequality keeps rising.* Paris: OECD Publishing.

OECD 2015. *In it together: Why less inequality benefits all.* Paris: OECD Publishing.

Office of the US Trade Representative. 1994. *1994 trade policy agenda and 1993 annual report of the president of the United States on the trade agreements program.* Washington, DC: US Trade Representative's Office.

Oka, Tokashi. 1970. "WAY SEEN TO END TEXTILE IMPASSE: Japanese Official Bids U.S. to Use Kendall Proposal." *New York Times*, March 27, pp. 49, 51.

Olson, Mancur. 1965. *The logic of collective action.* Cambridge: Harvard University Press.

Ostrom Jr., Charles W. 1978. *Time series analysis: Regression techniques.* Thousand Oaks, CA: Sage Publications.

Panitch, Leo, and Sam Gindin. 2013. *The making of global capitalism: The political economy of American empire.* New York: Verso.

Peetz, David, and Georgina Murray. 2012. "The financialization of global corporate ownership." In *Financial elites and transnational business: Who rules the world?* Georgina Murray and John Scott, 26–53. Cheltenham, UK: Edward Elgar Publishing.

Pennings, Johannes M. 1980. *Interlocking directorates: Origins and consequences of connections among organizations' boards of directors.* San Francisco: Jossey-Bass Inc.

Perrow, Charles. 2005. *Organizing America: Wealth, power, and the origins of corporate capitalism.* Princeton: Princeton University Press.

Peschek, Joseph. 1987. *Policy-planning organizations: Elite agenda and America's rightward turn.* Philadelphia: Temple University Press.

Pfeffer, Jeffrey. 1987. "A resource dependence perspective on intercorporate relations." In *Intercorporate relations: The structural analysis of business.* Edited by Mark S. Mizruchi and Michael Schwartz, 25–55. New York: Cambridge University Press.

Pfeffer, Jeffrey, and Gerald R. Salancik. 1978. *The external control of organizations: A resource dependency perspective.* New York: Harper & Row.

Phillips, Michael M. 2000. "Lawmakers are warned to back China trade or lose contributions." *Wall Street Journal*, February 9, p. A1.

Phillips-Fein, Kim. 2009. *Invisible hands: The making of the conservative movement from the New Deal to Reagan.* New York: W. W. Norton & Company.

Pierce, Justin R., and Peter K. Schott. 2012. *The surprisingly swift decline of U.S. manufacturing employment.* NBER Working Paper No. 18655. Cambridge, MA: The National Bureau of Economic Research.

Piore, Michael J., and Charles Sabel. 1984. *The second industrial divide: Possibilities for prosperity.* New York: Basic Books.

Polanyi, Karl. 2001. *The great transformation: The political and economic origins of our time.* Boston: Beacon Press. First published 1944 by Beacon Books.

Polanyi-Levitt, Kari. 1985. "The origins and implications of the Caribbean Basin Initiative: Mortgaging sovereignty?" *International Journal* 40: 229–281.

Poulantzas, Nicos A. 1973. *Political power and social classes.* Translated by Timothy O'Hagan. NLB. London: Sheed and Ward. First published 1968.

—1978. *State, power, socialism.* Translated by Patrick Camiller. London: Verso.

Powell, Colin L. 2001. "The promise of China trade." *Washington Post*, June 1, p. A31.

Prasad, Monica. 2006. *The politics of free markets: The rise of neoliberal economic policies in Britain, France, Germany and the United States.* Chicago: University of Chicago Press.

—2012. "The popular origins of neoliberalism in the Reagan tax cut of 1981." *Journal of Policy History* 24: 351–383.

Prechel, Harland. 1990. "Steel and the state: Industry politics and business policy formation, 1940–1989." *American Sociological Review* 55: 648–668.

—2000. *Big business and the state: Historical transitions and corporate transformations, 1880s–1990s.* Albany: State University of New York Press.

—2003. "Historical contingency theory, policy paradigm shifts, and corporate malfeasance at the turn to the 21st century." *Research in Political Sociology: Political Sociology for the 21st Century* 12: 311–340.

Preeg, Ernest H. 1998. *From here to free trade: Essays in post-Uruguay round trade strategy.* Chicago: University of Chicago.

Przeworski, Adam. 1990. *The state and economy under capitalism.* New York: Harwood.

Quark, Amy. 2011. "Transnational governance as contested institution-building: China, merchants, and contract rules in the cotton trade." *Politics & Society* 39: 3–39.

Raudenbush, Stephen W., and Anthony Bryk. 2002. *Hierarchical linear models: Applications and data analysis methods.* Thousand Oaks, CA: Sage Publications.

Robinson, William I. 2004. *A theory of global capitalism: Production, class, and state in a transnational world.* Baltimore: Johns Hopkins University Press.

Rockefeller, David. 1963. "International monetary reform and the New York banking community." In *World banking reform: Plans and issues.* Edited by Herbert G. Grubel, 150–159. Stanford: Stanford University Press.

Rodrik, Dani. 1997. *Has globalization gone too far?* Washington, DC: Institute for International Economics.

Rogowski, Ronald. 1989. *Commerce and coalitions: How trade affects domestic political alignments.* Princeton: Princeton University Press.

Ruggie, John G. 1982. "International regimes, transactions, and change: Embedded liberalism in the postwar economic order," *International Organization* 36: 379–415.

—1998. *Constructing the world polity: Essays on international institutionalization.* New York: Routledge.

Salant, Jonathan D. 1999. "Business groups ready for China trade debate." *Ocala Star-Banner*, December 19, p. 4B.

Salisbury, Robert H. 1992. *Interests and institutions: Substance and structure in American politics.* Pittsburgh: University of Pittsburgh Press.

Sanger, David E. 2000. "The China trade vote: Rounding out a clear Clinton legacy." *New York Times*, May 25, p. A23.

Sassen, Saskia. 1996. *Losing control? Sovereignty in an age of globalization.* New York: Columbia University Press.

—1999. "Making the global economy run: The role of national states and private agents." *International Social Science Journal* 51: 409–416.

Sayrs, Lois W. 1989. *Pooled time series analysis.* Newbury Park, CA: Sage Publications Inc.

Schattschneider, Elmer E. 1935. *Politics, pressures, and the tariff: A study of free private enterprise in pressure politics, as shown in the 1929–1930 revision of the tariff.* New York: Prentice Hall.

Schriftgiesser, Karl. 1967. *Business and public policy: The role of the Committee for Economic Development, 1942–1967.* Englewood Cliffs, NJ: Prentice-Hall.

Scott, John. 1979. *Corporations, classes and capitalism*. London: Hutchinson.

—1991. *Who rules Britain?* Cambridge: Polity Press, 1991.

—1997. *Corporate business and capitalist classes*. Oxford: Oxford University Press.

Scott, John, F. Stokman, and R. Zeigler, eds. 1985. *Networks of corporate power*. Cambridge: Polity Press.

Shoch, James. 2001. *Trading blows party competition and U.S. trade policy in a globalizing era*. Chapel Hill: University of North Carolina Press, 2001.

Shoup, Laurence H., and Minter, William. 1977. *The imperial brain trust: The council on foreign relations and United States foreign policy*. New York: Monthly Review Press.

Silva, Patricio. 2008. *In the name of reason: Technocrats and politics in Chile*. University Park: Pennsylvania State University Press.

Sinclair, Scott. 2015. "NAFTA Chapter 11 Investor-State Disputes to January 1, 2015." Ottawa: Canadian Centre for Policy Alternatives.

Sklair, Leslie. 2001. *The transnational capitalist class*. Oxford: Basil Blackwell.

—2002a. "The transnational capitalist class and global politics: Deconstructing the corporate-state connection." *International Political Science Review / Revue Internationale de Science Politique* 23: 159–174.

—2002b. *Globalization: Capitalism and its alternatives*. Oxford: Oxford University Press.

Skocpol, Theda. 1979. *States and social revolutions: A comparative analysis of France, Russia, and China*. Cambridge: Cambridge University Press.

—1992. *Protecting mothers and soldiers: The political origins of social policy in the United States*. Cambridge: Harvard University Press.

Skocpol, Theda, and Edwin Amenta. 1985. "Did capitalists shape social security?" *American Sociological Review* 50: 572–575.

Skocpol, Theda, and Kenneth Finegold. 1982. "State capacity and economic intervention in the early New Deal." *Political Science Quarterly* 97: 255–278.

Sonquist, John, and Thomas Koenig. 1975. "Interlocking directorates in the top US corporations: A graph theory approach." *The Insurgent Sociologist* 5(3): 196–229.

Sorauf, Francis J. 1991. "PACs and parties in American politics." In *Interest group politics*. Edited by Allan J. Cigler and Burdett A. Loomis, 87–105. Washington, DC: Congressional Quarterly Press.

Staples, Clifford L. 2006. "Board interlocks and the study of the transnational capitalist class." *Journal of World Systems Research* 12: 309–319.

—2007. "Board globalization in the world's largest TNCs 1993–2005." *Corporate Governance: An International Journal* 15: 311–321.

—2012. "The Business Roundtable and the transnational capitalist class." In *Financial elites and transnational business: Who rules the world?* Edited by Georgina Murray and John Scott, 100–123. Cheltenham, UK: Edward Elgar Publishing.

Stokman, F.N., R. Ziegler, and J. Scott, eds. 1985. *Networks of corporate power: A comparative analysis of ten countries*. Oxford: Polity Press.

Strange, Susan. 1996. *The retreat of the state: The diffusion of power in the world economy*. Cambridge: Cambridge University Press.

Sweezy, Paul M. 1953. *The present as history: Essays and reviews on capitalism and socialism.* New York: Monthly Review Press.

Thacker, Strom C. 2000. *Big business, the state, and free trade: Constructing coalitions in Mexico.* New York: Cambridge University Press.

TransPacific Partnership Embassies. 2013. News release, "TPP Ambassadors to the United States welcome congressional friends of TPP caucus." October 29. Washington, DC: TPP Embassies.

US Council for International Business. 1993. Annual Report. Washington, DC: USCIB.

US Council for International Business. 1994. Monthly News. Washington, DC: USCIB.

US House of Representatives. 1995. *Fast Track Issues.* Committee on Ways and Means, 104th Congress, 1st Session. Washington, DC: Government Printing Office.

US Senate. 1992. *North American Free Trade Agreement.* Committee on Finance, 102nd Congress, 2nd Session. Washington, DC: Government Printing Office.

US Senate. 2004. *U.S.-Australia and U.S.-Morocco Free Trade Agreements.* Committee on Finance, 108th Congress, 2nd Session. Washington, DC: Government Printing Office.

Uniworld Business Publications. *Directory of American firms operating in foreign countries*, 9th, 10th, 11th, 12th, 13th eds. New York: Uniworld Business Publications, Inc.

Useem, Michael. 1979. "The social organization of the business elite and participation of corporate directors in the governance of American institutions." *American Sociological Review* 44: 553–572.

—1984. *The inner circle: Large corporations and the rise of business political activity in the U.S. and U.K.* New York: Oxford University Press.

Vitali, Stefania, James B. Glattfelder, Stefano Battiston, and Alejandro Raul Hernandez Montoya. 2011. "The network of global corporate control." *PLoS ONE* 6(10): 3–18.

Vogel, David. 1989. *Fluctuating fortunes: The political power of business in America.* New York: Basic Books.

Walker, Jack L. 1991. *Mobilizing interest groups in America: Patrons, professions, and social movements.* Ann Arbor: University of Michigan Press.

Wallach, Lori, and Michelle Sforza. 1999. *Whose trade organization? Corporate globalization and the erosion of democracy.* Washington, DC: Public Citizen.

Weber, Max. [1921] 1978. *Economy and society.* Edited by Guenther Roth and Claus Wittich. Berkeley: University of California Press.

Wilcke, Gerd. 1967a. "U.S. backs Javits on trade protectionism: A coalition is urged." *New York Times*, November 1, p. 63, 67.

—1967b. "Protectionist moves in Congress assailed: The 54th Convention of NFTC." *New York Times*, November 2, p. 71, 79.

—1967c. "Trade camps vie for favor: Support urged on opposing interests." *New York Times*, November 10, p. F71.

—1967d. "Watson of I.B.M. heads group opposing import quota moves." *New York Times*, November 16, p. 69, 78.

Williams, Albert L. 1971. *United States international economic policy in an interdependent world*. Washington, DC: Commission on Interim Trade.

Wilson, Michael G. 1993. "The North American Free Trade Agreement: Ronald Reagan's Vision Realized," Executive Memorandum. Washington, DC: The Heritage Foundation.

Woodall, Patrick, Lori Wallach, Jessica Roach, and Katie Burnham. 2000. *Purchasing power: The corporate–White House alliance to pass the China Trade Bill over the will of the American people*. Washington, DC: Public Citizen.

Woods, Tim. 2003. "Capitalist class relations, the state, and New Deal foreign trade policy." *Critical Sociology* 29: 393–418.

Woods, Tim, and Theresa Morris. 2007. "Fast tracking trade policy: State structures and NGO influence during the NAFTA negotiations." *Research in Political Sociology* 15: 177–204.

Yarbrough, Beth V., and Robert M. Yarbrough. 1992. *Cooperation and governance in international trade: The strategic organizational approach*. Princeton: Princeton University Press.

Zeitlin, Maurice. 1974. "Corporate ownership and control: The large corporation and the capitalist class." *American Journal of Sociology* 79: 1073–1119.

Index